# HOME LANDSCAPING

## in the Northeast & Midwest

### by Ken Smith

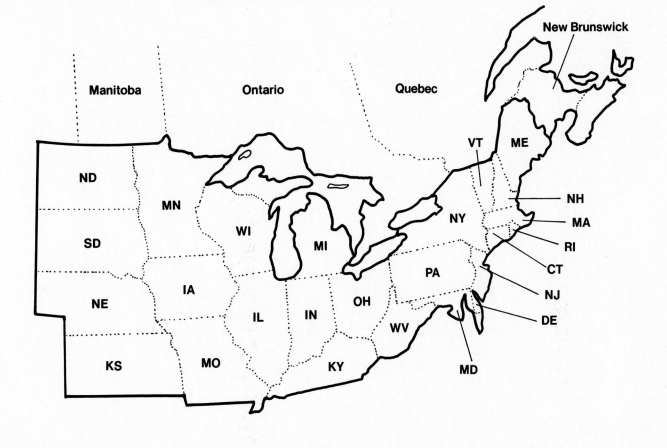

Publisher: Rick Bailey; Executive Editor: Randy Summerlin
Editors: Roberta Janes, Judith Schuler; Art Director: Don Burton
Book Assembly: Lisa Ortmann; Managing Editor: Cindy J. Coatsworth
Typography: Michelle Carter; Director of Manufacturing: Anthony B. Narducci

**Published by HPBooks**
**A division of HPBooks, Inc.**
P.O. Box 5367, Tucson, AZ 85703 (602) 888-2150
ISBN: 0-89586-311-1
Library of Congress Catalog Card Number: 84-62856
©1985 HPBooks, Inc.   Printed in U.S.A.
3rd Printing

Notice: The information in this book is true and complete to the best of our knowledge. All recommendations are made without guarantees on the part of the author or HPBooks. The author and publisher disclaim all liability in connection with the use of this information.

# TABLE OF CONTENTS

# Landscape and You

Imaginative development of outdoor space can make a small house seem like a large one. Patios, fences, lawns and trees cost less than floors, walls, carpet and a new roof. And you don't have to be an expert to work in outdoor spaces.

It takes common sense, hard work and some guidance to design outdoor space. That's what this book is all about. Garden construction and planting are fun if they're done right. Do-it-yourself projects are satisfying, and they can save you money.

Anyone can benefit from good landscape ideas, even if your estate is limited to a small condominium patio, a mobile-home lot or a balcony. In fact, the smaller the area, the more important it is to make the most of limited space.

## PURCHASING OR BUILDING A HOME

It takes a lot of time and effort to select a new home. A house may be the most important purchase made by a family. Your choice can have a profound effect on your health and happiness.

Let's assume a house is well built and a pleasing design. It should have enough space for your needs and be located in a desirable neighborhood. It should be close to shopping, fire and police services, schools, recreation areas and transportation. A house must also be within your financial reach, with some money left for outdoor work. There are many landscape considerations that can make a house a good purchase or an unsound one.

Carefully check the house and

**Raised deck nestles between existing trees to make best use of sloping Long Island property. Landscape architect: Raymond J. Rolfe, ASLA.**

property. Evaluate existing trees, views, soil conditions and drainage. Talk to other residents to see if there are seasonal or prevailing winds that could be a problem or an asset. If you're building a house, choose an orientation suited to the specific climate. In most northern states, it is preferable for major glass areas to face south. A sufficient roof overhang should block high, summer sun and allow low-angle winter sun to warm the house.

You don't have any choice when a house is already built. It is a matter of designing the landscape to fit the situation. The information beginning on page 16 describes ways to modify climate with plantings.

Determine what needs different areas will serve. See if there is room for a patio or screened porch, swimming pool, spa, game court, vegetable garden or anything else that is required. Look for good indoor-outdoor relationships so outdoor

**Left: A well-planned landscape can transform a house and lot into a pleasing, comfortable living environment. Design/build: Theodore Brickman Co., Long Grove, Illinois.**

living areas are convenient and part of the house.

Decide what needs to be done first. Establish a budget for some immediate landscape costs, such as paving, lawn, fencing and trees.

Check to see if there is a sewer or septic tank, reliable water supplies or above-ground power lines. Find out about easements, deed restrictions, architectural committee guidelines or other requirements that might limit property development. Verify property lines—there should be surveyor's stakes marking the corners.

Study site plans and zoning maps to determine what may be built on adjacent property. Will the upstairs windows of a neighboring house look down on your back yard? Will there be apartments or a gas station across the street? Consider room additions and future developments. Be sure there is sufficient area and access to make additions.

If the house is to be built or isn't completed, ask the builder to provide high-pressure hose-bibbs for convenient portable watering or a supply line for permanent sprinklers. Install electrical stub-outs with indoor switches for garden, pool or spa lighting. Protect paving from damage during construction, or pave after work is done.

If building is underway, erect temporary fences around existing trees and other plants for protection. Remove and stockpile existing topsoil from the construction area to use later for lawn and planting. Thoroughly clean up plaster, wood, concrete and other trash, and remove it from the site.

If landscaping is included in the cost of the home, ask the builder for an itemized breakdown of what is included—you're paying for it. Builder landscaping is usually not done very well. It's often better to get a credit for the work than to end up having to do it over.

Investigate the workmanship of subcontractors before they do any paving, wall construction, lighting, grading or other custom work for you.

Try to picture the completed living environment of house and garden. Will the finished house and landscaping be "just what you want" or will it always be an unsatisfactory compromise?

You may have to settle for a little

This back yard is a great outdoor room. A carpet of dark-blue water contrasts with a floor of brick. Walls are covered with lush foliage. There's room for lounging under the handsome shade structure or for sunbathing on the brick deck.

Front yards can be beautiful and functional. Low fence subtly creates a gracious entry court in this Connecticut garden. Landscape architect: CR3 Inc.

Sound, basic planning lasts a long time. Many changes have been made in this yard, but the major elements of my original design for Dr. and Mrs. Jerry Sievers remain intact after 18 years.

less than your ideal. No property is perfect. You can probably live with some small items or handle them yourself. Try not to overlook major problems—they may cause a property to be unlivable for you.

It's easy to panic when you find yourself surrounded by a barren yard with weeds, dust or mud to look at. The temptation is to call a concrete man to pour a patio or a landscape company to put in a lawn. Stay away from the phone, and resist the urge to rush outside to start planting.

There is a logical order that a landscape professional follows when a complete garden is installed at one time. This is shown in the box in the next column. There is considerable overlapping and coordination, but the general order prevails.

You are more likely to dine outdoors when the area is private, pleasant and convenient to the house. Landscape architect and contractor: Theodore Brickman Company.

Do you have a problem with a narrow side yard? Beauté la terre Designs transformed a bleak space into a pleasing scene. Photo: Kala Busby.

### Logical Order of Installation

1. Design
2. Rough Grading and Retaining Walls
3. Spas and Swimming Pools
4. Paving
5. Topsoil, Finish Grading and Drainage
6. Fencing
7. Sprinkler Systems
8. Lighting and Electrical Work
9. Shade Trellises and Patio Roofs
10. Miscellaneous Construction
11. Soil Preparation and Weed Killers
12. Planting
13. Lawns
14. Furniture and Finishing Touches

The logical order of installation here is to first build walls and fences for pets and children. Wide side yards allow easy access for patio and other future construction.

Installing your own landscaping is easier and more fun when the entire family participates. Jason isn't old enough to sweep or mix mortar, but he's good with a hose.

Budget restrictions, site conditions and special priorities may modify this sequence. You may want to install fencing or a hedge as soon as you move in. A pool or screened porch can be a future addition if the budget won't stand the strain right away.

When you modify this sequence, allow for work you plan to do later. Install pipes or sleeves that must go under paving. Include footings for posts in a patio. Keep plants and piping clear of future construction, and leave room for equipment access. A little foresight now can save a lot of time, effort and money later.

## TOLERANCES

You may notice I use *most, many, probably, often, generally, could, sometimes, if, but, however, about, usually* and other qualifying words in this book. That's because there are many variables in garden design, especially personal preference and requirements of living plants.

Rigid formulas are difficult to apply to landscaping. Gardening is an art, not a precise science. It helps to keep good records and general schedules, but be flexible, consider alternatives and be aware of constantly changing conditions.

Don't try to apply exacting standards to landscape design. You'll only be frustrated. It's impossible to impose a hundredth-of-an-inch tolerance to bricks or planks when they may each vary 1/4 inch. Overall straightness, level, plumb (verticality) and pattern are *usually* more im-

portant than precision of individual parts. When installing any landscape work, stand back occasionally to see if it looks "right." This is often a better test than a tape measure or level.

## FIRST STEP

A garden is complex and has many interrelated parts. Make a list of specific requirements and what you want your garden to be. Drive around, look at other homes and see what appeals to you. Search garden magazines, and clip photos of what you like. Study descriptions of various

garden styles, and decide what overall feeling you want to achieve. Restrain yourself a little longer. It's time to start designing, not digging.

## GARDEN STYLES

There isn't a particular type of garden that can be classified as Northeast or Midwest. Lawns are the predominant factor. Shade trees, foundation plantings, windbreaks, hedges and flowering trees are common, but they aren't necessarily arranged in a particular way. The best design is one created for your specific site,

This Illinois landscape has dignity and repose without being ostentatious. If there were such a style, I guess it could be called Northeast/Midwest.

Above: Set in an Ohio wood, brick-on-sand paving and a casual, relaxed feeling contribute to an *Informal* style. Design/build: Land Techniques. Landscape architect: Andrew L. Sparks, ASLA.

Left: Even without the definitive Japanese stone lantern, this delightful garden has an *Oriental* flavor.

neighborhood, architecture, climate, budget and lifestyle.

A garden *can* borrow from other eras and achieve a flavor of what is admired from the past. The following descriptions of various styles or motifs serve as general guides, not specific historical formulas. Most successful present-day gardens combine elements from more than one style. When these elements are skillfully blended, a new style evolves. It may be more practical and appropriate and as beautiful as its predecessors.

**Formal**—Formal gardens are symmetrical, axial, geometrical, rigid or precise. These gardens include masonry walls, balustrades, terraces, stairways, fountains, statuary, gazebos, sheared hedges and large pots. Slate, brick, tile, crushed rock and cut stone are also used. Plants used most often include boxwood, yew, Canadian hemlock, privet, roses, poplar, arborvitae, spruce, ivy, pachysandra, annuals and manicured lawns.

**Informal**—Informal gardens are a-symmetrical, casual, relaxed and unpolished. These gardens include brick and flagstone paving, wood decks, stone walls, board and stake fences and pergolas. Plants used most often include forsythia, lilac, spirea, abelia, bearberry, honeysuckle, periwinkle, perennials, dogwood, flowering crab apple, silk tree, honey locust and rolling lawns.

An outstanding example of classic *Colonial* style in historic Williamsburg.

Above: John Clayton Thomas, ASLA, of TKA Landscape Architects, created this *Natural* landscape for Mr. and Mrs. William Chambers of Indianapolis, Indiana.

Right: This is really *Formal.* It is appropriate for the Louvre, but I doubt if you'd want to keep your yard this way.

Below: Matching American hollies flank the front door and lend a *Formal* touch. Landscape architect: Claire Bennett Associates, FASLA.

**Natural**—Natural gardens are irregular, rambling, flowing, rough textured or gently contoured. These gardens include waterfalls, ponds, streams, meadows, boulders, flagstone, pebble concrete, railroad ties, wood tubs and barrels. Dry stone walls, split rail, grapestake and stockade fences may also be used. Plants used most often include prairiegrass, crown vetch, native plants, junipers, mountain laurel, snowberry, birch, sycamore, redbud, wildflowers and spring-flowering bulbs.

**Colonial**—Colonial gardens are balanced, with straight lines, angles and rectangles. These gardens include white-picket fences, sundials, brick paving and walls, crushed-rock paths and arbors. Plants used most often include boxwood, holly, periwinkle, ivy, dogwood, sweet gum, tulip tree, bulbs, flowers, vegetables, herbs and fruit trees.

Sophisticated materials and forms were used in this pool garden. I didn't have a specific style in mind when I designed it, but if it has to have a name, I guess it is *Contemporary.*

This is a "real" Japanese garden designed by famed professor Nakane of Osaka University. But it is in Singapore, and the plants, such as the striking yellow flame tree, are tropical. It shows you can adapt any style to almost any locality and still have a successful design.

**Oriental**—Oriental gardens are serene and natural but neat and orderly. These gardens include ponds, bridges, pavilions, earth forms, boulders, wood decks, pebbles, stone lanterns and bamboo tubs. Plants used most often include black and other types of pine, Japanese maple, junipers, azalea, bamboo, liriope, iris, yew, winged euonymus, wisteria, ginkgo, weeping willow, flowering cherry and mosses.

**Contemporary**—Contemporary gardens are dramatic, sophisticated and organized, with contrasting textures. Various paving and construction materials are combined in a striking manner. Many plants are used in bold masses and exciting ways, including colored and variegated foliage, specimens and accents.

A curving walkway, gentle contours and boulders give an *Informal* and *Natural* atmosphere. Note how the flagstone carries out the entrance stonework. Design/build: Landscape Services Inc., Hockessin, Delaware.

# The Design Comes First

Every garden is designed by someone. Complex projects call for the services of a professional, but an average yard may be successfully designed by an amateur—with proper guidance. If you want to design your own garden, sift through advice of friends, relatives, neighbors and anyone who has laid a brick, built a fence or planted a tree. Some of their suggestions are helpful; others are disastrous.

This book should answer most of your questions. See *Sources of Information* pages 188 and 189 for other books and places to get assistance. If you get stuck, consult a professional.

## PLANNING

There is a general procedure to follow regardless of who is designing the garden. First, prepare an accurate plan of your land at a scale of either 1/8 or 1/4 inch equal to 1 foot. Graph paper makes it easier to convert measurements to the plan. Show existing conditions, such as the house, property lines, easements, utility lines, sewer lines, septic tanks, leach fields, top and toe (bottom) of slopes and nearby neighbors. Include house doors, windows, overhangs, existing paving, walls, fences and plants—especially trees. Mark the direction of seasonal winds, the north arrow, drainage flow and similar items.

Lay a piece of tracing paper over the plan. Explore, experiment, dream, reject and erase while you try to picture the completed garden. Involve family members in your planning. They have to use the space and may have specific needs or desires.

Begin with a diagrammed layout of use areas, as shown at right. Integrate circulation, privacy, wind, noise, views, drainage and sun-shade patterns with the overall organization.

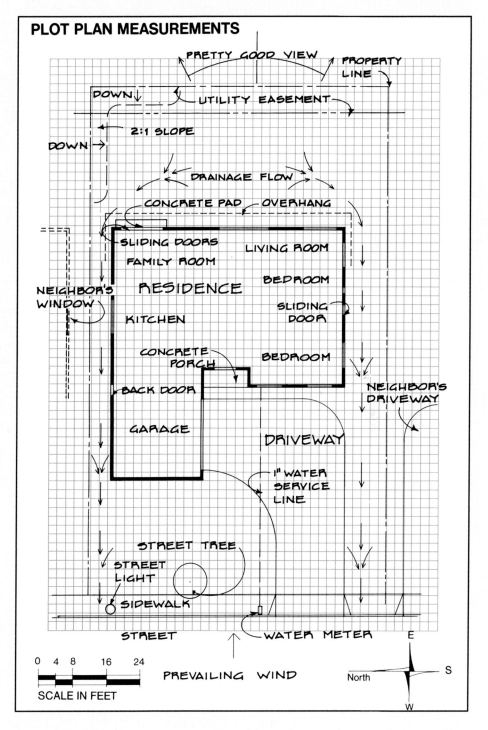

**PLOT PLAN MEASUREMENTS**

**Left: Beautiful design compostions require a skillful blending of form, color and texture along with a knowledge of construction and plants. Landscape architect: Lee Sharfman. Photo: William Aplin.**

As ideas begin to form, draw in paving and structures, such as walls, fences and shade trellises. Decide what uses plants will serve, where they should go and how big they should grow. Shade, privacy, noise reduction, windbreak and erosion control are some important uses for plants. Make tentative selections based on the *Plant Lists* beginning on page 86.

## BEAUTY

Sadly enough, a garden can be functional but not pleasant to look at or be in. Try to apply basic art principles to your designs. Proportion, color, texture, unity and rhythm are important in a garden. Think of your garden as three-dimensional—even four-dimensional—when movement through time and the ever-changing nature of living plants is considered. Along with practical factors, a garden is more difficult to create than other art forms. But don't be overwhelmed. Limit the number of construction materials, and repeat materials used in the house where possible. Use the same colors that are in and on the house. Don't try to use one of every plant in the nursery. Think in terms of areas, groups and masses. One-of-this and one-of-that can look terrible.

Start with simple, restrained plans. Many plants provide a bonus of seasonal displays that may not be evident when they're first planted. Add accents later if you feel something is lacking. Concentrate on the *overall concept*. Avoid fussy details and gaudy gimmicks. Be bold—if in doubt, make it larger, not smaller.

## CHECKING YOUR PLAN

Look closely at your design. If you have trouble picturing it, go outside and make a "mock-up" with stakes and string. Pretend you're having friends over for a party or you're one of the children. Does the proposed plan serve everyone well? Will you be able to take care of it? Does it accomplish your desired uses?

Involve the entire family. If the plan passes the test at this stage, you're on the right track. Make sure your plan meets local building codes and deed restrictions. It should not violate setback or easement requirements.

Technical plans for structures, sprinklers, lighting and drains don't

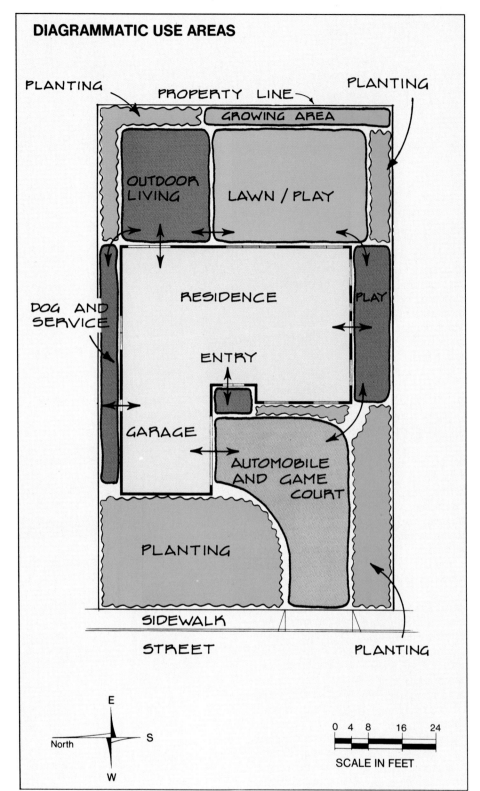

**DIAGRAMMATIC USE AREAS**

**Famous "Sand Garden" in Kyoto, Japan is for meditating, not family entertaining or touch football. Decide what functions your garden must accommodate before you design.**

**Front entrance was laid out first with stakes and string to get a feeling of size. Footing was then dug for railroad-tie wall.**

have to be completed until you're ready to install them. But rough them out at this time. This allows you to include sleeves, stub-outs and footings where they are needed. Consider possible future additions, such as a swimming pool, spa, playhouse or extra bedroom.

Prepare an overall cost estimate before making final decisions on materials, size of plants and the extent of paved areas. If you plan to have all or part of the work done by others, call several reputable contractors, and ask for competitive bids. If prices are much higher than you can or want to invest, this is the time to consider substitutions.

The patio may have to be made of concrete instead of brick. Plants may have to be smaller to start with. The lawn may have to be planted from seed instead of being sodded. Rather than cutting basic quality, set aside some items as future phases, and install them when finances allow. One advantage of a good plan is everything fits together, even if it isn't installed at the same time.

## HOW MUCH WILL IT COST?

There isn't much you can do about house payments and property taxes. Furniture, carpet and drapes are usually essential. With the outdoors, you have more choice. It's nice to have a completed landscape the day you

move in. More often, it's a matter of setting priorities. You may do the most important items first and wait to do other phases until your budget allows for additional expenditures.

When you have a plan worked out, estimate the cost. It may differ from the chart below, but the basic items and general costs are similar. The chart is based on the *average* builder-constructed house in the $75,000 to $125,000 price range on a level 7,500-square-foot lot. All materials and labor are assumed to be provided by a landscape contractor. Do-it-yourself items can usually save about 50% of the contracted figure.

Few homeowners have the time, capability or desire to do everything. Leave certain items to experts unless you've had previous experience or can get experienced help. Attempt concrete paving, masonry walls, chain-link fences, 110-volt electrical work, gas lines, spas, swimming pools and planting large-specimen trees *only* after careful consideration.

You can probably handle brick-on-sand paving, wood fences, sprinkler systems, minor construction, simple trellises, low-voltage lighting and most planting. Get the family involved—it's fun and can speed up a project. It can also be a rewarding ex-

| Landscape Costs | | | |
|---|---|---|---|
| Type of Work | Typical Cost Range in $ | | |
| Design | 500 | to | 1,000 |
| Rough Grading | 300 | to | 500 |
| Paving | 1,500 | to | 2,500 |
| Finish Grading & Drainage | 300 | to | 500 |
| Fencing (Assumes cost split with neighbors) | 500 | to | 2000 |
| Sprinkler System | 500 | to | 2,000 |
| Lighting | 200 | to | 500 |
| Miscellaneous Construction | 300 | to | 500 |
| Soil Preparation | 300 | to | 500 |
| Planting | 1,000 | to | 3,000 |
| Lawn | 500 | to | 1,000 |
| Furniture & Finishing Touches | 500 | to | 1,000 |
| Total | $6,400 | to | $15,000 |

It takes considerable skill to construct a 6-foot masonry wall. There are many other landscape projects better suited to doing-it-yourself.

perience for children to help.

Ten to fifteen percent of the cost of the house and property is considered a reasonable investment for basic landscaping. The cost of a screened porch, spa, swimming pool, retaining wall or other major construction is additional.

Financing may be available for construction work, but it may be more difficult to get for planting. One solution is a home-improvement or personal loan. With these loans, you usually pay interest on the total amount borrowed for each year of the loan. This can be expensive. If you have a large equity, consider refinancing or a second mortgage. Either way, you pay simple interest on the *declining* balance, so finance costs are less. Doing the work in phases and paying as you go can save the money you'd pay in interest. But if it takes years to complete a livable landscape, you've lost a lot in enjoyment and use. Explore different alternatives before making a final decision.

## CAPITALIZE ON YOUR CLIMATE

Indigenous architecture usually takes advantage of the best characteristics of a site and helps overcome disadvantages. The prairie-sod house, arctic igloo and tropical thatched hut are suited to their location. They are also oriented to benefit from desirable sun and breezes and to exclude unwanted environmental elements.

The typical mass-produced house is often set on the lot with no regard for exposure. Sliding glass doors may face west. A wide overhang may be found on the north side, where it is least beneficial. Even with good insulation, in some homes heating or air-conditioning must be run most of the year to make them livable.

Few people have the opportunity to start from scratch and design a house to fit a particular site and climate. But most of us *can* do something with the landscape, such as locate the patio in the most desirable exposure. For most areas, this means the southeast or east side of the house. Where cool breezes are a daily occurrence in summer, such as along the ocean, the south side may be more comfortable. A northern exposure, although shaded in summer, is chilly in spring and fall. The west side heats up in late afternoon and evening when you want to relax.

The most logical location for a patio is usually at the back of the house, with privacy and access from the family room or kitchen. When this location is in a hot exposure, a shade trellis, patio roof or screened porch can make it livable, especially when combined with well-placed shade trees. Sometimes a small, secondary sitting area can be a sun-trap for winter warmth. Shaded, it's an escape from summer heat. A sun room or solar greenhouse can add a comfortable, semioutdoor room to use during chilly weather, and it helps conserve heat.

In our desire for year-round foliage, we often overlook the advantage of deciduous trees. They shade the house and patio during the hot months and then allow the welcome sun to enter during the winter. Use small trees to shade the east wall from morning sun, tall trees on the south to shade the roof when the sun is

Traditional "Spring House" provides shade and protection from rain and insects for pleasant back yard relaxing in this Edina, Minnesota garden. Design/build: Landshapes Inc. Landscape architect: Paul H. Barton, ASLA.

high, and low-branching trees on the southwest and west to block low, afternoon sun. Exact placement should be based on the angle of the sun in your latitude, roof height and location of major grass areas.

Lawn and ground covers can reduce glare and radiation, significantly cooling the surrounding area. Windbreaks and fences on the north and northwest can filter strong winter winds and reduce their intensity, saving considerably on heating costs. See *Hedges, Screens and Windbreaks,* pages 68 and 118.

Make the most of your climate by emphasizing seasons rather than concentrating only on spring or summer. Sun-belt residents shiver at the thought of freezing temperatures and blankets of snow. But where else, except the Northeast and Midwest, can you find such a brilliant display of fall color? The beauty of a silent snow scene, accented with berries and bare branches, is unique to the north. When spring arrives, it comes with an exuberance and contrast unknown elsewhere. The heat of summer is even welcome when tempered by shade trees and cool lawns.

Planting with four seasons in mind can extend the beauty of your garden throughout the year, instead of only

**This house in Borneo works *with* the climate. The high-peaked, thatched roof permits hot air to escape and provides protection from torrential rains. Stilt construction allows cool air and high water to flow under the house and discourages cobras from entering—not something everyone has to worry about.**

## STAR PERFORMERS FOR SPRING

*Flowers. Some have attractive new foliage.*

Forsythia
Flowering Almond
Crocus
Narcissus
Red Maple
Cornelian Cherry
Star Magnolia
Daffodil
Tulip
Hyacinth
Flowering Cherry
Flowering Crabapple
Redbud
Azalea
Pea Shrub
Saucer Magnolia
Flowering Dogwood
Mountain Ash
Flowering Quince
Iris
Creeping Phlox
Lily-of-the-Valley
Bradford Pear
Shadblow/Serviceberry
Fringe Tree
Purple-leaf Plum
Horsechestnut

**Forsythia**

**Azalea**

## STAR PERFORMERS FOR SUMMER

*Mostly flowers.*
Yellowwood
Tree Lilac
Japanese Dogwood
Wisteria
Russian Olive
Tulip Tree
Hosta
Ajuga
Deutzia
Mock Orange
Cinquefoil
Pyracantha
Cockspur Thorn
Washington Hawthorn
Viburnum Species
Rhododendron
Abelia
Kerria
Weigela
Trumpet Creeper
Kolkwitzia
Roses
Daylily
Catalpa
Littleleaf Linden
Smoke Tree
Bigleaf Hydrangea
Anthony Waterer Spirea

## STAR PERFORMERS FOR FALL

*Some flowers, mostly fruit and fall color.*
Silk Tree
Japanese Pagoda Tree
Goldenrain Tree
Rose-of-Sharon
Peegee Hydrangea
Viburnum Species
Cotoneaster
Pyracantha
Barberry
Autumn Crocus
Boston Ivy
Burning Bush
Chrysanthemum
Holly
Sugar Maple
Red Maple
American Sweet Gum
Sour Gum

Japanese Dogwood

Bigleaf Hydrangea

Peegee Hydrangea

Viburnum

Washington Hawthorn

American Sweet Gum

## STAR PERFORMERS FOR WINTER

*Fruit, twigs, branches and bark.*
Snowberry
Redosier Dogwood
Yellowtwig Dogwood
Winterberry Holly
Japanese Barberry
Winged Euonymus
Crabapple
Amur Corktree
Viburnum Species
European Mountain Ash
Russian Olive
American Bittersweet
Cockspur Thorn
Korean Barberry
Kentucky Coffeetree
Amur Chokeberry
Bayberry

for a few months. The lists of *Star Performers,* found on this page and pages 17 and 18, are in *approximate* order of peak display. Plants with outstanding flowers, foliage color, fruit and ornamental branches are included. Choosing several plants from each season will ensure year-around interest, and you'll never have to say, "If only you'd been here last month —the garden was beautiful then."

### LEGAL CONSIDERATIONS

In our complex society, even landscaping is subject to restrictions, codes and laws. As in all business transactions, it is advisable to deal only with properly licensed, insured companies. Secure signed contracts that clearly define the work. Receive labor and material releases *before* making final payment.

Verify property lines before starting any work. Check for easements or right-of-way that might limit use of property. Locate septic tanks and leach lines if there is no sewer service. Find out about deed restrictions. Find out if there is an architectural committee that must approve plans. Cooperation with neighbors on fencing, planting and views may not be required legally, but it is usually mutually beneficial. Be careful in placement of large trees that might block views, cause root damage, cast excessive shade or drop piles of leaves on the yard next door.

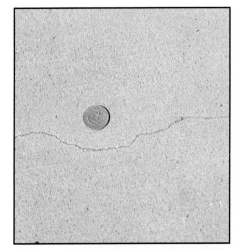

Don't be concerned if a few hairline cracks appear in your concrete—they won't hurt anything. In the past we used a dime to indicate scale, but it's up to a quarter now.

### BUILDING CODES

Most cities and counties have building codes that require permits for landscape work. *Check with the agency having jurisdiction in your area.* Below is a list of common restrictions.

**Grading**—Cuts exceeding 5 feet, fills exceeding 3 feet or movement of more than 50 cubic yards of material may require a permit. Most lots must drain into the street or storm drain, not over banks or onto neighboring property.

**Banks**—Approved erosion control, such as ground cover, shrubs and trees, may be required.

Japanese Barberry

Winterberry

Kentucky Coffeetree

**Spas and Swimming Pools**—Engineering and installation require permits. Power lines may not cross over spas or pools. The location of pumps and other equipment may be restricted.

**Fences**—There is usually a 3-1/2-foot height limitation within a front-yard setback, 6 feet for side and rear yards. Many communities have an ordinance requiring pools and spas to be fenced, with self-closing gates and lockable latches.

**Retaining Walls**—Many agencies have standard designs for walls less than 4 feet high, including the footing. A structural engineer may be required to design retaining walls higher than 4 feet.

**Sprinklers**—Supply lines must be of approved size and material. Anti-siphon devices, to prevent backflow of possibly contaminated water into potable water supply, are required by health departments.

**Lighting and Electrical**—Permits are required for all work, except low-voltage types. Conduit must be buried or protected under paving. Direct-burial cable is now accepted by some departments.

**Parkways**—Property lines normally begin 6 inches back from the sidewalk. This leaves 3 to 10 feet of parkway owned by the city or county to be maintained by the property owner. Paving and plantings are usually restricted within this area. For example, street trees cannot be removed or changed without permission of the city or county. Where the sidewalk is adjacent to the street, the property line or easement is located in the yard to allow for street trees.

**Patio Roofs and Screened Porches**—Design and installation need approval. Aluminum, canvas awnings and detached pergolas of 400 square feet or less are usually exempt. No power lines can pass overhead.

**Gas**—All piping, valves and equipment must be approved.

**Wood Decks**—Footings, spans and railings must conform to building codes for raised decks and decks extending out over a slope.

## CONTRACTOR'S RESPONSIBILITY

Poor drainage, concrete cracks and plant guarantees can become legal problems.

**Water**—Small amounts of standing water are almost unavoidable, especially after a heavy rainstorm. However, large areas that don't drain or paving and planting areas that obviously slope toward the house, usually indicate the need for correction by the contractor.

**Cracks**—Hairline cracks in concrete, as shown in photo on page 19, are inevitable and do not indicate defective work. Some shifting and cracking may occur in expansive soils, even if proper precautions are taken. Large cracks caused by too-thin a pour, laying over dry clay soil with no precautions and lack of required expansion joints are usually considered the contractor's responsibility.

Why can't you cut down a street tree or plant one you like better? Because it's really not on your property. But, in most cities, you have to take care of it. The ginkgo tree is an excellent choice for this narrow parkway.

I was impressed by the excellent and appropriate shearing job the gardener is doing on these shrubs in Hartford, Connecticut. The same treatment could be a disaster on a natural planting.

**Plant Guarantees**—Maintenance is almost always assumed by the homeowner as soon as planting is complete. The question often arises as to who killed a plant—the contractor when planting it or the owner when caring for it. The contractor usually gives a 30- or 60-day guarantee and will replace a few plants, regardless of the cause. If the garden is extremely dry or wet and many plants die, the responsibility may lie with the owner, especially if watering needs were properly explained. Failure of seed to germinate is usually due to improper watering.

## THE LANDSCAPE INDUSTRY

Few people know the difference between the several professions in the landscape industry. Various roles used to be played by one person—now it takes an entire cast. To complicate matters, there is considerable overlapping of parts. The following information helps you know whom to call for what.

**Landscape Architect**—This is an expert qualified to design outdoor areas. He is required to be licensed in most states. Training is comparable to that of an architect or engineer. He usually holds a degree from an accredited university and often has additional experience in other phases of the industry. The initials *ASLA* signify membership in the American Society of Landscape Architects. The initials *FASLA* signify a member is a Fellow, which is an honorary title.

A landscape architect does not sell a specific plant or product but strives to create the best living environment possible for the client. He receives payment through professional fees instead of discounts or profits. A landscape architect considers total site development, including structural elements, along with plantings and

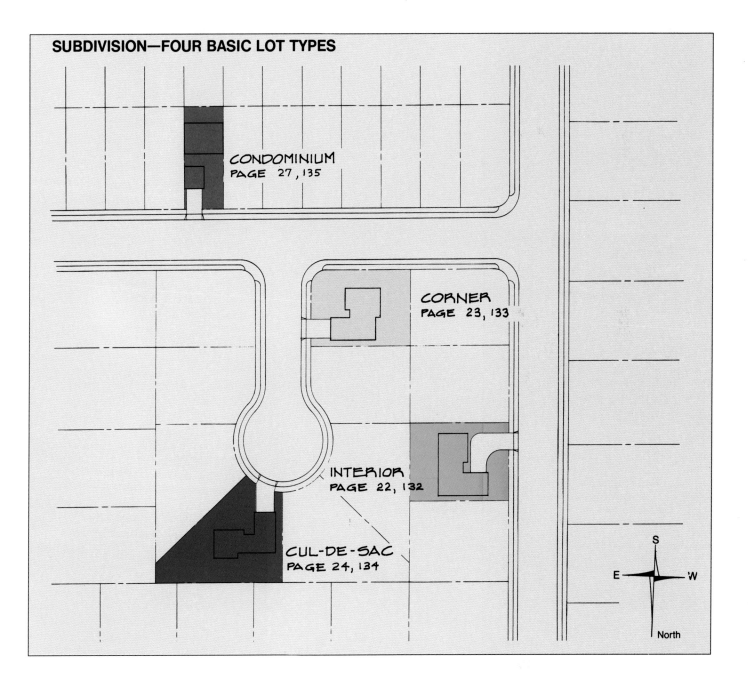

SUBDIVISION—FOUR BASIC LOT TYPES

CONDOMINIUM
PAGE 27, 135

CORNER
PAGE 23, 133

INTERIOR
PAGE 22, 132

CUL-DE-SAC
PAGE 24, 134

If you find it difficult to plan a large area, such as the one shown above, contact a landscape architect or landscape designer. Lanscape architect: Andrew L. Sparks, ASLA, with Land Techniques.

sprinklers. When possible, call one while a tract house is still under construction. On custom houses, the landscape architect should collaborate with the architect when the house is being designed.

**Landscape Contractor**—This person is also licensed in most states. The landscape contractor installs the garden based on plans of the landscape architect. He handles planting and usually installs paving, sprinklers and outdoor structures. Sometimes his own crew does all the work. At other times, he functions as a general contractor, making sure subcontractors perform their work properly. Most landscape contractors belong to an association, such as the *ALCA* (Associated Landscape Contractors of America) or a state organization. These organizations help them keep abreast of the latest developments and methods.

**Nurseryman**—The nurseryman is charged with the important job of supplying plant material for a garden. He often grows some of the plants himself and orders the rest from wholesale growers. He tries to keep a stock of healthy, well-grown plants of suitable size.

A nurseryman does not make substitutions for difficult-to-find plants on a plan. He advises the owner to ask the landscape architect if a substitute is in order. A nurseryman is usually qualified to offer general planting and maintenance advice and often is an expert on local climatic conditions.

In some states, a nurseryman may have *certification*. This means he has satisfied specific requirements of competency and experience. Many nurserymen belong to the *AAN* (American Association of Nurserymen), a state organization or various horticultural societies.

**Gardener**—The highly complex art of gardening takes many years of training and experience. Unfortunately, there is no state registration that assures a homeowner a gardener is qualified. City licenses are for tax purposes only. Most good gardeners are in such fields as golf course, park, cemetery, commercial and estate maintenance.

As a homeowner, carefully assess the ability of an individual gardener. Keep close watch on the work and be prepared to pay a fair price for his time. Clarify if watering is to be the gardener's responsibility or if you intend to do it. Partial services—cutting and edging lawns, general cleanup and weeding—are more common than complete care.

When a gardener is totally in charge of a garden, he receives the finished product from the landscape contractor. The gardener guides it to its ultimate form. He must be receptive to the intent of the landscape architect and owner. He may make many interpretations of his own as years pass. If you are thinking of a casual, natural effect, and your gardener shears everything into a sphere or cube, there's bound to be trouble. Explain what your personal preferences are *before* hiring anyone.

**Landscape Designer**—This title is often used by people engaged in landscape design but unlicensed as landscape architects. Some are well-qualified; some are not. You have no way of knowing from the title alone. A landscape designer may be in business for himself or work though a contractor or nursery.

**Multiple Roles**—Confusion is caused by overlapping services. Some nurserymen and gardeners design and install gardens. Some landscape contractors offer planning services. Some landscape architects are also landscape contractors. With proper licensing, this is not illegal. There is much to be said in favor of efficiency under multiple businesses. Small towns may not be able to support a design specialist. Many design/build firms have qualified people in both roles and do outstanding work.

Commercial interests can limit the availability of these services. Spreading talent and energy over several fields can result in lower-quality services. Take time to look at completed jobs. Check out the reputation of anyone you decide to hire.

## LANDSCAPE-DESIGN SERVICES AND FEES

There are three reasons why many homeowners don't hire a landscape architect to design their property. First, they think it is too expensive. Second, they're afraid their own ideas will be disregarded. Third, many landscape architects are involved in large projects and are not available for residential design.

**Expense**—Fees vary with the job and each landscape architect. Most charge a consultation fee of $50 to $100 to visit the site and offer ideas and advice. This is an inexpensive way to get a professional's input without being obligated any further. If additional consultation or a plan is desired, many landscape architects charge for their services on an hourly basis. This usually includes an estimated range of time for specific work. Others charge a percentage of construction cost or a lump-sum fee.

Typical costs for an average residence can be as little as $200 for a planting plan to over $1,000 for a total basic plan service that includes design of outdoor living areas. Price depends on the size and complexity of the site, amount of structure, overall budget and the client-designer relationship. The basic-plan service normally includes an initial meeting on the site, one preliminary plan, a cost estimate, site review and construction drawings based on the approved preliminary plan. Preparation of the basic plot, major revisions or changes in the scope of the work, securing of bids and supervision are usually additional.

For a small property, a portion of a garden or a simple development, some landscape architects provide a one-trip service. They do a rough design at the site. Drafting and details are completed at the office, and final prints are delivered by mail. This method eliminates a lot of drafting and travel time while providing the essential design concept. This efficient way of working ranges in cost from $200 to $500.

A landscape architect can also provide valuable services in addition to drawing plans for a new garden. Among them are property selection; siting of the house; collaboration with the building architect on basic house design; selection of a house already built; general consultation; addition of a patio roof, shade trellis, swimming pool or spa; design of part of a garden; remodeling an existing garden; and maintenance advice.

**Your Wishes**—Most landscape architects encourage as much client participation as possible. Having a list of things desired and a portfolio of pictures and drawings is helpful.

**Architect Availability**—This may be a problem. Spring and fall are usually busy seasons. It may be easier to find a landscape architect during summer or winter. When a registered landscape architect isn't available, it may be possible to get help from a landscape designer. Fees are usually lower than a landscape architect, although in many cases, charges and methods of operation are similar.

## INTRODUCTION TO MASTER LANDSCAPE PLANS

My mathematically minded son tells me if I took the four basic lot types, shown on the next four pages, with four basic styles, four basic climates and four different orientations to the sun, the total equals 256 possible master plans. If you add the factors of family composition, budget and maintenance preference, the figure could be astronomical.

The overall feeling of a certain style and the family's needs determine garden uses. Climate and orientation also influence design, especially plant selection. The climate zone mentioned at the bottom of each plan refers to the map on page 81.

Sample plans in this book are designed to help you choose ideas and solutions that apply to your specific situation. Plans may appear complicated and confusing at first, but after looking at them several times, they should become clearer. If you're lucky, you might discover you're someone who can project the plan into three dimensions in your mind.

## MASTER PLAN—Interior Lot

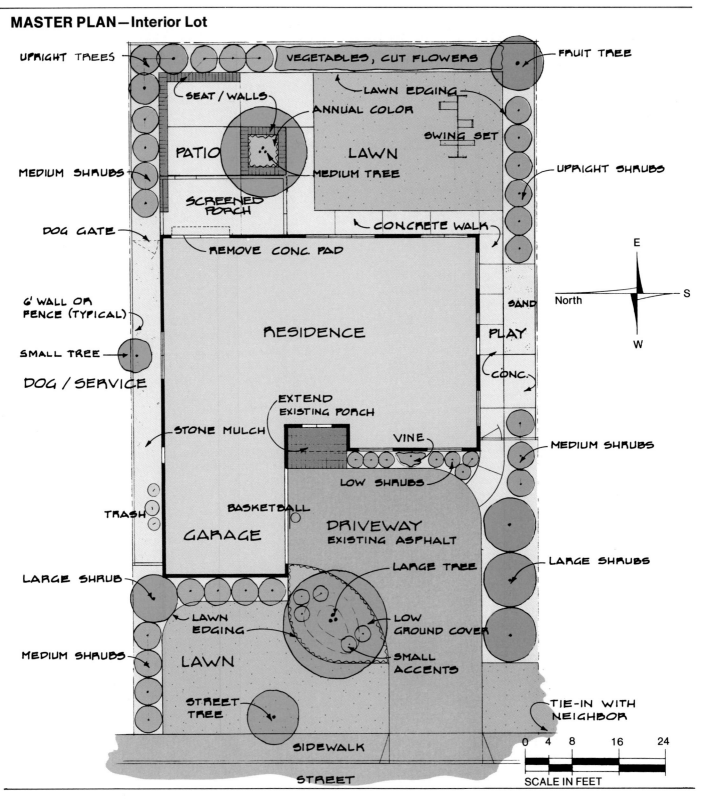

Labels on plan:

UPRIGHT TREES
VEGETABLES, CUT FLOWERS
FRUIT TREE
SEAT / WALLS
LAWN EDGING
ANNUAL COLOR
PATIO
LAWN
SWING SET
MEDIUM SHRUBS
UPRIGHT SHRUBS
SCREENED PORCH
MEDIUM TREE
DOG GATE
REMOVE CONC. PAD
CONCRETE WALK
6' WALL OR FENCE (TYPICAL)
RESIDENCE
SAND
PLAY
E / North / S / W
SMALL TREE
DOG / SERVICE
CONC.
EXTEND EXISTING PORCH
STONE MULCH
VINE
MEDIUM SHRUBS
LOW SHRUBS
BASKETBALL
DRIVEWAY EXISTING ASPHALT
TRASH
GARAGE
LARGE TREE
LARGE SHRUBS
LARGE SHRUB
LAWN EDGING
LOW GROUND COVER
MEDIUM SHRUBS
LAWN
SMALL ACCENTS
STREET TREE
TIE-IN WITH NEIGHBOR
SIDEWALK
STREET
0  4  8  16  24
SCALE IN FEET

### Assumed Conditions

- Zone 6.
- Young family with small children.
- Modest budget.
- Medium to low maintenance.

### Design Considerations

- *Combination* style.
- No particular style is emphasized. Overall effect is neat, simple and organized.

- Children have ample play area in side and back yards, with front basketball area and separate side entrance for when they get older.
- Screened porch provides rain and insect protection for outdoor dining; patio is shaded by tree.
- Ample paving, stone mulch and restrained planting is easy to maintain.

See Planting Plan for Interior Lot, page 132.

## MASTER PLAN—Corner Lot

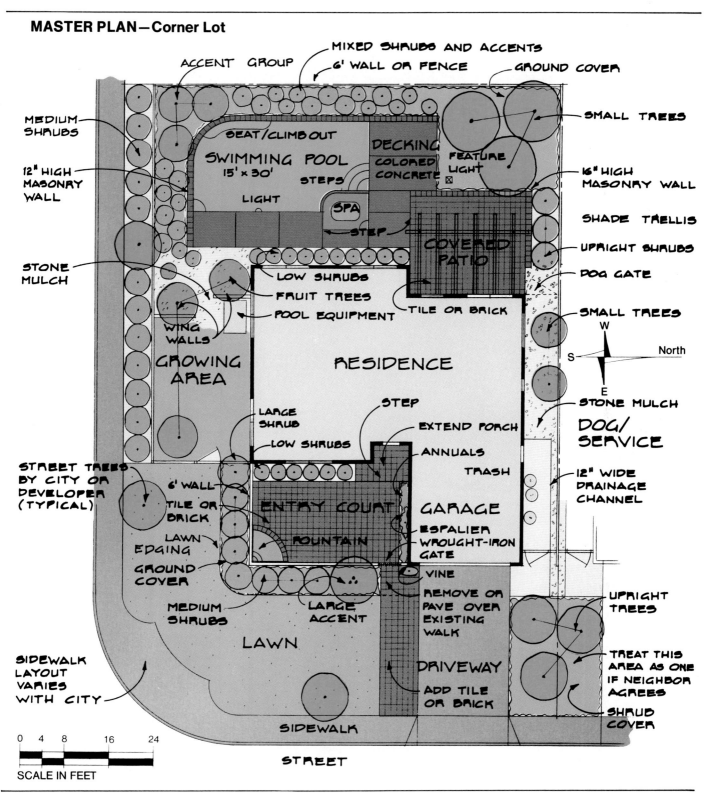

**Assumed Conditions**

- Zone 5.
- Active couple with no children. Frequent parties and entertaining.
- Ample budget.
- Medium to high maintenance.

**Design Considerations**

- *Contemporary* style.
- Dramatic use of paving, structure, lighting and bold plant materials carry out the contemporary theme.
- Covered patio and small swimming pool with built-in spa are ideal for entertaining.
- Paving added to driveway allows room for both cars and people. Enclosed entry court is comfortable for evening sitting.
- Growing area makes use of large, sunny side yard.

See Planting Plan for Corner Lot, page 133.

# MASTER PLAN—Cul-de-sac Lot

## Assumed Conditions

- Zone 4.
- Family with teenage children, lots of relatives.
- Average budget.
- Medium maintenance.

## Design Considerations

- *Natural* style.
- Contours, boulders, stone walls and paving, wood path lights, stone mulch and free-flowing lines contribute to natural effect.
- Extra parking is included for RV and teenagers' cars.
- Multi-use game court and open lawn are ideal for family games.
- Patio has choice of sun or shade. Fire pit extends use into evening.

See Planting Plan for Cul-de-sac Lot, page 134.

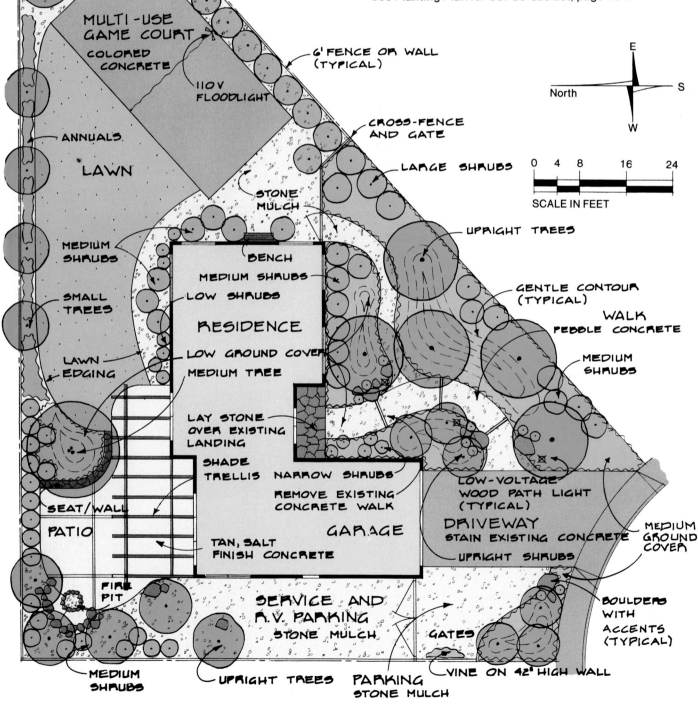

UPRIGHT TREES

MULTI-USE GAME COURT
COLORED CONCRETE

6' FENCE OR WALL (TYPICAL)

110V FLOODLIGHT

CROSS-FENCE AND GATE

ANNUALS.

LAWN

LARGE SHRUBS

STONE MULCH

UPRIGHT TREES

MEDIUM SHRUBS

BENCH
MEDIUM SHRUBS
LOW SHRUBS

RESIDENCE

GENTLE CONTOUR (TYPICAL)

WALK
PEBBLE CONCRETE

SMALL TREES

LAWN EDGING

LOW GROUND COVER
MEDIUM TREE

MEDIUM SHRUBS

LAY STONE OVER EXISTING LANDING

SHADE TRELLIS   NARROW SHRUBS

REMOVE EXISTING CONCRETE WALK

LOW-VOLTAGE WOOD PATH LIGHT (TYPICAL)

SEAT/WALL

PATIO

GARAGE

DRIVEWAY
STAIN EXISTING CONCRETE

MEDIUM GROUND COVER

UPRIGHT SHRUBS

TAN, SALT FINISH CONCRETE

FIRE PIT

SERVICE AND R.V. PARKING
STONE MULCH

BOULDERS WITH ACCENTS (TYPICAL)

GATES

MEDIUM SHRUBS

UPRIGHT TREES

PARKING
STONE MULCH

VINE ON 42" HIGH WALL

E
North   S
W

SCALE IN FEET
0   4   8   16   24

# MASTER PLAN—Condo Lot

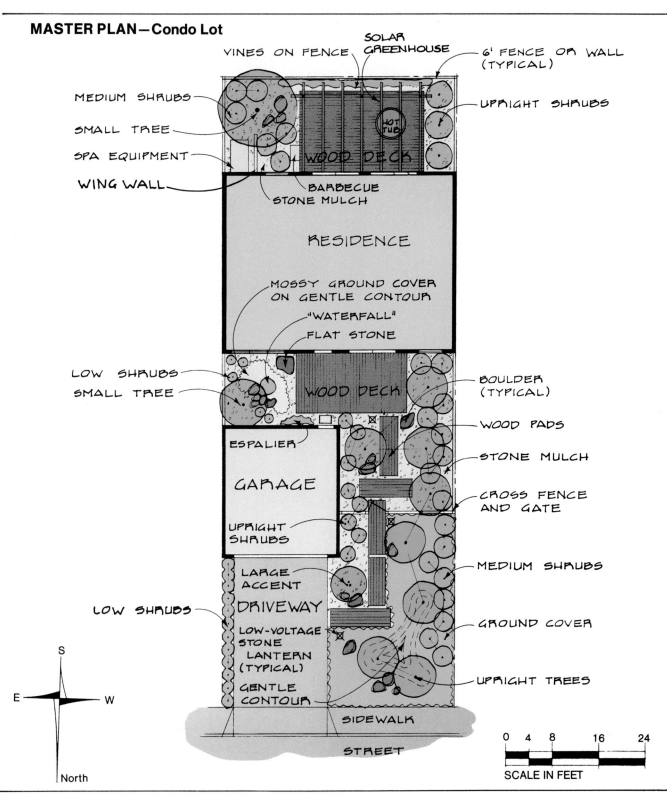

VINES ON FENCE

SOLAR GREENHOUSE

6' FENCE OR WALL (TYPICAL)

MEDIUM SHRUBS

SMALL TREE

SPA EQUIPMENT

WING WALL

UPRIGHT SHRUBS

HOT TUB

WOOD DECK

BARBECUE STONE MULCH

RESIDENCE

MOSSY GROUND COVER ON GENTLE CONTOUR

"WATERFALL"

FLAT STONE

LOW SHRUBS

SMALL TREE

WOOD DECK

BOULDER (TYPICAL)

WOOD PADS

STONE MULCH

CROSS FENCE AND GATE

ESPALIER

GARAGE

UPRIGHT SHRUBS

MEDIUM SHRUBS

LOW SHRUBS

LARGE ACCENT

DRIVEWAY

LOW-VOLTAGE STONE LANTERN (TYPICAL)

GENTLE CONTOUR

GROUND COVER

UPRIGHT TREES

SIDEWALK

STREET

S
E W
North

0 4 8 16 24
SCALE IN FEET

## Assumed Conditions

- Zone 3.
- Retired or working couple, no children.
- Ample budget.
- Low maintenance.

## Design Considerations

- *Oriental* style.
- Wood decks, boulders, stone mulch, natural water feature, contours and lanterns give Oriental feeling.

- Front wood walk and deck provide a gracious entry and sitting area.
- Water feature can be viewed from both inside and outside.
- Back deck with hot tub and barbecue is protected by solar greenhouse. Fences, shrubs and vines are used for privacy.

See Planting Plan for Condo Lot, page 135.

# Relaxing and Entertaining

Travel with a family is expensive. Lakes, beaches, campgrounds, parks and other vacation spots are often crowded. Home recreation is convenient, inexpensive and more restful than harried trips.

Consider your yard an outdoor room that needs a floor, walls and a partial roof. Incorporate into your design some of your family's favorite activities. Allow for cooking and gracious entertaining areas. Then you will have a garden that not only looks good but also serves living and recreational needs.

Begin with the entrance. Most arrivals are by automobile, so be sure there is enough parking and unloading space. Standard driveways can be widened to allow for easier walking and extra parking. If you have a boat, trailer or camper, store it out of sight, such as next to the garage.

Guests appreciate a walkway next to the curbing. A wide, gracious walk is an inviting approach to the front door. When your home has a typical 3-foot-wide walk, consider adding to it so it's more in scale with the house and property. If the only path from the street to the front door is the driveway, it may be better to build a separate walkway. But this could cut up a small yard. If it does, it might be better to use the driveway as part of the walkway, then branch off for a special entrance treatment close to the house.

A generous landing or porch with a convenient bench is good for saying hello and goodbye to friends. You'll probably have to expand what's already there to improve scale and usability.

Landscape architect Paul H. Barton, ASLA, of Landshapes Inc., turned this difficult entry into a dramatic feature with timber steps.

Bold, sweeping driveway makes an impressive approach to this Indianapolis home. Owner: Fred Grumme. Landscape Architect: Claire Bennett Associates, FASLA.

Brick stairs are well-lighted at night for safety. They impart a warm, welcome feeling to visitors.

Left: A gracious entry walkway welcomes guests to the front door.

**Appropriate furniture is important. This white wrought-iron set seems perfect for this secluded patio.**

**Rocking chairs and carefully placed plantings can turn a covered porch into a bonus sitting area. Landscape architect: Steve Coenen.**

## PATIOS AND TERRACES

The terms *patio* and *terrace* are used interchangeably. For convenience, we'll call them patios. Patios should be pleasing to look at, but they are mainly for people to use. Situate patios to make the most of climate and orientation. You may need more than one patio if the choice is between warm-and-protected or cool-and-breezy.

There's nothing wrong with using a lawn instead of a patio, but it does have limitations. Grass is often wet, furniture sinks in and heavy use in a concentrated area causes compacting and eventual deterioration. You usually need some solid paving, then use the lawn for overflow from family picnics and large groups.

A successful patio must be large enough for entertaining guests but should have an intimate feeling for family use. An 8x10' space can hold a table and chairs, but it would be cramped. A 15x25' space is a minimum size. This allows for furniture, a barbecue, storage and room to move about without stubbing a toe. Consider privacy, wind protection and the relationship to the kitchen or family room. If a patio is too far from the house, in the prevailing wind or within view of the neighbors, it may not get much use.

A properly located patio shaded by the house or existing trees may be comfortable without additional shade. However, a shade tree or roof is almost essential. A shade trellis of

**Low brick wall defines outdoor living terrace. Well-chosen furniture, pots of geraniums and handsome light fixtures complete the setting. Landscape architect: Claire Bennett Associates, FASLA.**

open latticework filters sun without excluding light from adjacent rooms. A solid roof costs more but provides protection from the elements. Add screened-in areas where mosquitoes and other insects are bothersome. Glass porches and solar greenhouses are a good way to extend the outdoor living season into colder months.

## PATIO ROOFS, TRELLISES AND SCREENED PORCHES

Many general building contractors find building patio roofs too small a job—they'd rather build houses. Many landscape contractors consider the job a nuisance and try to avoid getting involved. Most homeowners don't want to build one themselves.

These shade trellis posts are set on top of the retaining wall. The built-in wood bench eliminates the need for space-consuming furniture.

By repeating materials and colors from the house, a screened porch can look like an integral part of the original house.

Three choices for outdoor living: lawn, wood deck or screened porch. Landscape architect: Paul H. Barton, ASLA, with Landshapes Inc.

Try to find a company specializing in patio construction. If you can't, one solution is to work with a carpenter, contributing as much as you're able.

Basic framing is the same, whether the roof is solid or open. Lumber costs about $300 for an overhead area of 200 square feet. Add $100 for 2x2s or $200 for 1x6 sheathing and mineral-coated roll roofing. A good price from a contractor doing all the work is $5 per square foot for a shade trellis and $10 per square foot for a shed-type solid roof with open walls and roll-type roofing. Screen and glass walls obviously cost more. The patio floor and staining or painting are additional. Shingle and tile roofs require a steeper pitch and cost more than roll-type roofing.

Most experienced carpenters are strong on construction and weak on design. If you can show a carpenter the example you like, have him look at it before giving you a bid.

By using one wall of the house for support, it's a simple task to attach a patio roof or trellis. A screened porch is similar but built more like an actual room. The trick is to make the addition look like part of the original construction and not an unrelated afterthought. Repeat existing house materials and colors to make it more harmonious. See *Highlights of Construction,* page 33.

Oversized rafters, beams and posts are more in scale with the outdoors than minimum dimensions. Use 3x6 or 4x6 rafters instead of 2x6s. Enhance standard 4x4 posts and 4x8 beams with *plant-ons* of 1x2 or larger strips for a built-up effect. Most building departments have span charts indicating minimum lumber sizes. They can offer over-the-counter advice. A building permit is required by most agencies, and footings must be inspected before pouring concrete. Setback distances from property lines must also be complied with.

Rafters alone seldom provide sufficient shade. Usually, a covering made of 2x2s or lath is added on top, at right angles to rafters. Spacing determines the amount of shade. The closer together the covering, the less sunlight gets through. Grapestakes, 2x3s, 1x2s, bamboo poles, netting and various types of shade cloth can also be used.

Removable panels allow for more sun during the cool months, but they are a nuisance to take off and store. The best way to determine how much shade you need is to first finish the framework. Then lay whatever material you've selected on top, without

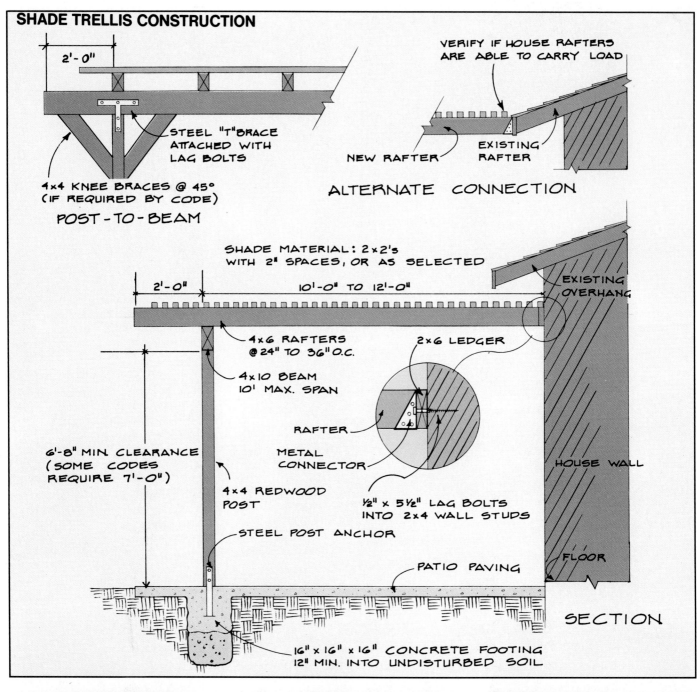

## SHADE TRELLIS CONSTRUCTION

2'-0"

STEEL "T" BRACE
ATTACHED WITH
LAG BOLTS

4x4 KNEE BRACES @ 45°
(IF REQUIRED BY CODE)

POST-TO-BEAM

VERIFY IF HOUSE RAFTERS
ARE ABLE TO CARRY LOAD

NEW RAFTER

EXISTING
RAFTER

ALTERNATE CONNECTION

SHADE MATERIAL: 2x2's
WITH 2" SPACES, OR AS SELECTED

2'-0"        10'-0" TO 12'-0"

EXISTING
OVERHANG

4x6 RAFTERS
@ 24" TO 36" O.C.

2x6 LEDGER

4x10 BEAM
10' MAX. SPAN

RAFTER

6'-8" MIN CLEARANCE
(SOME CODES
REQUIRE 7'-0")

METAL
CONNECTOR

HOUSE WALL

4x4 REDWOOD
POST

½" x 5½" LAG BOLTS
INTO 2x4 WALL STUDS

STEEL POST ANCHOR

PATIO PAVING

FLOOR

SECTION

16" x 16" x 16" CONCRETE FOOTING
12" MIN. INTO UNDISTURBED SOIL

This built-up post is made using two 2x8s
with a 4x4 inside.

Another way to build up a post is to nail
1x2s on all four sides of the 4x4.

*Knee braces* can be turned into a design
feature with a little fancy sawing.

# HIGHLIGHTS OF CONSTRUCTION

Post anchor was set in concrete patio with footing below. Bolts will be put through the post to prevent shifting. If you must leave a post anchor unused for any period, cover it to avoid accidents.

Connect rafters to the house with steel fasteners lag-bolted directly to a ledger plate. This is stronger and usually preferable to attaching to an existing roof overhang. Existing fascia is notched to receive the rafters.

Steel fasteners are also used for post-to-beam and rafter-to-beam connections. They are stronger than toenailing. Bolts are stronger than nails for anchoring fasteners.

The 2x3s are shifted to test desired shade density before nailing permanently.

This *knee brace* is required by most building departments to eliminate side sway or *shear.* The steel "T" brace is too small to do the job alone.

Effectiveness of 2x3s is shown by the shade pattern on the previously sun-drenched wall.

Lath strips make an attractive and relatively inexpensive shade covering.

Sometimes an open framework is all that's needed if there's a tree to help out.

nailing it down. Determine if you like it or want a different shade density.

Other structural considerations are footings, size of posts, connection to house, shear bracing and sheathing. A 16-inch square concrete footing, extending below the frost line with a steel post-strap to receive the post, is adequate for most situations. If the patio may be enclosed as a room some day, include a continuous footing at the future wall line.

Post size is seldom an engineering problem. A decay-resistant 4x4 or a 2-1/2-inch steel-pipe column is enough to support most patio roofs. You may want to use 6x6 posts if you're looking for a heavy-timber effect. Pipe columns look better if encased in brick or stone. Decorative wrought-iron supports give an airy effect.

Attach only a light shade structure to an existing overhang. The best procedure is to bolt a 2x6 *ledger* to the house wall, directly underneath the existing overhang. Attach rafters to the ledger with metal connectors.

Shear bracing is needed to keep the roof from moving sideways, parallel to the house wall. This can be accomplished with *knee braces* at the posts. They do the job but look terrible. A better way is to bolt steel *"T" braces* to the post and beam if your local building department allows this. Steel-pipe columns set 3 feet deep in concrete provide shear support and eliminate the need for braces.

Ferns thrive under this shade cloth stretched over 4x6 rafters.

Beauté la terre Designs used a handsome wood trellis to tame the Kansas summer for people and plants. Photo: Kala Busby.

Sheathing is important for patio roofs because it is seen from below. Tongue-and-groove 1x6s are a standard size and easy to install.

## SHADE TREES

One disadvantage of using a shade tree to cool a patio is growing time. Fast growers, such as honey locust, fruitless mulberry and green ash, will take 4 or 5 years to do the job, even if you start with a 5- to 6-foot tree. Where there is access, you can plant a large-specimen tree for about the same cost as constructing a shade trellis. You'll be able to sit under the spreading branches the day the tree is planted.

## PERGOLAS AND GAZEBOS

Pergolas and gazebos are other ways to provide shade. A pergola is a free-standing structure, usually consisting of simple posts, beams and rafters of heavy timber. Vines, such as grape, wisteria, climbing rose and clematis, are frequently planted at each post for additional shade.

Gazebos are also free-standing but are lighter weight and semienclosed. Hexagonal shapes are most popular, although squares are easier to build. Lath is a common gazebo covering in a right-angle or diamond pattern for a Victorian look. Ready-to-assemble precut kits can simplify the job. You can have fun and save part of the cost by putting it together yourself.

Change materials and design to fit your chosen garden style. You can create an Oriental teahouse, an old-world iron cage or a modern geodesic dome. They all provide an inviting, shady sitting area.

If you can master the center connection, you can build almost any gazebo.

A nice place to sip a cool drink and enjoy the view of a sparkling beach in the Bahamas.

Precut gazebo kit was easy to install. Brick planter gives it a built-in look.

Old-world gazebo of iron grillework and stone columns is more of a sculpture than a place to sit.

A solid roof is worth considering if you want rain protection for sitting and outdoor dining.

## BARBECUES AND FIRE PITS

Cooking outdoors is natural for summer evenings. Prefabricated gas barbecues are convenient, or you can use charcoal. Move portable barbecues out of the wind, and store them out of sight when not in use. Built-in counters and storage spaces save repeated trips indoors. Fire pits extend comfort into chilly evening hours. It's great to gather around a friendly fire after a session in a pool or spa.

**Above: This fire pit uses radiant heat from volcanic rock to make the most of a natural-gas fire.**

**Left: Prefabricated gas barbecue is efficient and unobtrusive.**

**Right: Landscape architect Raymond J. Rolfe, ASLA, included counter space with storage below twin built-in gas barbeque units. Conveniently located next to a dining deck, the cook can be part of the fun while tending to the cooking.**

**Swing sets have almost universal appeal. This one is actually in far-off Malacca.**

## PLAY AREAS

Play areas and game areas can serve everyone in the family and provide activities to share with guests. Avoid creating an expensive, unattractive area that takes up space and is seldom used.

Family interests vary over the years. Children outgrow sandboxes and swing sets. Teenagers may play a certain game for months, then are bored by it. Adults are just as fickle in their preferences. Temporary, expendable, convertible, multiuse areas are often better than unchangeable, permanent installations.

Preschoolers may accept being fenced in for a while, with mother watching from the house. They soon outgrow the enclosure and are happier if allowed to play in the entire yard rather than one small area. Some children ignore elaborately contrived apparatus. They may end up digging a hole in the dirt or building a house out of boxes and scrap lumber. Imagination and creativity are more important than a sophisticated structure that pleases parents.

Don't overlook the ever-popular swing set. When placed on a lawn, it requires no garden remodeling after removal. A sandbox or pile of sand is also a favorite with young children. It's easily disposable when no longer used.

Standard-sized playing courts for badminton or volleyball take a lot of space, especially when proper clearance is allowed for safety and to avoid damage to nearby plants. The chart below shows the space required for specific activities. Make a cut-out the same scale as your plan, and move it around the layout to see where it fits best.

You may find you don't have the space required. Don't despair. Most playing courts can be scaled down and still be fun. Even as small an area as 20x40' can work well for badminton, volleyball, tetherball and half-court basketball.

If it's a choice between having a lawn or paving the back yard, badminton, volleyball and croquet can be played on a tough grass, such as tall fescue, hybrid bermuda or zoysia. Grass is also usable for mini-games of baseball and football.

If your driveway or motor court is wide enough, it may serve double-duty for games such as basketball and tetherball. It should be level and safe from street traffic. If you live in a classy neighborhood, you may want to use removable poles and a fold-down basketball backboard so you don't offend neighbors.

Table tennis is enjoyed by all ages. The table is easy to move around and store. The game can be played on a lawn, but paving is better. A garage is fine for the average game. Outside, locate it out of the wind, with some shade for daytime games.

Dancing, archery, catch and similar activities that require no special or elaborate installation are no problem. A horseshoe court can be installed at relatively small cost. Shuffleboard can be marked off on any long, relatively smooth concrete area. A full-size, specially constructed court is seldom worth the cost unless the game is played quite often.

A tennis court is a major investment, and it takes up a great deal of space. Build one *only* after careful investigation. A possible alternative is

A 30x60' game court turned this back yard into a popular recreation area for family and friends. Construction by Sport Court.

paddle tennis. It requires about half the space and is also a challenging game.

Give a swimming pool a lot of thought before building one. A discussion of pools, spas and hot tubs begins on page 72.

A shaded place where spectators

can sit is a welcome addition to any recreation area. It can be a low wall, steps or a bench. To save wear and tear on the kitchen, an outside drinking fountain is also a good idea. Provide adequate lighting for evening use, but avoid glare on neighboring property.

## Space Requirements For Outdoor Activities

| Activity | Actual Size in Feet | Total Space in Feet Required |
|---|---|---|
| Badminton | 20 x 44 | 30 x 60 |
| Basketball | 50 x 94 | 60 x 100 |
| Croquet | 30 x 60 | 40 x 75 |
| Horseshoes | 8 x 50 | 12 x 60 |
| Paddle Tennis | 20 x 44 | 35 x 70 |
| Table Tennis | 5 x 9 | 12 x 20 |
| Shuffleboard | 6 x 52 | 10 x 60 |
| Spa or Hot Tub | 6 (diameter) | 14 (diameter) |
| Swimming Pool | 16 x 36 | 28 x 52 |
| Swing Set | 6 x 12 | 16 x 20 |
| Tennis | 36 x 78 | 60 x 120 |
| Tetherball | 6 (diameter) | 20 x 20 |
| Volleyball | 30 x 60 | 45 x 80 |

## PAVING

A large part of a garden may be covered with a solid surface. Function should dictate the form and size the paved area takes. Don't skimp on size of paved areas. Large areas of well-designed paving increase the usability of a garden, reduce maintenance and can be attractive.

Use of the area determines which materials are most suitable. Appropriateness to site and personal preference narrow the choice, and cost influences the final decision. Cost can be reduced considerably if you do some of the labor yourself.

After you record the shape and extent of various paved areas on the plan, concentrate on selecting the type of paving to use. The following descriptions and the paving-materials chart on page 53 will help you wade through the bewildering number of options.

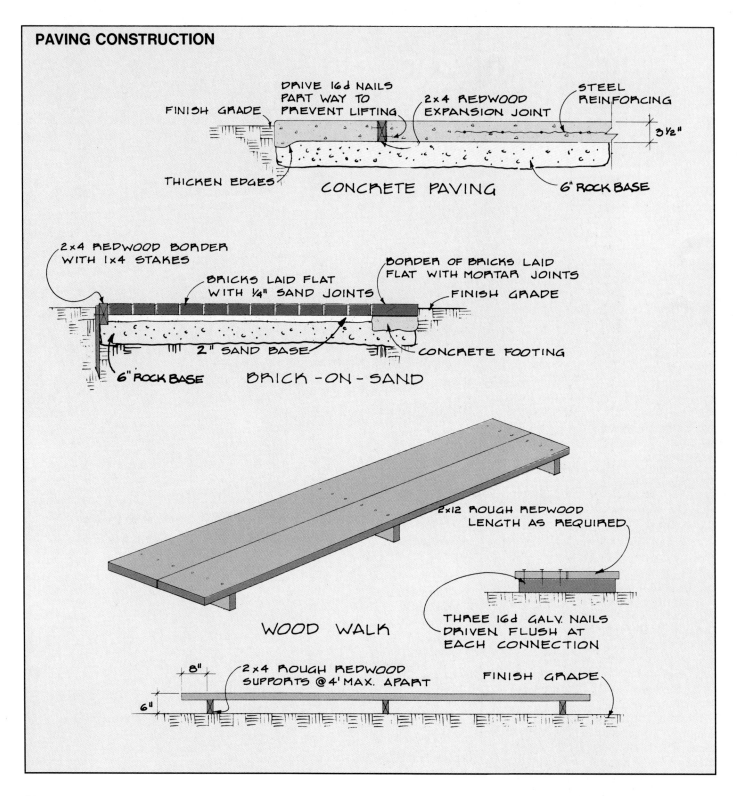

PAVING CONSTRUCTION

# LAYING CONCRETE

Forms made with 2x4s are easy to work with and strong enough to hold the fluid concrete in place. A 6-inch base of rock dust, decomposed granite or similar material helps prevent cracking on any soil but is essential on clay soils.

Right: Concrete is struck off or *screeded* with a straight 2x4. Low spots are filled in along the way.

Using a *bull-float* takes a delicate touch. A float with no handle, called a *darby*, is used for walks and small areas.

Right: An edger is used after initial troweling while concrete is still workable. Edges that aren't rounded look bad and break off easily. The surface texture will be determined by final troweling or brooming.

## CONCRETE

Concrete is the most widely used garden paving material. It is durable, practical, relatively inexpensive and available in a variety of types and treatments. Choose a surface that is non-skid and colored or textured to break glare. Divide it for design interest and to prevent cracking. Place expansion joints at corners, stress points and through areas larger than 200 square feet. Redwood 2x4s, vinyl dividers and deep-driven joints look better than commonly used fiber strips. Shallow scribe lines are of little value in preventing cracks.

In clay soils that expand when wet, soak the subsoil before laying concrete to avoid raising and cracking. A 6-inch-deep base, such as crushed rock, sand or cinders, minimizes frost heaving. Add wire mesh or steel-bar reinforcing as a safeguard against major cracks. Hairline cracks are almost unavoidable and are not cause for concern.

Concrete requires 1/8- to 3/16-inch pitch per foot for good drainage. Allow a little more for pebble and pattern finishes. Pouring concrete, especially large areas, is not a job for an amateur. If you want to do part of the job yourself, consider grading, laying forms and assisting an experienced finisher.

One cubic yard of ready-mix covers about 80 square feet, 3-1/2 inches thick. Order a little extra so you don't run short. You can also use redwood or other dividers to cut the job into small units that don't have to be done all at once. Ready-mix comes in minimum loads of 3 to 6 cubic yards. Mix it yourself in a wheelbarrow, or rent a mixer when doing only a few square feet at one time.

TIP—A good concrete mix:
- 1 part cement.
- 2-1/2 parts washed sand.
- 2-1/2 parts 3/4-inch crushed rock aggregate.
- 5 gallons of water per sack of cement.

# VARIATIONS WITH CONCRETE

Rock salt is sprinkled on wet concrete at a rate of 5 to 10 pounds per 100 square feet and tamped in with a wood float. It is dissolved with water after the concrete hardens. Post anchor is for 4x4 post.

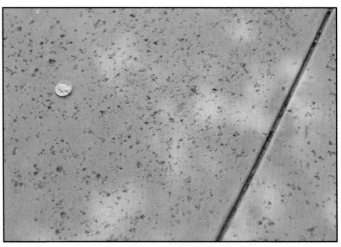

Tan, salt-finished concrete has a deep-driven joint.

Concrete is a fluid material. Its shape is determined by the forms. This entrance walkway has a stone-like quality. Landscape architect: Roy Seifert for Dr. and Mrs. George Zucconi.

Plain concrete, exposed-pebble concrete and railroad ties are combined in these handsome steps by landscape contractor Bill Peterson. Note louvered step lights recessed into railroad ties.

Troweled-on topping is cool to the feet. It is an excellent surface for pool decking in hot areas.

Owner John Mrak did a neat acid-staining job to give this concrete walk a flagstone-like appearance.

Colored concrete is impressed with a patented steel or plastic form to impart an antique-block paving effect.

# LAYING COBBLESTONE

Cobblestone paving is a good do-it-yourself project. First, large round stones are tapped into a 2-inch bed of sand until level.

Mortar is used to fill in between the stones and tooled until firm.

Surface is cleaned with a brush and water so that stones are visible.

Finished paving fits perfectly with railroad ties and looks a hundred years old. Landscape architect: Jack Smith, ASLA.

Pebble concrete with a redwood 2x4 divider. The crushed rock was part of the concrete mix. It was rough troweled then exposed with a fine spray of water.

Hand-set stone paving is fun to do yourself. The contracted cost is quite high because of the time involved.

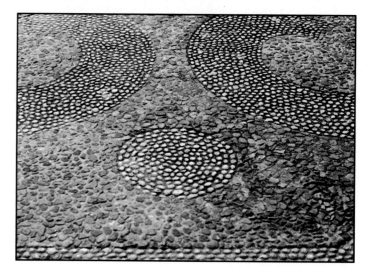

Brick-on-sand is set on a 2-inch sand base. A 2x4, notched the thickness of a brick, levels the sand to the proper depth.

Fine sand is swept into the joints to make a firm surface. No mortar is needed.

## BRICK

Brick is an outstanding garden paving because of the many sizes, colors and patterns available. Common red bricks are medium hard. They are about 4 inches by 8 inches and a little more than 2 inches thick. Allow five bricks per square foot. This amount allows for some breakage.

You can also use bricks that are smoother or harder, thinner or thicker, wider or longer. Bricks come in many colors, including light red, dark red, yellow, buff and brown. Lay them flat, on edge, side-by-side, diagonally, overlapping or many other ways. They can be laid on sand or concrete, the joints swept with sand, filled with mortar or ground cover. Brick paving is cool, glare-free and not slippery.

The installed cost of brick is more than concrete. However, about half of the cost is for materials. Do it yourself, and save the difference.

Unlike concrete, you don't have to finish it immediately when you start. Lay as many bricks as you want at one time, then work on it later. Another way to cut cost is to lay bricks over existing concrete. This way you don't have to tear out and haul away the old paving.

Square the pattern every 3 or 4 feet. If you don't, you may get an unpleasant surprise when you stop to admire the completed project.

## BRICK PAVING PATTERNS

Running Bond

Basketweave

Stacked

Herringbone

TIP—A good mortar mix:
- 1 part cement.
- 3-1/2 parts washed sand.
- 1/2 part lime or fire-clay.
- Enough water to bring to a plastic, workable consistency.

TIP—Brick paving absorbs water, which helps it dry out. A pitch of 1/8 to 3/16 inch per foot helps keep paving dry, especially in shaded areas.

If you're mixing a lot of mortar, use a full-sized *contractor's wheelbarrow*. It is also handy for mixing concrete and for hauling soil and other materials.

A professional brick mason brought this brick water-saw to the job. Some supply yards will saw bricks, tile, stone and pre-cast concrete for 10 to 25 cents per cut.

These bricks are laid over an old concrete patio and tapped into level position on a 1/2-inch mortar setting bed. Mortar joints will be filled later, all at one time.

## SETTING BRICKS WITH MORTAR JOINTS

A homemade grout bag is filled with mortar made from pre-mixed mortar.

Grout bag is used to squeeze mortar into joints like cake frosting. Used bricks with rustic joints require less precision than new bricks.

Professionals carefully line up brick courses with string and constantly check level.

Mortar is scrubbed into joints with a piece of burlap. Surface is immediately cleaned with a wet sponge, before mortar dries.

## ASPHALT

Don't rule out asphalt as valid paving for certain garden uses. If you've tried to keep grease spots off a concrete driveway, you know asphalt is more practical where cars are involved. Asphalt is also satisfactory for game courts and service yards. Softness and heat accumulation during summer and an uninspiring appearance make it unsuitable for uses on patios and entrances.

The main advantage of asphalt is saving money. Even with the increase in the cost of petroleum, asphalt costs much less than concrete. This is true *if* there is a clear access for large trucks and rolling equipment and *if* the area is large and open.

*Asphaltic concrete,* as it is correctly called, is laid 2 inches thick over a 6-inch rolled crushed-rock base for most residential uses. Soil sterilant keeps weeds from breaking through. Border edges with sturdy, decay-resistant 2x4s securely staked and laminated for curves. Concrete, brick or steel borders can also be used at added cost. Pitch should be at least 1/4 inch per foot. Have any depressions or dishes in the surface fixed before the final bill is paid.

This is not a do-it-yourself project unless you own a big, dirty dump truck and a 10-ton roller.

## FLAGSTONE

Flagstone is a beautiful paving but costs a lot of money. If you live near a quarry, it might cost the same as brick. With transportation costs, the price is often prohibitive.

Colors of flagstone range from almost-white to tan, pink and brown in sandstone, and gray and blue for granite and slate. Thickness ranges from 1/2 to 4 inches, and sizes of individual pieces can be several feet across. Variety and natural appearance make flagstone easy to fit into any garden. A concrete base with mortar joints is usually best for patio-type uses. For informal areas, lay flagstone in sand, or dig it into the ground with grass or creeping plants growing in the cracks.

Flagstone is not the easiest paving to lay. It's hard to get the feel of it, and amateur jobs can look awful. If you want to tackle it yourself, look at some good examples to see how joints were fitted and how mortar was installed. Lay out stones ahead of

**This asphalt driveway was widened with brick to make a more convenient and better-appearing entry.**

**A 3-inch-thick flagstone makes a sturdy and good-looking step.**

**Precision-cut slate walkway was planned by landscape architect Thomas W. Hill, ASLA, in Cleveland, Ohio.**

**Flagstone patio with rich brown tones is set in sand for casual effect. Design: Terry S. Wallace of Landscape Services Inc.**

time. Allow 1/4 inch per foot of slope for drainage, unless water can soak into a sand or soil base.

## TILE

Tile comes in more colors, shapes and sizes than brick. Textured, casual finishes fit better in most gardens than slick, precise types. Cost and installation methods are similar to brick. Tolerances are a little tighter, but if you can lay brick, you can lay tile.

## PRECAST CONCRETE

Using precast concrete is a good way to let the manufacturer take the worry out of trying to finish concrete. Of course, you pay for the advantage. There is a large range of shapes, sizes, colors and finishes available. Some are stepping-stone slabs of concrete. Others are special pavers with various methods of interlocking. Check them carefully, and you may find some are preferable to brick or tile. Lay out the design so you can use as many full-size pieces as possible, or you'll have to cut them with a masonry saw. Installation can be on a sand base or over concrete, similar to tile and brick.

## WOOD GARDEN FLOORS

Wood is a great garden-paving material. It can give many years of service when used properly. When wood is in contact with the ground or footings, use pressure-treated wood or a decay-resistant type, such as heart redwood, cypress or cedar. Preservatives applied without pressure are usually of little value.

Boards should be at least 2 inches thick. Thin boards may warp when subjected to outdoor conditions. Nail boards securely in place. Rough surfaces are less apt to be slippery when wet, and they don't show marks and defects as readily as smooth finishes. Slivers aren't always a big problem. Trim edges with a wood rasp. Sand the surface lightly with coarse sandpaper to make it more comfortable for bare feet.

Paints and shiny finishes deteriorate rapidly. It is better to apply a transparent water sealer or an exterior-type stain.

Use galvanized, aluminum or stainless steel nails. Drive them flush in a pleasing pattern rather than trying to hide them by setting.

Swirling pattern of brown tile is emphasized by the white mortar joints. Layouts like this take lots of cutting and setting skill.

Crab Orchard stone is almost tilelike in appearance. Landscape architect: Raymond J. Rolfe, ASLA.

Thin-set mix is easy to use for laying tile and brick. It can be spread less than 1/4-inch thick.

Interlocking precast concrete paving units fit together like a jigsaw puzzle. They can be installed on a 2-inch sand base with sand joints.

Redwood 2x4s hold the edges in place and define the planting areas. Designed and installed by landscape contractor Jim Keener.

Railroad ties, 2x4s on edge, cut logs, 6-inch-long end pieces cut from 4x4s and similar boards can be laid directly on a sand base. It is simple, effective and fun to do. Where excessive moisture and termites are a severe problem, avoid direct contact with the ground by building a raised deck.

Lumber is expensive. Material alone can be $1.00 a square foot or more. A cheap source of scrap lumber helps keep the cost down. Make sure wood is pressure treated or decay-resistant.

## LOW-LEVEL DECKS

Low-level decks are another way to use wood as garden paving. They are as easy to build as laying the wood directly on a sand base. In fact, there is usually less digging to do. Pressure-treated or decay-resistant 2x4 or 4x4 *stringers* are laid on concrete supports or directly on a sand or cinder base. Planking is nailed to stringers, and the weight holds it in place. Space stringers to suit the planking. Flat 2x4s span 2 feet with a little flexing. Placed on edge and nailed together, they'll reach 6 feet. Boards 2x6 and wider are acceptable for 3-foot spans.

As the deck gets higher, construction becomes trickier and may require a permit. You'll need a railing and steps for height above 18 inches. Work with a carpenter unless you have experience and confidence. Standard *pier and girder* support is satisfactory for most situations. For normal deck loading, 4x6 girders spaced 3 feet apart span 6 feet between piers.

Hillside decks are another story. Most agencies require a structural engineer to calculate spans and footings. Contractor's costs are high, and it is an overwhelming project for most homeowners. If you have enough level space on solid land to serve the need, it's usually better to avoid the complication and expense of a deck set precariously on a hillside. If usable space is limited and you have a sensational view, consider a dramatic deck to gain full use of your property.

## SEMIPAVINGS

What do you do with an area that doesn't require a solid paving, yet is unsatisfactory for lawn, ground cover or bare dirt? For example, a side yard to store firewood or a path to the back

A 16d galvanized nail is used as a spacer while two nails are driven flush with the surface of each 2x4.

Here is an easy way to build a curbside or other type of wood walkway. Two redwood 2x4s laid on edge support 2x4 planks.

Finished result is neat and simple. The low-voltage wood path light was designed to tie in with the angles of the 2x4s. Landscape architect: Ken Smith, ASLA.

corner that isn't worth doing in concrete or brick.

What you need is a low maintenance material that can be walked on, drains rapidly, is easy to install and is low in cost. It should be relatively free of mud and dust, fairly stable and pleasant appearing. There are many common granular, stone and bark materials you can use. You can grow shrubs and trees directly in them. When water conservation is crucial, some materials can also be used as lawn and ground-cover substitutes.

Semipavings need borders, such as curbings or edgings, to keep them in place. Use them on fairly level ground to prevent erosion. It is unnecessary to put plastic underneath. This impedes water penetration and usually becomes exposed to view. Weeds can be pulled by hand or controlled by sprays, as described on page 183. All it takes to install semipavings is

Landscape contractor Dave Geller designed and installed this walkway of redwood 4x6s. Note the piece tapered to fit the subtle bend in the walkway.

Wood deck adds valuable outdoor living space on a steep hillside lot and provides a beautiful view of the river below.

Right: Wood walkway steps down with the natural slope. Landshapes Inc. design and installation.

Below: What could be simpler? Two rough redwood 2x12s were nailed to 2x4 supports to create a fun walkway that took only a few minutes to build.

# LOW-LEVEL DECK CONSTRUCTION

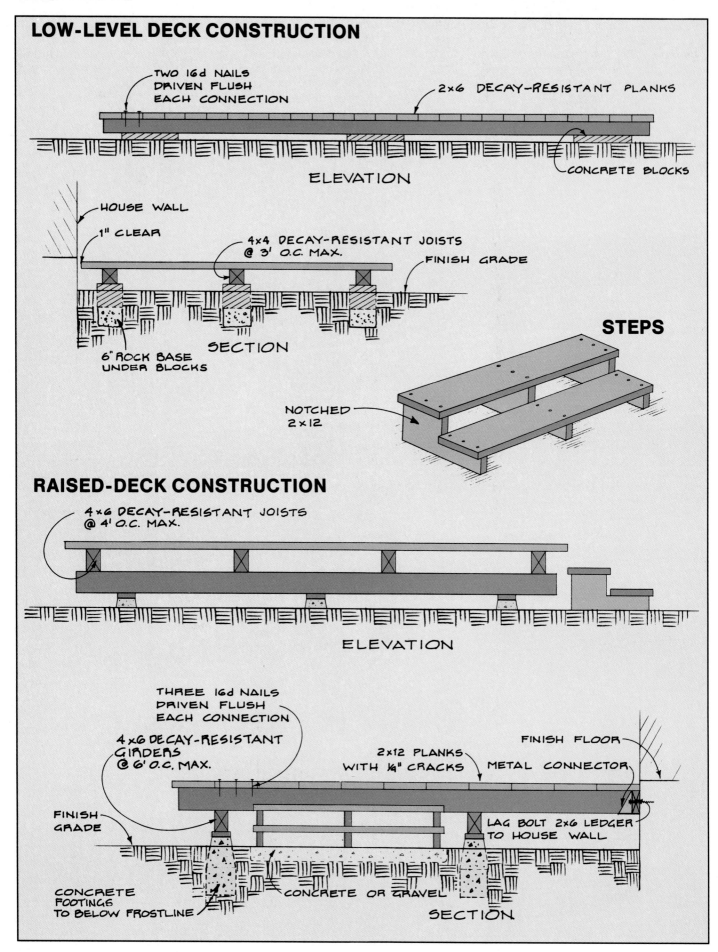

TWO 16d NAILS
DRIVEN FLUSH
EACH CONNECTION

2×6 DECAY-RESISTANT PLANKS

ELEVATION

CONCRETE BLOCKS

HOUSE WALL

1" CLEAR

4×4 DECAY-RESISTANT JOISTS
@ 3' O.C. MAX.

FINISH GRADE

SECTION

6" ROCK BASE
UNDER BLOCKS

## STEPS

NOTCHED
2×12

# RAISED-DECK CONSTRUCTION

4×6 DECAY-RESISTANT JOISTS
@ 4' O.C. MAX.

ELEVATION

THREE 16d NAILS
DRIVEN FLUSH
EACH CONNECTION

4×6 DECAY-RESISTANT
GIRDERS
@ 6' O.C. MAX.

2×12 PLANKS
WITH ¼" CRACKS

FINISH FLOOR

METAL CONNECTOR

FINISH
GRADE

LAG BOLT 2×6 LEDGER
TO HOUSE WALL

CONCRETE
FOOTINGS
TO BELOW FROSTLINE

CONCRETE OR GRAVEL

SECTION

# BUILDING A DECK

Jane and Billy join in as Bill Becher digs holes for precast concrete piers. The piers must be carefully leveled or the whole deck will be crooked.

Rough redwood 2x4 stringers are nailed to the piers and finished redwood 2x6 planks are laid across them. Planks are extended over the old concrete step, instead of tearing it out. Leave a 1-inch space between the wood and the house to protect against termites.

Left: String indicates where the 2x4 is underneath.

Right: Chalkline is snapped to mark a straight edge.

A portable rotary saw is used to trim excess wood. Edges are smoothed with a rasp.

Not bad for a day's work. They deserve a rest before doing the planting.

common sense and a strong back.

Products sold in sacks are convenient but expensive for large areas. Most semipaving materials are sold in bulk, by the cubic yard, ton or skip load at a much lower cost. You can haul them yourself in a pickup or trailer, or arrange for large deliveries with a dump truck. Cost varies with quantity, availability and distance of haul.

It takes a mathematician to calculate how much of which to cover what. The safest way is to measure how many square feet you have to cover. Convert that number to cubic feet by dividing by 6 for a 2-inch thickness. Then, divide that figure by 27 to get cubic yards. For materials sold by the ton, you'll need to find the ratio of weight to volume. Ask the supply yard to give you an equivalent amount. Add a 10% safety margin no matter how the material is sold.

**Granular Materials**—Common semi-pavings include decomposed granite, rock dust, select natural base and brick dust. Laid 2 or 3 inches deep, these pack solidly and can be raked easily. They're good for walks, parking areas and game courts. Colors include gray, tan, brown and red. Granular materials scratch floors, so keep them away from entrances to the house.

**Stones, Cinders and Gravels**—These start at pea size and go up to 2 inches and larger in diameter. Heavy, 3/4-inch mixed gravel stays in place the best and is easiest to walk on. Earth colors are most pleasing and don't show leaves and debris as much as white and light colors. Lay this material at least 2 inches deep for foot traffic and 4 to 6 inches deep for driveways. Keep it slightly below the border or adjacent paving to prevent scattering. Loose stones are a nuisance in parkways or along public sidewalks. Keep cinders and lightweight volcanic types well-confined.

**Bark Products**—These products can be walked on, and they make excellent mulches for plants when placed at least 2 inches deep. Large chunks look good, but they can float or wash away. Keep large pieces of bark away from moving water. Mix smaller sizes in with soil so they stay in place a little better. Shredded bark placed 6 inches deep is safe under swing sets and slides.

All types of bark decompose and need replenishing at least once a year.

An occasional raking keeps decomposed granite looking neat.

A layer of 3/4-inch mixed stone is walkable with shoes on. These rich colors are found in *rusty* types that contain iron.

Path of tan gravel helps create a woodsy feeling. Landscape architect: Eldon Russell, ASLA.

Grayish tones blend well with granite boulders in this composition by Theodore Brickman Co., Long Grove, Illinois.

Pecan and walnut shells serve a similar purpose and are longer lasting, but they have sharp edges that are hard on bare feet. Pine needles are a good, natural-appearing covering. They're free or sold as inexpensive pine straw. Avoid using pine needles where they'll dry out and be a fire hazard.

In some areas, bark products may be a problem, particularly if you have pets. Ticks and other undesirable insects sometimes take up residence there.

## COSTS

The chart on page 53 gives estimated costs of various paving materials. In general, assume flagstone costs three or four times as much as gray

Landscape architect Jeffrey A. Gebrian, ASLA, of CR3 Inc., felt that asphalt would be out of place in this lovely Connecticut wooded setting, so he chose gravel for the driveway and motor court.

concrete. Asphalt is usually the least expensive solid type. Actual cost often depends on how busy contractors happen to be and how much competition there is. Small areas—less than 500 square feet—are usually more expensive per square foot than large areas.

If you have hard soil, difficult access or need extra grading, footings and complex forming, you'll have to pay more. If a contractor's bid seems too high, get a comparison bid. If you plan to do it yourself, materials alone are about half the installed cost.

## GRADING

After you choose the kind of paving you want, you're almost ready to start installation. But first you must prepare the ground.

Rough grading of most lots is performed by the builder. The typical lot is graded to drain *away* from the house to the street. A building department inspector is usually needed to approve the work. Carefully preserve the existing drainage pattern during subsequent grading and construction to protect the house, prevent erosion and avoid damage to neighboring property. Earth *berms,* or low dikes at the top of banks, can usually be made less obvious by flattening them a little. Don't impair their function of keeping water from flowing over the bank.

If paving patterns, terracing, contouring or other features that might affect grading are anticipated, a few passes with the tractor can save a lot of work later. Be sure to reroute drainage flow if the old route is blocked when paving is added. Side yards are often a problem. One solution is to leave an open channel at least a foot wide along the property line. Make lawn and planting areas about 2 inches

Shredded bark is walkable and useful under play equipment.

Newly planted shrub areas look good right away when mulched with bark chunks.

Walnut and pecan shells make good paths. They're also good for mulches in planting areas and can even be rototilled into the soil as an amendment.

Gravel driveways can be beautiful. They also cost less than solid paving.

below adjacent paving, rather than flush. This allows for soil from planting holes and the addition of soil amendments.

Don't do any planting until you're sure your entire property drains properly. About 1/4-inch-per-foot slope is advisable for lawn and planting areas. This means 2-1/2 inches of slope for every 10 feet or at least 2 feet in 100 feet. Test the drainage first by observing the flow of rain or applied water, then correct low areas.

Stockpile topsoil to be replaced in planting areas. This is possible only if the house is built singly, rather than in a tract. Don't bury concrete, plaster, lumber or other debris. Look at boulders and rock outcroppings as potential features. They can often be incorporated into the design rather than hauled away at considerable expense.

Grading permits are often required for any cut exceeding 5 feet, any fill exceeding 3 feet or if more than 50 cubic yards of material are involved. When large portions of a garden are paved, rain water has no place to soak in. Water coming from a paved area can cause erosion and flooding,

unless drainage to the street or storm drain is provided.

If roof water must drain to the street, avoid unsightly surface gutters of asphalt or concrete. Walks and driveways can often serve as drainage channels, but underground lines are advisable. When there are existing drain lines, it's easy to tie into them at little expense.

Sloping and hillside lots require careful grading design. Strict ordinances must be followed. In most instances, some retaining walls are necessary to fully use the site. Ideally, the architect of the house considers grading as an integral part of his design. Collaboration with the landscape architect at this stage is important.

## LAYING PAVING

Below are some basic tips that are useful for laying any paving:
● Stake out the proposed area on the ground. Make any last-minute modifications that are necessary.
● Check the final elevation for the top of the paving. You may be able to raise or lower it a little and save digging or filling.

● Grade for the slope and thickness required by the specific paving. Allow extra depth for the subbase. Include footings and post anchors.
● Arrange for any required inspections.
● Build the forms, and mark where dividers and expansion joints will be.
● Install reinforcing, piping, conduits and sleeves that need to go under paving.
● Soak the ground thoroughly to minimize expansion of clay soils.
● Lay the paving of your choice, referring to the description, detail sketches and photos. Watch a professional for a few minutes on a job similar to your own—it's the next best thing to hiring him.

Painters, plasterers and other workers create problems with paving if it's installed too early during house construction. If possible, obtain an allowance from the builder. Have paving installed *after* other work is completed. This gives you time to consider the design more carefully. If loan requirements necessitate earlier installation, insist that the builder protect the paving against damage.

**Consider putting excess soil to use before paying to have it hauled away. These earth *berms* give privacy and reduce noise from adjacent road. Design/build: Theodore Brickman Co.**

# PAVINGS: COST AND COMPARISONS

| Paving | Installed Cost per Square Foot | Paving | Installed Cost per Square Foot |
|---|---|---|---|
| **CONCRETE** | | Concrete Base—Excellent for laying over existing concrete because of the thinness of tile. This saves the cost of a new base. | $5.00 to $7.00 |
| **Basic Gray**—Can be monotonous and will glare in sunlight. Broom, sweat and swirl finishes are safer and more interesting than smooth, slippery steel-troweled surfaces. | $2.00 to $3.00 | | |
| | | **PRECAST CONCRETE** | |
| **Colored**—It's easier to order color mixed in with the concrete direct from the ready-mix company, rather than dusting it on the poured surface. Select colors from samples, not just names. Colors will fade unless sealed or waxed. | $2.25 to $3.25 | **Sand or Earth Base**—Avoid thin types that will crack. | $1.50 to $3.00 |
| | | **Concrete Base**—Same advantages as tile. | $3.00 to $5.00 |
| | | **WOOD PAVING** | |
| **Salt-Finish**—Very popular because it's fairly easy to do. Just press rock salt into the troweled surface while it's still soft. The pitted effect adds interest and fits into most garden scenes. Often used with colored concrete. | $2.25 to $3.25 | **Railroad Ties**—Laid directly in the ground with 8-inch side up. Not a smooth surface. Can be spaced to include lawn or walkable ground cover between ties. | $3.00 to $5.00 |
| **Pebble or Exposed Aggregate**—Workmanship and types vary considerably. Be sure to look at samples before giving the go-ahead. The unevenness can be a problem for furniture and is difficult to keep clean. | $3.00 to $4.00 | **Log Cuts**—Odd shapes between cuts are a problem. Concrete looks bad; stone or bark moves around. Lawn or low ground cover works best and keeps logs moist, which helps prevent cracking. | $1.50 to $3.00 |
| | | **End Pieces**—Lots of labor involved, but very attractive. | $4.00 to $6.00 |
| **Patterned**—A steel form is used to impress soft concrete to give a brick, cobblestone or tilelike effect. | $3.50 to $4.50 | **Laminated 2x4s**—Parallel lines give it a sophisticated quality. | $2.50 to $5.00 |
| **BRICK** | | **DECKS** | |
| **Sand Base**—Quite stable when the sand is 1 to 2 inches deep and well-compacted. Best when held in place with a redwood 2x4 or other type of permanent border. One of the few materials you can practice with or start over if you don't like the results. | $3.00 to $5.00 | **Low-Level Decks**—Perfect way to eliminate the common 6-inch step-down from a sliding door. | $3.00 to $7.50 |
| | | **Medium-Height Decks**—Cost doesn't include steps or railings. | $6.00 to $10.00 |
| | | **Hillside Decks**—Costs may double if you have to include engineering, permits, footings and railings. | $20.00 and up |
| **Concrete Base**—Usually laid with mortar joints. This makes it easier to sweep clean than a sand base. Install on new or over existing concrete. This saves the cost of a new base. Used bricks are best laid this way to allow for irregularities. Cost of old bricks is even higher than new bricks in most areas due to limited supply. | $5.00 to $7.00 | **SEMIPAVINGS** | |
| | | **Decomposed Granite**—The best looking is tan or brown with a uniform texture about the same as coarse sand. | $.50 to $1.00 |
| | | **Rock Dust**—Mixed gravel with *fine mineral deposits* often used as a base under concrete or asphalt. Usually a neutral gray. Not very decorative. | $.40 to $.80 |
| **ASPHALT** | | **Select Natural Base**—Fine mineral deposits dug directly out of the ground. Looks like tannish-gray dirt but packs like concrete and isn't too muddy. More utilitarian than pretty. | $.30 to $.75 |
| The larger the area, the better the price per foot. Redwood edging, weed killer and 2-inch base are included. | $.75 to $1.50 | | |
| **FLAGSTONE** | | **Brick Dust**—Red color goes well with tile roofs and brick work. | $.50 to $1.00 |
| **Sand or Earth Base**—Grow lawn or walkable ground cover in the joints for a natural effect. Easy to change. | $3.00 to $4.50 | **Bark**—Brownish-red chunks available in 1/2-inch to 2-inch sizes. Use shredded bark where softness is important. | $1.00 to $2.00 |
| **Concrete Base**—Mortar joints make it more practical for furniture and general use. | $5.00 to $7.00 | | |
| **TILE** | | **Common Stones and Gravels**—Whatever you can find at the local building-material yard. Look for brown tones and non-garish colors. | $1.00 to 2.00 |
| **Sand Base**—Weak tile will crack unless firmly bedded. Sand joints are not as satisfactory as with brick. | $1.50 to $2.50 | | |

# Making a Private Retreat

As affordable lots continue to get smaller, privacy becomes more important. There used to be little need for a solid wall or fence when a neighbor was several hundred feet away. If you have this kind of property, you may want partial fencing or none at all. Today, it's a different situation with about 10 feet between houses. When this is the case, it means a solid structure or heavy planting if you're willing to wait a year or longer for it to fill in.

It isn't antisocial to enjoy freedom from the prying eyes of neighbors. It's nice to be able to relax and do your own thing. In most instances, privacy is as desirable for neighbors as it is for you. Because few people want to wait for plants to grow, a masonry wall or well-constructed wood fence is often the best solution.

Even with a 6-foot solid enclosure, plants may be needed to achieve total privacy. Shrubs that grow above a wall or fence add privacy and help block wind and noise. They also soften the harsh lines of the structure.

When width is limited, choose upright plants that can be kept narrow without constant trimming. Well-placed trees can screen a neighbor's second-floor window that looks down on your patio. When the situation is uncomfortable, consider putting in more mature trees rather than having to wait years for trees to grow.

Hillside lots are more of a problem, especially if you happen to be on the downhill side. Talk it over with neighbors before planting a forest that could block their view. With cooperation and careful plant selection, everyone is satisfied. For example, use a shade trellis as a horizontal screen to cut off a disturbing line of sight into your windows.

Walls and fences usually look better if tops are level. It is preferable to jog or slope the top of a fence to adjust to

Sometimes extra height is needed to achieve total privacy. The height of this wall is doubled by arborvitaes that also help block sound and filter the wind.

This fence is almost 8 feet high, but it looks lower because of the stone-wall base.

a grade change, rather than make it slightly slanted. However, informal rail fences, rustic stakes, see-through-wire and iron fences can usually follow the land.

Before you decide what kind of fence to build, there are several things to consider in addition to privacy. A wall or fence is usually needed to provide protection for children and pets, and it deters intruders. Walls help break the wind. A fence that filters the breeze works better than a solid wall that causes the wind to go up and over. Noise from neighbors, highways and other sources can be reduced by solid fences and walls.

Many gardens have a nice view in one direction but need privacy in another. By installing a section of see-through fencing, it's possible to have a view *and* privacy. In a small yard, see-through panels give an open feeling.

**Left: This secluded wooded setting requires no privacy fencing. Design/build: Land Techniques, Landscape architect: Andrew Sparks, ASLA.**

A horizontal screen and lots of container plants are used here to restrict the view from the higher lot into the bedroom.

Change in grade is turned into a design feature by jogging fence sections rather than precisely following the slope of the land.

A finely detailed fence designed by landscape architect Peter Muller.

Plantings can visually soften the bare expanse of a block wall.

Stockade fences require little maintenance and blend well with plantings.

## BEFORE YOU BUILD

Verify property lines before building *any* wall or fence. The maximum allowable front-yard height is normally 3-1/2 feet. Backyard height is usually limited to 6 feet. There are places where a 6-foot fence isn't quite enough. If you and your neighbor agree, you should not have a problem building a fence a little higher or adding to an existing one. Masonry walls over 6 feet high need extra reinforcing, so it's easier to use wood.

Some cities require permits for all walls and fences. Agencies may frown on *any* type of wall or fence over 6 feet high. Check regulations before you build. If there's a chance you may later add a swimming pool, hot tub or spa, plan all fences to meet applicable ordinances. You'll get a lower bid if several hundred linear feet or if several neighboring yards are done at one time. Good access can also lower cost, especially for concrete block. Material-to-labor ratio is close to 50-50

for most types of walls and fences. Cost doesn't include painting or staining. Add $50 to $75 for each 36-inch-wide gate.

## CHOOSING A STYLE

It's hard to believe problems can develop over fencing, but they can. Picture three adjacent neighbors who want three different types of fencing—all different from the kind you prefer. If you want to split the cost, it's worth the effort to come to a

**Concrete block walls enclosing condominium patios are plastered and painted white to match buildings.**

**House siding and trim colors are repeated in this imaginative fence. Design/build: Theodore Brickman Co.**

mutually agreeable choice *before* anyone begins building.

Often, style is set by what already exists in the neighborhood. Hopefully, it is compatible with all the houses. For example, stakes look fine with shingle roofs and wood siding. Brick walls are an obvious choice for a brick house, and white-picket fences are appropriate with colonial or Cape Cod architecture. The following descriptions of various types of walls and fences, and the cost chart on page 66, should help you make a choice.

## MASONRY WALLS

Masonry walls are sturdy, permanent and almost maintenance-free. They have the additional advantage of cutting out a lot of sound. Although brick, stone and poured concrete are used, concrete blocks—especially lightweight-cinder types, are the most common.

Blocks come in a wide range of sizes, colors and textures. They can also be plastered to match the house. Blocks 6 or 8 inches wide, 8 inches high and 16 inches long are standard. Blocks 4 inches wide are economical, but require pilasters every 16 feet and additional steel for extra support.

The two biggest drawbacks of block walls are their high cost and their tendency to create a closed-in feeling—especially in a small yard. Panels of grille blocks or wrought iron relieve the prison effect and allow welcome breezes to enter. Generally, it's better to have block walls installed by

an experienced contractor unless you have lots of time, experience and muscle. If you're undaunted by this warning, use the following construction procedure.

## BUILDING MASONRY WALLS

Locate property corners and set string lines *before* digging the foundation. For normal soils, dig a 12-inch-wide concrete footing at least 12 inches down into undisturbed soil, and add a 1/2-inch horizontal steel bar. Soft edges of fill slopes and soggy soils offer poor support for heavy walls. Settling and cracking can occur. Either increase the size of the footing,

or avoid masonry walls and use wood or chain-link instead.

The base row, called a *course,* is set in the wet footing or added later with a layer of mortar. Place vertical reinforcing bars 24 inches apart, and add another horizontal bar in the top course. Vertical bars are embedded in the footing and connected to the horizontal bars with tie wire. Fill all cells containing steel with concrete grouting.

When mixing grout by hand, use one part cement, two parts sand and two parts pea gravel. Pour this mixture into the cells. Some building departments require permits for all masonry walls. They may give advice and may supply free plans to follow. Construct retaining walls according to an engineered plan. Have adequate drainage behind the wall to avoid build-up of hydrostatic pressure that can cause the wall to fail.

The base course is embedded in concrete footing. The pilaster contains steel bars and will be completely filled with grout. Note step-up pyramid for holding string line.

It is important to get the base course level. This one is especially tricky because of the step down.

Build corners first, like step-up pyramids. This gives a handy ledge to stretch a guide line for filling in the blocks in between. Move the guide line up as you complete each horizontal course.

Make joints about 1/2 inch wide. By adjusting each one a little, blocks can be fitted with a minimum of cutting. Usually, joints are left open in the bottom course to allow water to flow through. Mix enough mortar to last about half an hour, using the mix on page 42. Butter the lower block and edge of the block to be set with mortar. Tap the block gently with the trowel handle until it is in line and level in both directions. It takes a while to get the hang of it. Try low planter walls before attempting the 6-foot-high variety.

Finish joints with a joint tool or piece of 3/4-inch pipe as soon as the mortar is firm but still workable. Or cut joints deep, called *raking,* for a shadow effect.

Fill the top cells for a flush or rounded concrete cap. You can also use a solid block for the top course or a matching concrete brick or clay brick. Another solution is to set a 2-inch-thick wood plank with bolts into the top cells. Brush on or mix concrete glue with the mortar to prevent dislodging of the cap course.

### BRICK WALLS

Structural bricks with hollow cells are as easy to lay as concrete blocks. A 4x8x12" brick costs about 75 cents each. This is about twice as much as a concrete block of comparable size. It's more economical to use structural bricks than building a brick wall or applying solid bricks as a veneer.

Walls of solid brick are more difficult to build because bricks are smaller than blocks. There are no convenient cells for steel reinforcing and concrete grout. The most common method is to lay two separate walls about 4 inches apart, and use the space between for reinforcing. Finish the top by troweling the grout flush or laying a 12-inch-long brick crosswise as a cap course for a neater effect.

Handling mortar is similar to hollow-block work. Mortar is laid on top of each brick and *furrowed* with the trowel point to form a setting bed. Because of the high cost, fewer brick walls are being built today. A good way to introduce brick into the garden

A curving brick wall is stronger than a straight one. Thomas Jefferson designed one like this for the University of Virginia.

Low planter walls are a good use of brick and well within the capabilities of an owner-builder.

is to use it as a covering for a concrete block wall or for seat-high planters.

### STONE WALLS

The most common way to use stone is to treat it as a facing veneer over a

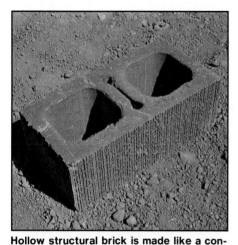

Hollow structural brick is made like a concrete block.

Well-laid, cut-stone wall is neat and sophisticated.

Steel reinforcing rod in the narrow space between two rows of brick adds strength to an 8-inch-wide wall.

Stones of various sizes and surface textures are skillfully blended. This is not an easy task, even for an expert.

Dry-laid roundish stones give an informal effect. House colors and stone colors are compatible. Landscape architects: CR3 Inc.

concrete wall. You might consider doing this, especially if the wall is low. Adding concrete glue to the mortar doesn't help during construction, but when dry, the wall is almost indestructible. Solid-stone walls require a large amount of material and skill. If you have a lot of free stone that you don't want to haul away, it might be worthwhile to use it. Consider a dry wall for heights up to 3 feet. They're easier to build and can be softened visually with planting. The vertical face of retaining walls should be *battered*—angled back—instead of building it straight up and down.

## CONCRETE WALLS

When properly laid, broken concrete can give a stonelike appearance at lower cost. It is heavy enough to be used for low terracing walls without mortar. This gives it a pleasing, casual effect. Laid in mortar with regular courses, concrete walls can be attractive.

Poured concrete is fine for curbings, seat walls and low retaining walls. But by the time you build sturdy forms to hold the weight of the fluid concrete, you could have built it from block at lower cost. Justifications for a concrete wall include creation of a freeform shape or a pebble-finish surface.

## WOOD FENCES

Wood is softer appearing and usually less expensive than masonry. Wood fences are available in many varieties and can fit many situations. You don't have to be a carpenter to build simple wood fences. This makes the project great for a non-professional. Wood fences require little maintenance when allowed to weather naturally. Redwood, cedar and rough textures are best. If color is desired, staining is preferable to painting, except for white-picket types.

Posts must be pressure treated or made from *decay-resistant* wood. Even then, posts are subject to deterioration, but no one seems to worry about it. Posts usually last for many years without falling over. Use steel pipes if permanency is important, but it costs more.

When you decide on the basic frame, you can choose from many materials and patterns. You can modify the framing for non-wood materials described under Other Materials, page 65.

## BUILDING WOOD FENCES

Start by lining up the fence with a string line. Don't encroach on other property lines. Locate the 4x4 posts *inside* the line, at a maximum of 8 feet apart. Boards laid across the space between posts are *stringers*. Stringers sag if they're farther apart than 8 feet. Unless your lot line is an exact multiple of 8, divide the length into equal spaces *not exceeding* 8 feet. This keeps you from ending up with an odd panel at the end. If you work with precut stringers, posts must be set carefully or pieces won't fit.

Steel pipe posts are advisable where soggy soils cause rapid deterioration of wood posts.

Dry-laid broken-concrete wall is visually softened by creeping thyme. Landscape architect: Jack Smith, ASLA.

A hand auger or clam-shell digger is fine for a few holes or soft soil. Use a power auger if many holes are involved or if digging is tough. The hole should not be larger than 6 inches in diameter, so don't use a shovel. A 2-foot-deep hole leaves 6 feet above ground if you start with an 8-foot post. Or use 7-foot posts, and let the boards extend 1 foot above the top stringer for a 6-foot height.

You can pack crushed rock around the posts, but concrete holds them more securely. A little extra depth and additional concrete is advisable for gate posts and at the top of slopes. Some building codes require banking the cement against the posts to form a mound above ground level.

Set the corner posts first, and brace them securely. Run a *taut* string to line up, and determine the top of the posts in between. Be sure the string doesn't sag. For long runs, it's better to set the posts high, and cut off excess.

Let the concrete cure for a day or more before nailing on stringers. Run the bottom 2x4 stringer on edge to add vertical strength. Use the top 2x4 stringer flat to help keep the fence in line. Nail the top stringer to the posts with two 16d nails. The bottom stringer is harder to attach because it is cut to fit between the posts and toenailed in place with two or three 8d nails. If you don't have a helper to hold the stringer while you nail, a temporary

A 2-man power auger is considerably faster than the clam-shell post-hole digger in the background on the right.

# WOOD FENCE CONSTRUCTION

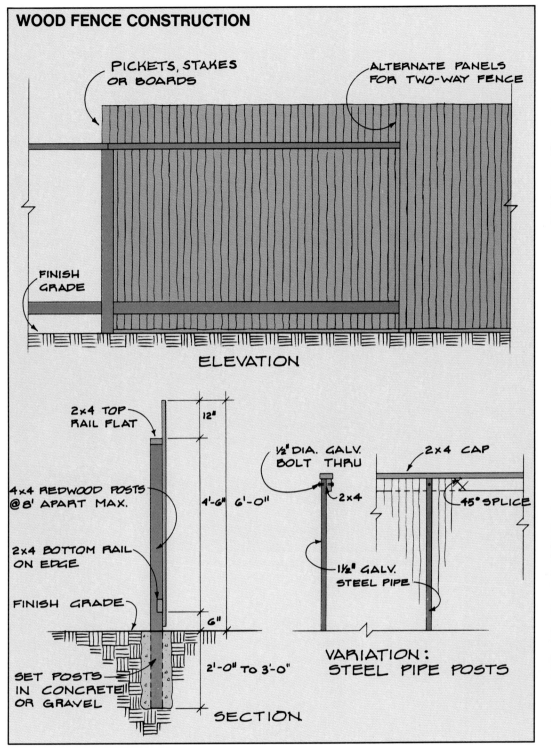

PICKETS, STAKES OR BOARDS

ALTERNATE PANELS FOR TWO-WAY FENCE

FINISH GRADE

**ELEVATION**

2×4 TOP RAIL FLAT

12"

½" DIA. GALV. BOLT THRU

2×4 CAP

45° SPLICE

2×4

4×4 REDWOOD POSTS @ 8' APART MAX.

4'-6" 6'-0"

2×4 BOTTOM RAIL ON EDGE

1½" GALV. STEEL PIPE

FINISH GRADE

6"

SET POSTS IN CONCRETE OR GRAVEL

2'-0" TO 3'-0"

**SECTION**

**VARIATION: STEEL PIPE POSTS**

The ends of the bottom stringer are cut-in and toe-nailed to the posts. The top stringer is nailed flat to lend rigidity.

Boards are nailed vertically. These extend above the top stringer for full 6-foot height.

block to rest it on saves frustration.

Attaching boards, stakes or panels is easy. Decide what size nails are needed and how far apart you'll space them. Two 6d nails are usually used at the top and bottom of 1x6 boards. One 8d nail at each connection point is common for stakes. To avoid rust streaks, use stainless-steel or alumi-num nails.

Most board or fencing material is applied vertically. Check frequently with a level to avoid tilting. Add a middle stringer for thin boards and fences more than 6 feet high. A 2x4 or 2x6 cap gives a clean top line. To do this, you need 8-foot or taller posts so they extend full height for nailing.

## WROUGHT IRON

Wrought iron is preferable to chain link for an open fence when close-up viewing is important. Hollow bars are commonly used, at a lower cost than the solid type. Cost of wrought iron is about *double* that of chain link. Use metal primer and high-quality paint to minimize the need for repainting.

# WOOD FENCE VARIATIONS

Board-and-board allows air circulation and looks the same from both sides. Gray stain soaks in and does not require restaining.

Board-on-board makes a solid fence. Panels must be alternated to avoid one-sided effect. Redwood can be stained or allowed to weather.

Picket fences keep intruders out without blocking the view.

Rustic rail fence defines yard boundary without looking heavy or unfriendly.

Grapestake fence has alternating panels. Water marks are sometimes a problem on unstained wood fences where sprinklers continually hit the same area.

Handsome fence of overlapping, horizontal boards is stained a weathered gray.

Wrought iron isn't for the do-it-yourselfer. Welding may be necessary at the site. However, prefabricated panels are available to use without welding if you measure carefully.

## CHAIN LINK

Chain link is a good solution when an immediate, solid enclosure is unnecessary or undesirable. Chain link costs much less than masonry or wood. To make it less obtrusive, leave off the top rail, and use black-vinyl-coated mesh. When semiprivacy is desired, insert wood strips. Aluminum or plastic strips are weatherproof but have a disturbing commercial appearance. Woven-wood panels wired to a low chain link fence make it higher and more private.

Chain link isn't difficult to install with proper tools, but it is not much fun. Installation prices are fairly low, so there's little to save by doing it yourself. Call a professional, and get the job done correctly.

Welded-wire fabric comes in a range of mesh sizes, from 1/2-inch squares and rectangles to 6 inch squares. This is easy to install on wood posts. Fabric can't be stretched as tightly as chain link, so it looks best when stapled to wood stringers, and it eliminates bulges. Chain link and wire fences provide excellent support for vines and supple shrubs that can be woven into the wire. Framework is eventually totally hidden by the foliage. See page 64 for *Plants for Chain-Link Fences.*

Climbing roses add color without obscuring the view through the wrought-iron fence. Concrete block columns appear substantial.

Owner Curt Reedy built this brick wall and added ornamental wrought-iron for a partially enclosed feeling.

Black-vinyl-coated chain link is less obtrusive than the standard galvanized type.

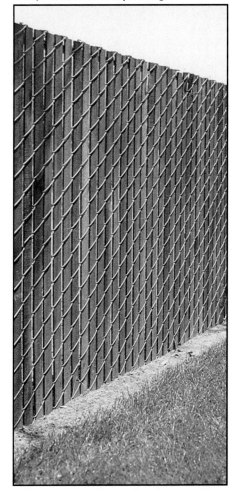

Redwood lath strips are slipped into chain link mesh for added privacy. Privacy isn't total, but the effect is pleasing.

# PLANTS FOR CHAIN-LINK FENCES

Listed in order of hardiness to cold. See Plant Lists beginning on page 86 for additional information.

| Common Name<br>*Scientific Name* | Degree of<br>Privacy | Remarks & Spacing |
|---|---|---|
| Grape<br>*Vitis* species | Partial | Rapid growth. Bare in winter.<br>Space 4 to 6 feet apart. |
| Hedge Cotoneaster<br>*Cotoneaster lucidus* | Solid | Moderate growth. Bare in winter.<br>Space 3 to 5 feet apart. |
| Yew<br>*Taxus* species | Solid | Slow growth. Evergreen.<br>Space 3 to 4 feet apart. |
| Bigleaf Wintercreeper<br>*Euonymus fortunei*<br>'Vegeta' | Solid | Slow to start. Evergreen.<br>Space 2 to 3 feet apart. |
| Sweetautumn Clematis<br>*Clematis paniculata* | Solid | Rapid growth. Bare in winter.<br>Space 4 to 6 feet apart. |
| Silver-lace Vine<br>*Polygonum auberti* | Solid | Rapid growth. Bare in winter.<br>Space 4 to 6 feet apart. |
| Climbing Rose<br>*Rosa* species | Open | Moderate growth. Bare in winter.<br>Thorns add security. Space 4 to 6 feet apart. |
| Hall's Honeysuckle<br>*Lonicera japonica* | Solid | Rapid growth. Semibare in cold winters. Needs<br>cutting back. Space 3 to 5 feet apart. |
| English Ivy<br>*Hedera helix* | Solid | Slow growth. Easy to control. Evergreen.<br>Space 2 to 3 feet apart. |
| Pyracantha<br>*Pyracantha coccinea* | Partial | Moderate growth. Semibare in cold winters. Thorns add security.<br>Space 4 to 6 feet apart. |

**Silver-lace Vine**

**Climbing Rose**

**English Ivy**

**Hall's Honeysuckle**

## OTHER MATERIALS

In special situations, materials such as glass, plastic, shingles, bamboo, plywood, canvas, expanded metal and precast panels may be an answer to a fencing problem. The limiting factor is cost. These custom fences are best used to enclose or divide a small area adjacent to the house rather than an entire lot. You can often use a wood frame similar to the one described under *Wood Fences,* pages 60 and 61.

Be sure spans fit the size of the material you select and the frame is strong enough to support the weight. Polyvinyl-chloride (PVC) white-rail fences eliminate the chore of repainting and are not subject to dry rot and insect damage.

**Cozy alcove is shielded by colorful canvas wind screen. Landscape architect Roy Seifert designed the panels for easy replacement every 5 years or so.**

**Railroad ties combine with pecky cypress 1x12 planks for a country effect.**

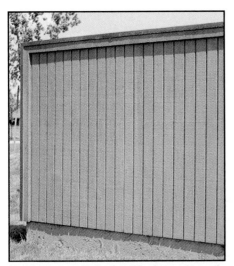

**Handsome and simple, this fence is made of exterior siding plywood that comes in 4x8' panels in various grooved patterns and textures.**

**Custom fence of 1x12 and 1x2 boards allows air circulation without loss of privacy.**

**Rather than introduce a new material, the house shingles were extended as a fence. It's a good do-it-yourself project if you're willing to take the time.**

**Lath is an easy-to-use screening material. This one was custom made on the site, but you can adapt prefabricated panels to most situations.**

# FENCES: COSTS AND COMPARISONS

|  | Installed Cost per linear foot for 6-foot height |  | Installed Cost per linear foot for 6-foot height |
|---|---|---|---|
| **WOOD FENCES** | | **Standard Brick**—Best for low retaining walls and low seats. | $8.00 to $10.00 |
| **Boards**—1x8 roughsawn redwood or cedar are quite common but boards come in various widths and many patterns. | $6.00 to $8.00 | **Stone**—First build concrete block wall, then apply stone veneer. | $5.00 to $10.00 |
| **Woven Boards**—Interlaced, flexible boards. Precut packages are easy to install. | $5.00 to $7.00 | **Poured Cement**—For retaining walls and low seats. | $5.00 to $10.00 (3 feet high) |
| **Grapestakes**—One of the most popular wood fences. Casual appearance. Rough texture requires no stain; ages well. Add 50 cents per linear foot for 2x4 cap. | $6.00 to $8.00 | **CHAIN-LINK FENCES** | |
| | | **Standard**—Looks commercial, but offers no privacy. Secure and maintenance-free. Vines and shrubs can be added. | $5.00 to $7.00 |
| **1x1s, 1x2s, Combed Stakes**—More sophisticated than grapestakes, but not as strong. 2x2s are sturdier, but cost more. | $6.00 to $8.00 | **Standard with Wood Inserts**—Looks surprisingly good. Privacy isn't total. Filters wind. | $7.00 to $9.00 |
| **Woven Palings**—Sturdy poles woven with wire. | $8.00 to $10.00 | **Colored Link**—Black vinyl is almost invisible when the posts are painted black. | $6.00 to $8.00 |
| **Plywood**—Use *textural exterior* types only. Neat, strong and easy to nail. Back is blank; not for situations where both sides will be seen. | $8.00 to $10.00 | **WROUGHT-IRON FENCES** | |
| | | **Standard**—The best answer for pool fencing. Especially appropriate with Mediterranean-style house. Embellishments are okay for gates, but simple uprights are usually preferable. | $8.00 to $12.00 |
| **Louvers**—Greatly overrated. Difficult to build; warp easily. For special uses only. | $10.00 and up | **Prefabricated**—Drop-in panels can be used if the spacing is correct. | $6.00 to $8.00 |
| **Lath**—Prefab panels and wired rolls save labor and are stronger than individual pieces. Good way to add height to an existing wall or fence. | $5.00 to $8.00 | **MISCELLANEOUS FENCES** | |
| | | **Glass**—For view and wind protection. Safety requires 1/4-inch-thick tempered plate glass. Plexiglass is less expensive but scratches. | $20.00 and up |
| **Shingles**—Great choice when the house has shingle walls. Can be applied over an existing wood fence. | $10.00 and up | **Plastic**—Corrugated fiberglass isn't very classy. Some flat panels are handsome but hard to obtain in exterior grades. Lets light through for small garden enclosures. | $15.00 and up |
| **Rail**—Obviously not for privacy or security. You can set the posts in gravel or directly in the ground. Looks good with ranch houses and shake roofs. | $3.00 to $5.00 (3 feet high) | | |
| | | **Bamboo**—Hard to install individual canes. Sometimes available in wire-woven rolls. Woven reed is inexpensive but temporary. | $15.00 and up |
| **Picket**—Better for keeping out animals and people than a rail fence. Looks best painted to coordinate with house. | $4.00 to $8.00 (3 feet high) | **Welded Wire**—Inexpensive see-through fence; easy to install. Needs frame on all sides or will wobble. | $5.00 to $7.00 |
| **Custom**—Tends to be gimmicky unless done tastefully. Have fun, but don't get carried away. | $10.00 and up | **Expanded Metal**—Can look commercial. Needs rust-proofing. | $15.00 and up |
| **MASONRY WALLS** | | **Canvas**—New vinyl coatings last for about 5 years. Nice colors available. | $15.00 and up |
| **Concrete Block**—Plain, colored slump, grille and textured. Avoid fancy patterns. | $10.00 to $20.00 | **Various panels**—Asbestos cement, pebble surfaces, pressed fibers and others. Good possibilities when well-designed. | $20.00 and up |
| **Plaster over Concrete Block**—Good way to tie in with a plastered house or to upgrade an old wall. The problem is to find a plasterer. | $10.00 to $20.00 | | |
| | | **Railroad Ties and Poles**—Striking when set vertically in the ground. Can be used as low retaining walls. Repeat clusters as accents. | $20.00 and up |
| **Structural Brick**—Available in several colors. Makes a handsome wall. Strong and costs less than solid bricks. | $15.00 to $20.00 | | |

This simple wood gate has no exposed latch on the front.

Z-brace resists downward pressure and keeps the gate from sagging.

Left: Wood gates don't have to be solid and heavy. However, intricate designs like this are not for a beginning carpenter.

Wrought-iron is ideal for wide driveway gates. These are electrically controlled for convenience.

This elegant wrought-iron gate enhances the entrance and provides security.

## GATES

Gates can be exasperating. No matter how solidly a wood gate is built, it always seems to sag or bind. Use lightweight dry wood, heavy-duty hinges and adequate bracing. Allow an extra 1/4 inch for swelling when the wood gets wet. Avoid wood gates more than 4 feet wide.

If you need a solid driveway gate, build it on a steel frame. Install a running wheel to relieve strain. Chain-link gates work fine, but they aren't pretty and afford no privacy. Wrought-iron gates are desirable for workability and appearance when seeing through the gate doesn't matter.

**English Boxwood**

## HEDGES, SCREENS AND WINDBREAKS

Plants can be used for privacy and protection. A tall, thick hedge keeps people and animals out of a yard. It also absorbs noise and softens wind. Hedges and screens are better looking than many types of fencing.

There are two major drawbacks to using plants. First, you must wait for a hedge or screen to grow and fill in. Second, plants require maintenance to keep them alive and looking their best.

Select a plant that naturally stays the height and width you want with minimal clipping and maintenance. This saves unnecessary labor, looks more natural and is often more pleasing. See pages 118 to 123 for plant lists and photos of hedges, screens and windbreaks. Additional photos are found on the following two pages.

**Vanhoutte Spirea**

**Alpine Currant**

**'Tallhedge' Buckthorn**

**Korean Littleleaf Box**

# HEDGES, SCREENS & WINDBREAKS

American Arborvitae

Zabel Honeysuckle

**Blue Arctic Willow**

**Clavey's Dwarf Honeysuckle**

**Redleaf Japanese Barberry**

## HOT TUBS AND SPAS

Many of us are comfortable at a crowded pool or the beach with thousands of people but dislike swimming or sunbathing in our own yard without total privacy. Full-sized swimming pools are difficult to screen from every angle. Small pools, hot tubs and spas are easier to tuck into a secluded corner beyond the view of neighbors. They take less space, are fairly inexpensive, don't require as much energy to heat or water to fill, are easy to cover, less work to keep clean and don't add much to your tax bill.

For sociable soaking and tension relief, a hot tub or spa is great. They're miniature swimming pools with aerated bubbles. Water is heated to 100F (38C). Because they use less than 1,000 gallons of water, gas and electric cost is only $10 to $20 per month with average use.

Complete-kit prices, including wood tub or fiberglass spa, heater, pump, filter and hardware, range

**Redwood hot tub blends beautifully with wood deck, railroad ties and barrel planters. Removable lid keeps water clean and conserves heat.**

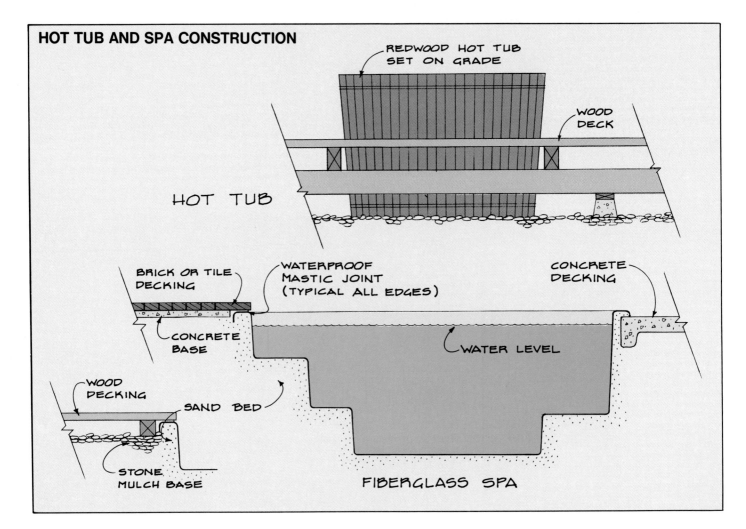

**HOT TUB AND SPA CONSTRUCTION**

REDWOOD HOT TUB
SET ON GRADE

WOOD DECK

HOT TUB

BRICK OR TILE DECKING

WATERPROOF MASTIC JOINT (TYPICAL ALL EDGES)

CONCRETE DECKING

CONCRETE BASE

WATER LEVEL

WOOD DECKING

SAND BED

STONE MULCH BASE

FIBERGLASS SPA

from $1,500 and $3,000 for most models. Double the kit price for an estimate of the total hook-up and installation package. Access, distance to gas and electricity, and other site conditions affect cost.

If you figure you can start soaking for as little as $3,000, you're only partially correct. Even if you have an existing garden in which to place a tub or spa, allow about another $1,000 for decking and additional plantings. The big expense could be whether or not you already have adequate fencing and if your building department has a

pool-fencing ordinance. Check before making any final decisions.

Gunite spas, made of sprayed-on, reinforced concrete, are only economical when constructed along with a swimming pool. The cost of a concrete spa is about twice as much as a comparable fiberglass type.

Hot tubs and fiberglass spas can be installed by a homeowner. Building departments require permits and inspections. It may be a good idea to hire licensed contractors for electrical and plumbing work if you lack experience in these areas. HPBooks' *Spas &*

*Hot Tubs* is an excellent resource, whether you do your own installation or hire a contractor.

A good way to achieve privacy for tubs and spas is to place them under a shade trellis or in a gazebo. Shade is welcome on hot days. The protection from wind and prying eyes is appreciated during evening use. A solar greenhouse is also a good spot for year-round use. Add some lush plants that thrive in the warmth and humidity, and you create a cozy, intimate spot.

Plan ahead and you can make your hot tub really work. This one is completely private, yet has a beautiful view. Photo courtesy California Cooperage.

It's fall outside but solar greenhouse allows use of spa all year round. Photo courtesy Four Seasons Greenhouses.

Interior designer Fran Elson wanted me to incorporate a work of art with a spa. We recessed a mural in a niche in the wall and selected brown fiberglass with tile trim to coordinate the colors.

**Blue-gray plaster and tile lend enchantment to this small pool. The angular shape was carefully contrived to make it look larger.**

**Stone wall built at the pool edge allows planting to arch gracefully over the water. Note underwater seat in corner for resting and safety.**

## SWIMMING POOLS

Don't rush into installing a full-sized swimming pool without carefully weighing advantages and disadvantages. No other garden element presents as many problems. Practical considerations, such as noise, glare, drainage and safety, impose rigid limitations.

The cost of the pool is only the beginning. If enough money isn't allowed for decking, fencing, planting, lighting, furniture, interest on the loan, taxes, operating costs and maintenance, the project may be a financial burden. The average pool costs $12,000 to $15,000. Vinyl-liner and fiberglass types usually cost less than concrete construction.

The simplest solution is a plastic pool on top of the back lawn. It isn't glamorous, but for about $600 to $700, including the filter system, you can have water for your family to cool off in on hot days. Take it down and store it in the winter, or sink it into the ground for a more-permanent installation. Add decking and it becomes more presentable.

If you have enough space, if the budget can stand the strain and if you're convinced a full-sized permanent pool will be enjoyed, go ahead. But do it right. You can trade in a lemon car, but you're stuck with a pool.

In terms of water conservation, it takes a lot of water to fill a pool—about 24,000 gallons for a 16x36' pool. With good maintenance, a pool rarely needs draining and refilling except in extremely cold climates. Logs and cushions along the perimeter reduce damage to the walls from freezing. Vinyl-liner pools are less subject to ice damage.

**Spa is separated from main pool by stone bridge. Dark-blue plaster gives a mountain-lake effect.**

**Landscape architect Eldon Russell and owner Marvey Finger carefully tucked this pool into the wooded setting to disturb as few trees as possible.**

A tire swing and slide for the children, and lounging and dining space for adults make this a real family entertainment center. I'll bet the adults use the tire swing after the kids have gone to bed. Design: Beauté la terre Designs. Photo: Kala Busby.

Situate the pool so it receives maximum sun and privacy, and shield it from prevailing winds. Keep it far enough away from the house so it doesn't dominate the view, or design it as part of the view. Provide enough space for lounging, sunbathing and entertaining, with easy access to dressing rooms and bathrooms.

Sprayed-concrete construction allows flexibility of shape, but choose a shape in relation to the setting. A rectangular pool placed within a rectangular area might be more pleasing than an unrelated form.

Vinyl-liner and fiberglass pools must be selected from a catalog. Most companies offer a wide variety of shapes and sizes.

Most activity takes place in the shallow area of a pool, even in families with expert swimmers. Make shallow areas the largest part of the pool space. Large, offset steps add interest and leave the main swimming area unobstructed. A 16x36' pool, with parallel ends, is large enough for serious swimming. An underwater-seat climb out can replace a ladder and serve as a convenient resting place.

A pool smaller than 16x36' is sufficient for most families. Try a friend's pool for size before you build your own. Lap pools 8 to 10 feet wide and about 40 feet long are great for exercise but require careful design to avoid a sterile look. Minipools, where you swim against a constant current, are a good compromise between a full-size pool and a spa.

Diving is great fun and can be included in some form in almost every pool. A professional, 16-foot-long, 1-meter board requires a 9-foot depth and a 20x40' pool. A 30-inch-high, 10-foot-long board is adequate for most divers. It is easier to fit into a smaller pool. Where space is limited, a 6-foot-long jump board or raised decking area is more challenging than just diving off the edge.

## POOL DECKS
Place the widest part of the decking in relation to the shallow area and steps of the pool. In some cases, it's possible to eliminate the walk area at the back side entirely. Concrete is often used because it's practical and economical. The surface should be non-skid, with expansion joints placed at frequent intervals. Deck drains and underground drain lines are desirable to keep chlorinated water away from adjacent plantings. Color and texture, such as swirl or broom finishes, help break glare and add richness. Changes in level and cantilevered decking that eliminates coping are effective design elements.

In expansive soils, take precautions to keep soil from cracking and shifting. Thoroughly soak soil before pouring. Mastic or plastic-expansion joints and a 6-inch-deep subbase of sand, gravel or cinders are advisable. This helps prevent frost heaving. Special engineering of the pool structure is required in expansive soils.

Other decking materials include flagstone and brick. On hillsides, wood decking is often used. These decking materials all cost more than concrete. One solution is to use them in small areas for a contrast to concrete. For areas with hot summers, a troweled-on *cool deck* to reduce surface temperature is a sole-saver. It is sold under various names and adds about 50 cents per square foot to the basic concrete cost.

## FILTERS
Pool maintenance is easier with a good filtering system. Position the skimmer where it will catch debris from summer breezes. Locate filter equipment as close as possible to the deep end of the pool for economy and maximum efficiency. Increase the size of the pipes so filter equipment can be moved to a less-obtrusive location.

Every pool builder has a favorite manufacturer, but most agree that a filter of 36-square-feet rating with a 1-horse-power motor is adequate for a 600-square-foot pool. This equals a 16x36' rectangle, with offset steps. A separation tank eliminates the nuisance of backwash water. An overflow pipe maintains proper water level even in areas with heavy rains.

Run the pool filter during the daytime, so noise is not a problem during sleeping hours. Place a spa-aerating motor close to the spa. Enclose it in a soundproof chamber because it is much louder than a pool pump.

Include three adjustable return lines for a 600-square-foot pool to improve water circulation and filtering efficiency. An automatic cleaning system reduces, but does not eliminate, pool care. It can be installed for about $600.

## HEATING AND LIGHTING
Solar heating is rapidly replacing gas heating for pool installations. At about $1,500 for installation, the cost is double that of gas, but you save

money because you don't use precious fuel. Using gas for pool heating may become restricted in the future.

You don't need to install an entire solar heating unit all at the same time. Include piping and stub-outs so it can be added later. Spas and hot tubs require higher temperatures and are often used at night. Backup heating is necessary. However, spas are easy to cover when not in use, which conserves heat and reduces maintenance.

Check solar heating companies carefully. Because these systems are fairly new, few people have much experience with them. Ask to see a completed system in operation—the older the better—and talk with the owner. This is good advice for solar heating and for any work you intend to contract out, whether it's a swimming pool, concrete patio or sprinkler system.

A 500-watt light under the diving board is usually standard equipment for a pool. If the main view from the house or patio is directly toward the light, shift the light to the side of the pool to reduce glare. An ink-blue lens on the light also reduces glare and adds interest. Locate a junction box for the light above grade outside the decking near the light. Plan additional lighting, phone jacks and outlets for appliances at this time to avoid installation problems later.

## PLANTING, WATER FEATURES AND FENCING

Protect plants around a pool from chlorine water with raised beds or deck drains. Some planting near the water that casts a reflection on the surface is dramatic. It helps relieve the flat plane of the water and decking. Building a raised planter directly at the pool edge is a good way to handle it. Stone or bark mulches adjacent to the paving are better than ground covers. They eliminate mud and dust, require little care and are not damaged by chlorine.

Plan waterfalls and fountains with caution. They can be effective but must relate to the design of the site and pool. A separate pump, which can be turned off without interfering with pool operation, is best. Slides are popular with children, but they look obtrusive.

Many cities and counties have laws requiring non-climbable fencing 4-1/2 to 5 feet high with self-closing

Bubble plastic pool cover is a good way to keep heat in and dirt out. Material cost is about 50 cents per square foot.

Swimming under the bridge in this elongated pool is fun.

Planting box raised to upper level is protected from chlorinated water. Blue Atlas cedar is pruned in a bonsai fashion.

Poolside waterfall by Beauté la terre Designs gives this Kansas landscape a mountainlike feeling. Photo: Kala Busby.

Reflecting pool gives a tranquil and dignified mood to this gracious garden designed by landscape architect C. C. Pat Fleming.

Balcony with open railing offered no privacy for sunbathing.

Solid panels were added to block the wind and prying eyes. Plant in corner is *Acmena Smithii*—one of the few named after a Smith.

gates around any body of water more than 1-1/2 feet deep. This is usually interpreted to include spas and tubs. Even a door at the back of a garage that opens onto the pool area requires a self-closing device.

When there are small children in a family, consider placing fencing around the pool itself rather than at property lines. This provides protection for family members as well as the public. Or include an openable or temporary fence within the yard, and remove it when children are older.

With a little imagination, an interior safety fence can be turned into an asset rather than an eyesore. Wrought iron, expanded metal or welded wire make attractive look-through barriers and still provide protection.

## SUNBATHING

Sunbathing is another activity that calls for privacy. Because it is often associated with a pool or spa, place part of the decking where it gets sun without being in the neighbors' view. Of course you don't have to have water to sunbathe. Walk around the house and choose a spot that is out of the wind and gets sun during the time of day you want it. Be sure you don't block the sun when you build high fences or plant trees.

Rooftops and balconies are always potential sunning areas. Sometimes a partial screen is all that is necessary for privacy and wind control. Use a few container plants to dress up the area.

## PLAN AHEAD

If a pool is to be built at a later date, leave room for heavy equipment access. Do as little as possible in the entire area. Unless a carefully considered master plan is drawn for the complete project, major changes and damage can occur when the pool is finally constructed. Water, electric and gas service lines may have to be stubbed out to avoid costly breaking through pavement.

## CAUTION

Pool contracting is a competitive business. Question "free design services." The ideal way is to have a plan before getting bids from several companies. Carefully compare bids before signing any agreement. Clarify exactly what is included in the contract. Unforeseen extras can turn a low bidder into the high bidder.

Many pool companies have declared bankruptcy. This has left homeowners with an unfinished pool or with a new installation that requires repairs or adjustment. To make matters worse, you can be required to pay twice if the pool company doesn't pay its bills. Never pay for more than what has been installed. Secure material and labor releases for all work. A completion bond or payment through a bank provides added protection.

Making a pool blend in rather than intrude upon its setting takes considerable design skill. Landscape architect: Raymond J. Rolfe, ASLA, Centerport, New York.

# Foolproof Plants

Furnishing your "outdoor room" is important. Suggestions and lists in this section are designed to help you select the *best* plants for your needs and location. *Plant Lists,* beginning on page 86, contain the kinds of plants to use for basic planting. Plants properly selected for a specific location will serve the intended purpose with a minimum of care and low rate of failure.

There are no totally *foolproof plants.* There *are* many rugged, reliable plants that come close. The *Plant Lists* can't include every plant that meets these requirements. If you know of an outstanding performer, use it if you wish. If you are adventurous and like the challenge of growing temperamental or exotic plants, use them sparingly. Hide them around a corner so a failure won't be a catastrophe.

## GET THE MOST FROM YOUR PLANTS

Before you decide where to put a plant, you must know what you want it to do for you. Plants have many important functions in addition to their natural beauty. Below is a discussion of common uses.

**Shade**—It's wonderful to sit on the lawn under a large tree on a hot, summer afternoon. Don't overlook shade trees to also cover driveways, parking areas, patios, work areas and the house. Well-placed trees can transform a scorching site into a cool oasis.

**Privacy**—If space is narrow, a clipped hedge may be necessary. Careful selection can change a hedge into a screen of natural growth that requires less care. If privacy from a specific point is a problem, such as a neighbor's window, a shrub or tree in the right spot can often take care of it.

**Screening**—You can mask a service

Dwarf red-leaf barberry, Chinese holly and juniper form an impenetrable barrier.

A majestic oak shades the roof and front of this stately home.

Thick growth behind a concrete block wall gives privacy, provides a windbreak and reduces traffic noise.

Left: Flowering dogwood, azaleas, pines and lawn in a simple and pleasing composition.

Lilac serves multiple purposes: privacy, screening, windbreak and property barrier.

**Herb border makes good use of a narrow planting bed.**

area, blot out a bad view or hide a telephone pole with plantings. Don't look at a meter or pile of firewood when you can hide them with plants.

**Windbreak**—Most properties do not have room for several rows of large trees. Sometimes an undesirable prevailing or seasonal wind can be modified with heavy plantings. Large shrubs or small trees that extend above a solid fence are effective in changing a wind to a gentle breeze.

**Traffic Barrier**—Tough plants can encourage dogs, children and adults to walk where you want them, rather than cutting across lawn and planting beds. If the situation is severe, don't hesitate to use prickly or thorny plants.

**Carpet**—Lawn or lawn substitutes can provide a soft, safe, cool area to play or sit. They also look good. Selecting the right kind of lawn is as important as picking out a shade tree.

**Erosion, Mud, Dust and Fire Control**—If you live on a hill, erosion may be your first concern. Ground covers and shrub covers can provide this control and help cool the soil and surrounding air. They also reduce glare.

**Noise Reduction**—The more plantings you have to absorb sound, the quieter your garden will be. To block noise from a busy street or highway would take a forest several hundred feet thick, so don't expect a single row

to be much help.

**Food and Flowers**—You can grow cut flowers, herbs and vegetables in the traditional patch. Or mix some effectively with ornamental shrubs. Many fruit plants look good enough to place anywhere in the garden.

After you decide what a plant is supposed to do, think of its size. Consider what exposure and other conditions it will be subjected to.

## CLIMATE ZONES

The Northeast and Midwest states have a range of average annual minimum temperatures from 0F (-18C) to -40F (-40C). This is shown on the United States Department of Agriculture (USDA) map on page 81. The map is helpful as a general guide. However, there can be a large variation within a few square miles.

A south-facing hillside lot can be as much as 10 degrees warmer in winter than one on the valley floor a few hundred feet away. There are even warm and cold pockets within an individual yard. Wide shifts in temperature are common in some areas, with frost at night followed by a 70F (21C) day.

Plants in the following lists should perform satisfactorily within their designated climate zones. Extreme conditions, such as low-lying air drainage basins, high-altitude mountain

areas, sites tempered by large lakes and rivers and those close to the ocean call for a careful check of plants that thrive locally. Find out if the Cooperative Extension Service has a climate map for your state that breaks down the USDA zones into detailed subzones. See page 188 for a list of Cooperative Extension Services.

## EXPOSURE

Few plants survive in all degrees of sunlight from deep shade to reflected sun. Most plants have a definite requirement that must be satisfied. For simplicity, the four basic wall exposures of your house are a good guide.

The north side—N—is the coolest and shadiest. It gets direct sun only in the early morning and for a short time in the late afternoon during the longest summer days.

The east side—E—gets the morning sun, but is protected from the afternoon sun when temperatures are high. This is not the same as the filtered sunlight of a lath-covered porch or under a tree, but it is similar.

# PLANT HARDINESS ZONE MAP

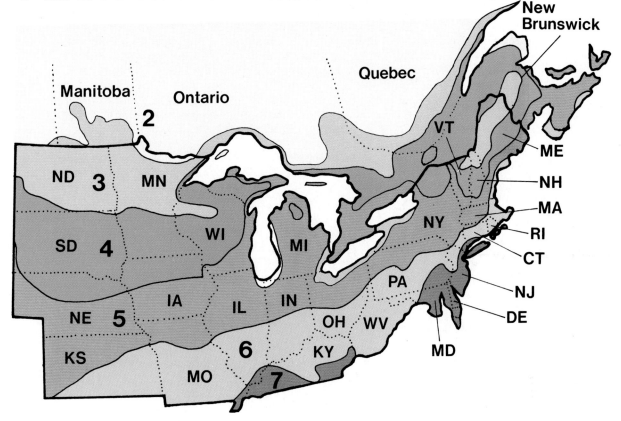

## Approximate Range of Average Annual Minimum Temperatures

**Based on information from the
United States Department of Agriculture**

| ZONE 7 | 0F to 10F (−18C to −12C) |
|---|---|
| ZONE 6 | −10F to 0F (−24C to −18C) |
| ZONE 5 | −20F to −10F (−29C to −24C) |
| ZONE 4 | −30F to −20F (−35C to −29C) |
| ZONE 3 | −40F to −30F (−40C to −35C) |
| ZONE 2 | −50F to −40F (−45C to −40C) |

The south side—*S*—gets the most sun and is comparable to full sun out in the open. With a normal 3-foot overhang, the house wall is shaded during the hottest months because the sun angle is higher. During the winter, the wall is exposed to more sun because of the lower angle. The overhang also provides additional protection from cold.

The west side—*W*—is probably the most difficult exposure to select plants for. It is cool in the morning and hot in the afternoon. In some areas, reflected heat can cook the leaves of plants. Keep an air space between the wall and plants.

All plants aren't planted directly against a wall, and all houses aren't oriented exactly north and south. Another way to determine exposure is to equate *N* with full shade, *E* with partial shade, *S* with full sun and *W* with reflected sun. Nearby fences, neighbors' houses, trees and large shrubs may modify the amount of sun a plant receives.

Plants may adapt to more or less sunlight than is considered typical for the species. If *E* and *N* are indicated as the best exposures for a plant, it means the plant requires a shady location. Don't try to grow it against a west wall in a hot climate. A sun-loving plant, listed as *S* and *W*, may dwindle away in the shade.

## SHADY SITES

As shade trees reach maturity, or if your property has large trees, you'll discover many plants do not grow well. Selection of shade-tolerant plants is crucial for areas of deep shade. Use only plants marked *N* in the lists. You may have to remove sun-lovers. Plants that grow in part shade, or marked *E* in the lists, have a better chance if trees are pruned to allow more light.

Dig a circle at the outside foliage spread of a shrub to temporarily limit invading tree roots. This may have to be repeated every year to prevent regrowth. Water deeply—shallow irrigation can be soaked-up by tree roots, which robs underplantings of an adequate supply. Apply fertilizer for trees and other plants. However, overfertilization can result in lanky, spindly growth that can be a problem in shady sites.

If moss grows in your area, appreciate its unique beauty instead of trying to eliminate it. Try growing some hardy maidenhair, deer, cinnamon, fragile, Alaska and fancy ferns. Throw in some sweet woodruff, wild ginger, galax, Canada mayflower, Christmas rose, liverleaf, alumroot, Solomon's-seal, mayapple and snow trillium for a natural, wooded scene. For densely shaded areas, where even the best choices have failed, mulches, pavings and semipavings may be the only solution.

**Caution**—Even though some plants may be adapted to summer sun, many broad-leaved and coniferous evergreens suffer damage from winter sun. Cell growth is started by warming rays, then subjected to freezing from cloud cover and night temperatures. In the severe climates of Zones 3, 4 and 5, some shade and wind protection is needed for many plants during the winter. Azalea, rhododendron, boxwood, holly, lily-of-the-valley shrub, yew, hemlock and arborvitae are especially susceptible to winter damage. Tender-bark deciduous trees also need protection, as described on page 127.

## SELECTING PLANTS

Plants in the following plant lists are easy to grow and will give consistent results in your landscape. They tolerate a wide range of conditions and thrive under normal garden situations when given reasonable care.

The general organization of plant lists is by type and expected approximate size at *young maturity*. This may take as little as 1 or 2 years for rapid growers, 5 to 10 years for most plants and 20 years or more for slow-growing plants.

Older plants may exceed the listed size, especially when grown under ideal conditions. I've seen English boxwoods 10 feet high, rhododendrons that are tree size and a silk tree that measured 81 feet wide. But don't plant them with that size in mind.

Some plants can be used in a smaller space because they are slow-growing or narrow. They can be kept under control with a minimum amount of pruning. Varieties termed *compact* or *dwarf* stay smaller but not forever.

There is a certain amount of overlap. If you're looking for a low shrub, check out medium shrubs, shrub covers and accents. You might also find a tree that is large enough to suit your needs listed under medium trees or narrow, upright trees.

Plants are arranged in order of tolerance to cold. If you live in a severe climate, start at the top of the list, and match the climate zone with your own.

## COMPATIBILITY

If you're consistent in your preferences, most of the plants you select will look good together. If you like pines, you probably also like

**Landscape architect Raymond J. Rolfe, ASLA, used a grove of Japanese black pines along with earth contouring to screen house from street. Low junipers and lawn combine subtly with the pines.**

# FLOWERING TREES

Silk Tree/Mimosa, see page 100.

Red Horsechestnut, see page 100.

Fringe Tree, see page 97.

Saucer Magnolia, see page 99.

## FLOWERING TREES

*Many trees not only have handsome foliage and a pleasing shape but the added bonus of flowers as well. The plants below display dramatic blossoms. Arrangement is in approximate order of blooming period.*

Flowering Cherry
Shadblow/Serviceberry
Flowering Crabapple
Fringe Tree
Eastern Redbud
Saucer Magnolia
Purple-leaf Plum
Flowering Dogwood
Bradford Pear
Red Horsechestnut
European Mountain Ash
Hawthorn
Japanese Tree Lilac
Japanese Dogwood
Goldenrain Tree
Silk Tree/Mimosa
Smoke Tree
Japanese Pagoda Tree

junipers, hemlocks and yews. The resulting combination is harmonious. If you like everything, you may be tempted to use too many different kinds. You could end up with a hodge-podge of textures, forms and colors. A design based on simplicity, repetition and restraint is usually more pleasing than an overly complex one.

Horticulturally, plants in the lists are compatible when placed according to their exposure requirements. They should grow together satisfactorily in normal soil when given similar care and watering. As you become more acquainted with specific needs, you'll know a certain plant responds to more water or another needs an occasional extra application of fertilizer.

Plants in the lists require regular amounts of rainfall and watering, unless otherwise stated. When a plant is well-established and has a deep root system, it won't die if there's a temporary drought or if you miss a watering. Plants able to withstand dryness are noted to be *drought tolerant.* If you live in an area where water conservation is a consideration, a discussion of the subject begins on page 178.

In the Plant Lists, outstanding features, important characteristics and additional varieties and species are listed in the right column. If good drainage or special soil conditions are required, these are noted under *Culture,* along with zone adaptation, best exposure, uses, growth rate and habit. Most plants in the lists do well in moderately acid, neutral or slightly alkaline soil with a pH range of 6.5 to 7.2. Plants termed *not fussy* or *widely adapted* do well in an even wider pH range. Those that require more acidity or tolerate higher alkalinity are noted.

## MINIMUM TEMPERATURE

You must know if a plant can survive the lowest temperatures likely to occur frequently in your area. If you're new to the area, ask a local nurseryman or weather expert what low temperatures can be expected at your site. The *approximate* sustained minimum temperature a plant can tolerate is indicated by reference to zones corresponding to the USDA map on page 81. But there are complications. Sometimes plants propagated from those grown in the southern extent of their range are less resistant to cold than the same species grown in the north. Or a plant shipped from a warmer area may not be sufficiently hardened-off or dormant to withstand the rigors of the north. Buying plants grown in a climate similar to your own helps avoid these problems.

## OTHER FACTORS

If minimum temperatures were the only factor, *all* plants would perform well as long as they were tolerant of the lowest temperature encountered in each zone. There are other climatic conditions that affect how a plant performs. Heat, wind, rainfall, humidity, fog and air quality are also important. When a plant is known to have requirements beyond minimum temperature or has a special tolerance, this is noted.

Another consideration is salt applied to pavement for deicing in winter. Keep plants back from areas where salt accumulation or spray is likely to occur. In borderline areas, avoid sensitive plants, such as pin oak, littleleaf linden, crabapple, dogwood, sugar maple, Eastern white pine, yew, spirea and barberry. Instead, use Russian olive, mountain ash, Norway maple, honey locust, Japanese black pine, pagoda tree, white ash, snowberry and rugosa rose. They are more salt tolerant but not totally immune to injury. Fultsgrass has been used with good results along roads where soil is highly contaminated.

## USING THE LISTS

The best way to start choosing plants is visit a local nursery to familiarize yourself with what is available. Plants at the nursery are probably best suited to your specific area. Take a drive, and look at the plants. If you don't know a plant's name, take a few leaves back to the nursery to find out.

Refer to the lists, and make a tentative selection based on your planting design. Try to stick with plants recommended for your zone or a colder zone. If you're in a borderline area, you may want to try a few less-hardy ones that appeal to you. Make sure you place them all in the proper exposure. The best exposure is listed first.

Use the plant lists carefully, and you may be able to avoid the gardening problems you find in your neighborhood. There is no need for you to make mistakes, such as planting a wide-spreading shrub too close

## PLANT NAMES

Plants usually have two scientific or Latin names. Names may look difficult to pronounce, but you can avoid costly mistakes if you are careful about them. The first word is the *genus* name. The second is the name of the *species.* A third name, which is not always applicable, is the *variety* or *cultivar* name. Cultivars are shown in single quotes. Each scientific name designates only one type of plant. The same common name can be applied to many different plants. Be sure both or all three names of a plant are exactly what you want.

To complicate matters, botanists are constantly reclassifying plants and changing names. Often a nursery lists a plant by its former name, so you may find some plants have two or more scientific names.

**Wards yew can be kept within this planting bed with a minimum of pruning.**

to a sidewalk, a large shrub in front of a view window or a giant tree where it rips up paving and drop leaves all over the yard. The right plant in the right place the *first* time is what you're after.

Study the planting plans beginning on page 132 before deciding on your plant choices. Pay attention to plans based on the climate that's closest to your own. You can't use all the plants shown on the plans nor should you want to. But find several plants you like, and try to get the feel for proper use and spacing.

## TREE TRUNKS

Certain tree trunks have a distinctive beauty. Some trees, like the white birch and American sycamore, are vertical accents of white in a landscape. Others, such as the tulip tree, river birch and katsura tree, have intriguing textures and a feeling of age. My favorites are the ancient appearance of English yew and the startling luminous effect of amur chokeberry.

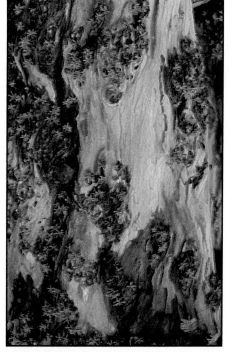
It took many years for this yew to develop such fascinating texture.

Smooth, shiny bark of the Amur chokeberry glows in the sun.

Distinctive mottled trunk of the American sycamore adds interest to the landscape.

Amur cork tree is distinguished by its sinewy, textured branches.

Striking trunk of the European white birch makes a strong vertical accent in the garden.

# LOW SHRUBS—1-1/2 to 3 feet

For small planting areas, foreground planting and in front of low windows. Space 2 to 4 feet apart. Also see Shrub Covers, page 112.

| Common Name<br>*Scientific Name* | Climate Zones/Best Exposure<br>Culture/Growth Rate & Habit/Uses | Description/Remarks<br>Similar Varieties & Species |
|---|---|---|
| Cinquefoil<br>*Potentilla fruticosa*<br>Photo pages 87 and 182. | Zones 3-9. W, S, E.<br>Widely adapted. Tolerates dryness.<br>Pest and disease resistant.<br>Moderate. Some compact, others upright to 4 feet.<br>Flowering border, clipped or unclipped hedge,<br>shrub cover. | Deciduous. Small, fernlike, green leaves. Covered with flowers all summer. 'Katherine Dykes' soft yellow. 'Abbotswood' white. 'Royal Flush' rosy-pink. 'Red Ace' orange. 'Klondike' golden-yellow. |
| Dwarf American Arborvitae<br>*Thuja occidentalis*<br>'Globosa'<br>Hetz Midget<br>Photo page 87. | Zones 3-8. E, S.<br>Foliage brown in severe winters.<br>Best in cool location with moist, fertile soil.<br>Subject to mites.<br>Slow. Compact, rounded.<br>Formal accent, hedge. | Evergreen. Dark-green, fanlike leaves. 'Nana' and 'Pumila' similar. 'Hetz Midget' very slow dwarf. 'Woodwardii' faster and larger. 'Rheingold' has golden foliage. Oriental arborvitae, *T. orientalis (Platycladus),* tolerates more heat, zone 6. 'Berckman's'/'Aurea nana' and 'Westmont' conical form with yellow-tipped leaves. |
| Dwarf Japanese Yew<br>*Taxus cuspidata*<br>'Nana'<br>Photo pages 84 and 176. | Zones 4-8. N, E.<br>Protect from winter sun in severe climates. Prefers well-drained, organic soil. Best planted in spring.<br>Subject to black-vine beetle, scale, mites.<br>Slow. Horizontal, compact.<br>Hedge, edging, shrub cover. | Evergreen. Thick, shiny, dark-green, needlelike leaves. Tiny, red fruit on female plants in fall and winter. Leaves and fruit poisonous. Ward's yew, *T. media* 'Wardii' faster, larger. |
| Bird's Nest Spruce<br>*Picea abies*<br>'Nidiformis' | Zones 4-8. E, S.<br>Moist, well-drained soil. Salt sensitive.<br>Slow. Dense, flat-topped globe.<br>Mass planting, rock garden, Oriental effect. | Evergreen. Short, dark-green needles. 'Maxwellii' rounded, even more dwarf. 'Pendula' low trailing, can be staked to weep. 'Remontii' wide cone, eventually to 10 feet. |
| Gold Coast Juniper<br>*Juniperus chinensis*<br>'Gold Coast'<br>Photo pages 87 and 165. | Zones 4-9. E, S, W.<br>Widely adapted. Well-drained soil.<br>Subject to scale and mites.<br>Moderate. Compact.<br>Foliage accent, shrub cover. | Evergreen. Yellow-tipped foliage, brightest in spring. 'Old Gold' similar. 'Parsonii' grayish-green. 'Compacta' light-green. |
| Anthony Waterer Spirea<br>*Spirea bumalda*<br>'Anthony Waterer'<br>Photo page 87. | Zones 5-9. S, W, E.<br>Widely adapted. Pest and disease resistant. Blooms longer where cool.<br>Prune before new growth begins in early spring.<br>Fast. Broad and flat.<br>Informal hedge, border. | Deciduous. Medium, serrated leaves, red fall color. Flat heads of rose-pink flowers in summer. 'Goldflame' similar with red flowers and bronzy-gold spring foliage, turning yellow in summer. 'Froebelli' taller, bright-pink flowers. *S. nipponica* 'Snowmound' very hardy with dark-green foliage, white flowers late spring. |
| Rose Daphne/Garland Flower<br>*Daphne cneorum* | Zones 5-8. N, E.<br>Needs snow cover or winter mulch in severe climates. Cool, well-drained soil. Transplant with care.<br>Slow. Very low and compact.<br>Patio, rock garden, container plant. | Evergreen. Small, needlelike, shiny green leaves, duller in winter. Sweet scented, rose-pink flower clusters in spring. All parts poisonous. 'Eximia' holds foliage better, not as fussy. |
| Slender Deutzia<br>*Deutzia gracilis*<br>Photo page 87. | Zones 5-8. E, S.<br>Neutral or alkaline soil. Thin out old branches after blooming.<br>Slow. Natural graceful, arching habit.<br>Spring accent. | Deciduous. Oblong, green leaves. Many white flowers late spring. 'Rosea' similar with pink flowers. |
| Emerald 'N Gold<br>*Euonymus fortunei* | Zones 5-9. S, W, E.<br>Widely adapted. Subject to mildew and scale.<br>Slow. Compact mound.<br>Border, low hedge, foliage accent. | Evergreen. Medium, yellow and green leaves. 'Emerald Gaiety' similar with white variegated leaves. 'Golden Prince' new leaves tipped with gold, hardier. |
| St. John's Wort<br>*Hypericum patulum* | Zones 5-8. S, W, E.<br>Widely adapted. Tolerates dryness and sandy soil.<br>Moderate. Compact, rounded.<br>Flower border. | Semievergreen. Small, shiny green leaves. Many yellow flowers in summer. 'Sungold' hardier than 'Hidcote'. *H. kalmianum* and *H. prolificum,* taller, hardy zone 4. |
| Kurume Azalea<br>*Rhododendron obtusum*<br>Photo page 17. | Zones 6-9. E, N.<br>Well-drained, acid soil with iron, moisture and mulch. Protect from hot, dry winds and winter winter sun. Northeast exposure best, heavy shade limits flowers.<br>Slow. Compact.<br>Shade, border, mass plantings, containers. | Evergreen. Small, dark-green leaves, bronzy-red winter color. Profuse white, pink to red flowers in spring. Very many varieties and species. 'Hino-Crimson', 'Snow', 'Hinodegiri' and 'Coral Bells' widely grown. Kaempferi hybrids hardier, faster, taller, larger flowers, usually semievergreen, include orange-red forms. |
| Dwarf Japanese Holly<br>*Ilex crenata* varieties<br>Photo page 87. | Zones 6-9. N, E.<br>Protect from winter sun in severe climates. Subject to nematodes.<br>Slow-moderate. Dense and compact.<br>Hedge, border, shrub cover. | Evergreen. Small, shiny leaves, not prickly. Blue-black berries on female plants. 'Helleri', 'Stokes' and 'Convexa' ('Bullata') most common. 'Helleri' smallest. 'Black Beauty' very hardy. |

**Anthony Waterer Spirea**

**Cinquefoil**

**Slender Deutzia**

**Hetz Midget Arborvitae**

**Dwarf Japanese Holly**

**Gold Coast Juniper**

# MEDIUM SHRUBS—3 to 6 feet

Consider these before using large shrubs that may require constant cutting back. Space 4 to 5 feet apart.

| Common Name / *Scientific Name* | Climate Zones/Best Exposure / Culture/Growth Rate & Habit/Uses | Description/Remarks / Similar Varieties & Species |
|---|---|---|
| Rose / *Rosa* varieties / Photo page 158. | Zones 3-9.  S, E, W. / Light shade OK in hot areas. Responds to fertilizer, mulch and water. Annual pruning necessary. Subject to aphids and mildew. / Fast. Upright canes. / Cutting garden, informal hedge. | Deciduous. Foliage and form not outstanding. Hybrid teas grown mainly for flowers. Grandifloras and floribundas fit into landscape better. Thorny branches. Countless varieties and species available. |
| Mugo Pine / *Pinus mugo* / Photo pages 89 and 130. | Zones 3-8.  E, S, W. / Slightly acid, well-drained soil with iron. Best where cool. Subject to pine tip moth and scale. / Slow. Variable globe forms from very compact to five-footers and larger. Good way to repeat feeling of pines in smaller form. Will stay in container for years. | Evergreen. Dark-green needles. Several other dwarf pines available. Tanyosho, *P. densiflora* 'Umbraculifera'. Dwarf White, *P. strobus nana*. Dwarf Scots, *P. sylvestris* 'Beuvronensis'. All choice, but quite expensive. |
| Snowberry / *Symphoricarpos albus* | Zones 4-9.  E, S, N. / Widely adapted. Tolerates poor soil, alkalinity, dryness. Pest and disease resistant. / Fast. Irregular, upright, arching branches. Spreads by suckers. / Planted mainly for attractive berries. | Deciduous. Medium, blue-green leaves. White berries in clusters early fall into winter. Indian Currant, *S. orbiculatus*, upright, red fall color, purplish-red berries, zone 5. *S. chenaulti*, compact, red-speckled, white berries, good low hedge, zone 5. *S. c.* 'Hancock' and Creeping Snowberry, *S. mollis*, dwarf, spreading shrub covers. |
| Pfitzer Juniper / *Juniperus chinensis* / Photo page 165. / *Mint Julep/Sea Green* / Photo page 89. | Zones 4-10.  S, W, E. / Widely adapted. Well-drained soil best. Subject to bagworms, twig blight and mites. / Fast. Wide spreading. / Mass plantings, natural screens and hedges. | Evergreen. Feathery, gray-green foliage. Many varieties. 'Aurea' gold-tipped foliage. 'Mint Julep'/'Sea Green' bright-green, vase shaped. 'Armstrongii' blue-green, compact. 'Glauca' and 'Hetzii' silvery-blue, taller, vigorous, arching. 'Ames' blue-green, broad pyramidal. 'Maney' blue-green, semierect. |
| Dwarf Flowering Almond / *Prunus glandulosa* | Zones 4-9.  S, E, W. / Well-drained soil. Prune after flowering or cut while in bloom for bouquet. / Fast. Upright, arching branches. / Spring accent, cut flowers. | Deciduous. Narrow, light-green leaves. Thick clusters of single or double white or pink flowers closely set on branches in spring spring before leaves appear. |
| Drooping Leucothoe / *Leucothoe fontanesiana* | Zones 5-8.  E, N. / Rich, acid soil with moisture. Protect from wind and winter sun. / Slow. Spreading and arching. / Shady foliage border. | Evergreen. Semievergreen in cold. Large, shiny, dark-green leaves. Bronze-purple in winter. Small, fragrant, white, bell-shaped flowers in spring. 'Rainbow' has leaves splotched with yellow and pink. 'Nana' to 2 feet. Coast Leucothoe, *L. axillaris* similar with narrow, pointed leaves. |

Flame Azalea

Kerria

Blue Holly

| Common Name<br>*Scientific Name* | Climate Zones/Best Exposure<br>Culture/Growth Rate & Habit/Uses | Description/Remarks<br>Similar Varieties & Species |
|---|---|---|
| Koreanspice Viburnum<br>*Viburnum carlesii* | Zones 5-8.  S, E, W.<br>Fertile, well-drained soil with moisture best,<br>but not fussy. Subject to borers. Transplant<br>with care.<br>Slow-moderate. Stiff, upward growth.<br>Border or accent shrub. | Deciduous. Medium, textured leaves, whitish underside. Tight heads<br>of very fragrant, pink buds open in spring, change to white.<br>Variable, red-maroon fall color. Red to black fruit in summer,<br>attracts birds. 'Compactum' to 2 feet. Hybrid Burkwood<br>viburnum is faster and taller, less subject to borers, narrow<br>leaves are semievergreen where protected in winter. |
| Beauty-Berry<br>*Callicarpa dichotoma* | Zones 5-8.  S, W.<br>Rich soil best. Prune heavily in early spring<br>for best berry crop.<br>Moderate. Spreading, flat growth.<br>Planted mainly for attractive berries. | Deciduous. Coarsely toothed leaves. Luminous violet-purple berries<br>fall into winter. *C. japonica* similar. |
| Kerria<br>*Kerria japonica*<br>Photo page 88. | Zones 5-8.  E, S, W.<br>Freezes to ground in cold. Easy, any well-drained<br>soil. Best with mulch and water. Prune after<br>flowering.<br>Moderate. Slender, upright branches.<br>Filler shrub, can be espaliered. | Deciduous. Long, bright-green leaves, yellow fall color, green<br>branches in winter. Single yellow-orange flowers at ends of<br>branches in late spring. 'Pleniflora' has double flowers. |
| Blue Holly<br>*Ilex meserveae*<br>Photo page 88. | Zones 5-9.  E, N, S.<br>Tolerant, but best with slightly acid, well-drained<br>soil, regular watering and winter protection.<br>Slow-moderate. Upright.<br>Hedge, specimen or unclipped screen. | Evergreen. Dark, blue-green, glossy, holly leaves with purple<br>stems. Large, red berries in fall and winter on female plants.<br>Include male types as pollinator. 'Blue Angel' slow and compact,<br>not as hardy. The others will eventually reach 10 feet or more<br>if unclipped, but can easily be kept to 6 feet. 'Blue Maid' and 'Blue<br>Princess' best berries. 'Blue Prince' and 'Blue Stallion' no berries, use<br>as pollinators. Chinese Holly, *I. cornuta* varieties faster, hardy to zone<br>6. 'China Boy' and 'China Girl' possibly zone 5. |
| Flame Azalea<br>*Rhododendron*<br>*calendulaceum*<br>Photo page 88. | Zones 6-8.  E, S, N.<br>Well-drained, acid soil with iron, mulch and<br>moisture. Protect from hot, dry winds.<br>Moderate. Upright.<br>Flowering border, natural plantings. | Deciduous. Medium, bright-green leaves with good fall color.<br>Tubular flowers, orange to scarlet tones in early summer. Chinese<br>Azalea, *R. molle* similar with yellow, orange, salmon flowers.<br>Many other species and hybrids. |
| Big-leaf Hydrangea<br>*Hydrangea macrophylla*<br>Photo page 18. | Zones 6-9.  N, E.<br>Freezes to ground in severe cold.<br>Rich soil with moisture. Good coastal but protect<br>from wind to prevent leaf damage. Subject to<br>to powdery mildew.<br>Fast. Rounded form.<br>Shade accent. | Deciduous. Large, heart-shaped, pleated leaves. Very large blue,<br>purple, pink or white flower clusters in midsummer. Choose<br>variety for preferred color. Acid soil needed for deep blue.<br>*H. arborescens* 'Annabelle' and 'Hills of Snow', *H. a.*<br>*grandiflora,* similar with white flowers, hardier to zone 4. |
| Glossy Abelia<br>*Abelia grandiflora*<br>Photo below. | Zones 6-10.  E, S, W.<br>Widely adapted. Pest and disease resistant.<br>Can be sheared, but better pruned to retain<br>natural form.<br>Moderate. Graceful, arching.<br>Foreground shrub, informal hedge. | Semievergreen. May freeze to ground in cold, but resprouts. Small,<br>pointed, glossy, dark-green leaves, bronzy in fall. Small, tubular,<br>pinkish flowers in summer. |

Glossy Abelia

**Mint Julep Juniper/Sea Green**

Mugo Pine

# LARGE SHRUBS—6 to 15 feet

Place carefully with ultimate size in mind. Plant away from walls and paving. Space 6 to 10 feet apart. Regular pruning can limit overgrowth.

| Common Name / *Scientific Name* | Climate Zones/Best Exposure / Culture/Growth Rate & Habit/Uses | Description/Remarks / Similar Varieties & Species |
|---|---|---|
| Winterberry / *Ilex verticillata* / Photo page 18. | Zones 3-8. E, N. / Rich soil with moisture. Tolerates poor drainage. / Subject to mildew. / Slow. Upright pyramidal. / Screen, natural planting. | Deciduous. Deep-green foliage with yellow fall color, become shiny black with frost. Bright-red berries on female plants along with leaves in fall and into winter. Attracts birds. 'Sparkleberry' heavy fruiting hybrid. Inkberry, *I. glabra,* hardy evergreen with black fruit, best in sandy soil. |
| Redosier / *Cornus stolonifera* / *(C. sericea)* | Zones 3-8. S, W, E. / Best in moist soils. Tolerates poor drainage. / Subject to scale, borers and canker. / Moderate. Upright branches, spreads by suckers. / Winter accent. | Deciduous. Medium, oval, green leaves with red fall color. Small, white flowers in early summer followed by white berries. Bright-red stems striking against snow. Yellowtwig, *C. s.* 'Flaviramea', similar with yellow stems. 'Kelsey Dwarf' to 2 feet, subject to leaf spot. 'Isanti' compact, makes good hedge. Siberian, *C. alba* 'Sibirica' quite similar to redosier. |

**Rhododendron**

| Common Name / *Scientific Name* | Climate Zones/Best Exposure / Culture/Growth Rate & Habit/Uses | Description/Remarks / Similar Varieties & Species |
|---|---|---|
| Common Lilac / *Syringa vulgaris* / Photo page 80. | Zones 3-8. S, W. Widely adapted. Neutral or slightly alkaline, well-drained soil. Subject to scale, borers, mildew. B&B establish and bloom sooner than bareroot. Prune after flowering. Moderate-fast. Upright. Background, hedge or feature shrub. | Deciduous. Large, heart-shaped, blue-green leaves. Showy clusters of fragrant flowers, white through purple shades in late spring. Numerous varieties, French hybrids most popular. Chinese lilac, *S. chinensis*, not as tall, more graceful, smaller leaves. Persian lilac, *S. persica*, to 6 feet with narrow leaves, violet flowers. Chinese and Persian hardy zone 5, good hedges. |
| Sweet Mock Orange / *Philadelphus coronarius* | Zones 4-8. S, W, E. Widely adapted. Well-drained soil with iron best. Pest and disease resistant. Prune after flowering. Slow. Irregular, sprawling. Flowering background. | Deciduous. Medium, toothed leaves. Many fragrant, white flowers in late spring are the outstanding feature. Gets leggy, rangy and straggly. Golden mockorange, *P. c.* 'Aureus' smaller with yellowish foliage. Lemoine mockorange, *P. lemoinei*, more compact. Virginal mockorange, *P. virginalis*, double flowers in summer-fall. Virginal variety 'Minnesota Snowflake' very hardy with 6 foot, arching branches to ground. 'Dwarf Minnesota Snowflake' 2 to 3 feet. |
| Doublefile Viburnum / *Viburnum plicatum tomentosum* / Photo pages 92 and 131. | Zones 4-8. S, W, E. Moist, well-drained soil best, but not fussy. Aphids not a problem as with *V. opulus*. Difficult to transplant. Moderate. Horizontal branches. Background, screen, hedge, accent. | Deciduous. Large, dark-green, serrated leaves. Purplish-red fall color. Flat, white flower heads on top of branches in late spring. Red to black berries late summer. Japanese snowball, *V. plicatum*, similar with round flowers. Common snowball, *V. opulus*, 'Roseum' greenish-white, ball-shaped flowers. Arrowwood, *V. dentatum*, rapid, very hardy to zone 2, tolerates wet soil, shade and clipping. Nannyberry, *V. lentago*, upright to 20 feet. Leatherleaf, *V. rhytidophyllum*, evergreen with protection zone 6, sprouts from base when frozen back zone 5. Long, crinkly leaves, yellowish flowers. |

**Beauty Bush**

**Weigela**

| Common Name<br>*Scientific Name* | Climate Zones/Best Exposure<br>Culture/Growth Rate & Habit/Uses | Description/Remarks<br>Similar Varieties & Species |
|---|---|---|
| Peegee Hydrangea<br>*Hydrangea paniculata grandiflora*<br>Photo pages 18 and 93. | Zones 4-9.  E.<br>Widely adapted. Easy, appreciates moisture.<br>Pest and disease resistant.<br>Prune back to control size.<br>Fast. Open form.<br>Background. Specimen. | Deciduous. Large, coarse leaves. Very large, pointed, pinkish-white snowballs in late summer, darken in fall. Oakleaf hydrangea, *H. quercifolia,* large, oaklike leaves, purple fall color. Flowers similar to Peegee. Grows to 6 feet, hardy zone 5. |
| Mountain Laurel<br>*Kalmia latifolia*<br>Photo below. | Zones 4-9.  E, N.<br>Cool, well-drained, sandy, acid soil with moisture and mulch. Pest and disease resistant.<br>Slow. Rounded.<br>Entrance feature, natural planting. | Evergreen. Large, shiny, dark-green leaves. Clusters of pinkish-white, cup-shaped flowers in late spring. Aristocratic shrub, combines well with ferns and rhododendrons. |
| Beauty Bush<br>*Kolkwitzia amabilis*<br>Photo page 91. | Zones 4-8.  S, W.<br>Poor, sandy, well-drained soils.<br>Tolerates dryness and alkalinity. Pest and disease resistant. Prune after flowering to prevent legginess.<br>Slow. Upright with arching branches.<br>Background with facer shrubs to cover bareness. | Deciduous. Large, oval, gray-green leaves, red fall color. Profuse, deep-pink buds, become paler in early summer. Brownish, peeling bark adds winter interest. |

**Doublefile Viburnum**

**Mountain Laurel**

| Common Name / Scientific Name | Climate Zones/Best Exposure / Culture/Growth Rate & Habit/Uses | Description/Remarks / Similar Varieties & Species |
|---|---|---|
| Forsythia<br>*Forsythia intermedia*<br>Photo page 17. | Zones 5-8. S, W.<br>Flower buds susceptible to frost damage. Neutral soil with mulch.<br>Needs water during hot spells.<br>Rapid. Upright, arching.<br>Spring accent, hedge. | Deciduous. Medium, yellow-green leaves. Profuse, yellow flowers along branches in early spring before leaves. 'Beatrix Farrand' large, 2-inch flowers. 'Karl Sax', flower buds hardier. 'Lynwood Gold' erect branches. Weeping forsythia, *F. suspensa*, branch ends droop to ground. Early forsythia, *F. ovata*, smaller, zone 4. Bronx forsythia, *F. viridissima* 'Bronxensis' to 2 feet, good shrub cover. 'Arnold Dwarf' similar, but few flowers. |
| Weigela<br>*Weigela florida*<br>Photo page 91. | Zones 5-8. S, W.<br>Some die-back in coldest zones. Well-drained soil.<br>Tolerates alkalinity, but may need iron. Pest and disease resistant. Prune after flowering.<br>Rapid. Rounded.<br>Background, hedge, accent. | Deciduous. Medium, pointed leaves. Covered with pink, tubular flowers in early summer. Attracts bees and hummingbirds. *Rosea*, deep pink. 'Vanicekii' dark red, hardiest. 'Variegatum' pink with yellow and green leaves. 'Bristol Ruby' red to 5 feet. 'Java Red' dark-purple leaves to 3 feet, pink flowers. |
| Catawba Rhododendron<br>*Rhododendron catawbiense*<br>Photo pages 90 and 164. | Zones 5-8. E, N.<br>Well-drained, acid soil with iron, moisture and mulch. Protect from hot, dry winds and winter sun. Northeast exposure best, heavy shade limits flowers. Main problem is root rot. Provide good drainage and plant high.<br>Slow-moderate. Broad, rounded.<br>Specimen, natural planting, large container. | Evergreen. Large, handsome foliage. Striking heads of white and rose-lilac to purple flowers in early summer. 'Roseum Elegans', 'Album Elegans' and 'Ignatius Sargent' are reliable and readily available. 'PJM' Carolina hybrid tolerates more sun, has good, maroon-red fall color, magenta flowers late spring, is more compact. Rosebay, *R. maximum*, blooms later than catawba, grows to 15 feet and more. 'PJM' and Rosebay hardier to zone 4. |
| Pyracantha/Firethorn<br>*Pyracantha coccinea*<br>Photo page 156. | Zones 5-10. E, S, W.<br>Protect in cold zones.<br>Widely adapted. Well-drained soil.<br>Tolerates alkalinity, but needs iron.<br>Subject to fireblight and mites.<br>Moderate. Irregular and rangy.<br>Hedge, barrier, espalier. | Deciduous to evergreen. Small, dark-green leaves. Covered with clusters of tiny, white flowers in late spring. Orange-red berries into fall. Thorny branches. 'Lalandei' and 'Kasan' most common. 'Low Boy' shrub cover to 4 feet. |

**Peegee Hydrangea**

# UPRIGHT SHRUBS—for narrow places

Most shrubs grow about as wide as they do high. Here are some that can be kept narrow with a minimum of effort.

| Common Name<br>*Scientific Name* | Climate Zones/Best Exposure<br>Culture/Growth Rate & Habit/Uses | Description/Remarks<br>Similar Varieties & Species |
|---|---|---|
| Northern Bayberry<br>*Myrica pensylvanica*<br>Photo page 95. | Zones 2-8. S, E.<br>Sandy, acid soil, dry or with moisture. Good coastal, salt tolerant.<br>Transplant carefully in early spring.<br>Slow-moderate. Wide upright, to 8 feet, spreads by suckers.<br>Hedge or background. | Semievergreen. Oblong, dark-green, glossy, aromatic leaves. Grayish berries on stems into winter on female plants. Withstands shearing. |
| Upright Junipers<br>*Juniperus* species<br>Photo page 152.<br>Twisted/Hollywood<br>Photo page 95. | Zones 3-9. S, W, E.<br>Hardiness and susceptibility to scale, bagworm, cedar-apple rust, mites and twig blight vary with species and locality.<br>Most are slow, dense. 10 to 20 feet.<br>Screens, hedges, formal accents. | Evergreen. Scalelike foliage, color range from dark-green to silver-blue. Most have bluish berries. Chinese junipers, *J. chinensis*: 'Blaauw' blue-green, vase to 4 feet, slow, good hedge zone 4. 'Columnaris' gray-green, narrow, fast, zone 4. Twisted/Hollywood, 'Torulosa'/'Kaizuka' dark-green, picturesque, excellent coastal. 'Robusta Green' bright green, dense, irregular. 'Keteleeri' light-green, loose, pyramidal. All zone 5. Rocky Mountain Junipers, *J. scopulorum*, zone 3 with reddish-brown bark. 'Pathfinder' blue-gray, broad pyramid. 'Cologreen' bright-green, cone, subject to cedar apple rust. 'Gray Gleam' silvery, gray-blue, columnar. 'Medora' bluish-green, narrow, vertical, slow. 'Tolleson's' weeping, graceful, arching miniature tree form, blue-gray and green selections. |
| Purpleleaf Sand Cherry<br>*Prunus cistena*<br>Photo page 95. | Zones 3-9. S, W, E.<br>Widely adapted. Well-drained soil.<br>Moderate. Vertical branches to 8 feet.<br>Specimen, shrub border, foliage accent. | Deciduous. Purple-red leaves all season. Fragrant pale-pink to white flowers in spring. Small purple fruit. |
| Virginia Cedar<br>*Juniperus virginiana* | Zones 4-9. S, W, E.<br>Widely adapted, thrives in Northeast.<br>Well-drained, gravelly soil with moisture best.<br>Subject to cedar-apple rust, twig blight, scale, mites.<br>Slow. Dense. 10 to 20 feet.<br>Specimen, hedge, screen, windbreak. | Evergreen. Scalelike foliage, color varies with selection. Most get brown in severe winters. Blue berries attract birds. Hillspire, 'Cupressifolia' dark-green, fine texture, broad pyramid, resists blight. 'Burkii' steel-blue, plum color winter, broad, resists blight. Dundee, 'Hillii' gray-green, purple winter, compact, resists blight. 'Manhattan Blue' blue-green, compact pyramid, 8 feet. 'Skyrocket' silver-blue, narrow column, fast. *J.* 'Canaertii' bright-green, good winter color, broad. |
| Rose of Sharon<br>*Hibiscus syriacus* | Zones 4-9. E, S.<br>Widely adapted. Tolerates dryness, good on coast.<br>Subject to leaf spot, mildew, aphids.<br>Slow-moderate. Vase shape. 8 to 10 feet.<br>Accent, hedge or screen. | Deciduous. Large, toothed leaves. Showy white, pink, red, purple, and blue flowers in late summer. |
| American Holly<br>*Ilex opaca*<br>Photo pages 10 and 169. | Zones 5-9. E, N, S.<br>Acid soil with coolness and moisture.<br>Protect from wind and severe winter cold.<br>Slow. Pyramidal. 20 feet and up.<br>Screen, hedge, formal specimen, holiday decoration. | Evergreen. Medium, green leaves with spiny edges. Small, red berries in fall and winter on female plants. 'East Palatka' fast with small, glossy leaves, abundant dark-red fruit. 'Christmas Carol' fast and hardy. 'Variegata' has creamy leaf margins. English holly, *I. aquifolium*, dark-green, glossy foliage, very spiny. Bright-red berries. 'Balkans' hardy zone 6. |
| Sarcoxie Euonymus<br>*Euonymus fortunei*<br>'Sarcoxie' | Zones 5-9. E, W, S.<br>Widely adapted. Subject to euonymus scale.<br>Slow. 6 feet.<br>Clipped hedge, large container, espalier. | Evergreen. Medium, dark-green leaves. Spreading euonymus varieties, *E. kiautschovica (patens)*, 'Manhattan' and 'Pauli' are taller with glossy, dark-green leaves, retain good winter color. |
| Oregon Grape<br>*Mahonia aquifolium*<br>Leatherleaf Mahonia<br>Photo page 95. | Zones 5-9. N, E.<br>Protect from winter sun and wind in severe climates. Well-drained soil with moisture best.<br>Watch for looper caterpillar.<br>Slow-moderate. 4 to 6 feet.<br>Accent, natural screen. | Semievergreen. Glossy, hollylike foliage on vertical stalks, purplish-red fall and winter. Yellow flower clusters in spring, blue berries summer. 'Compacta' to 2 feet, shrub cover. Leatherleaf, *M. bealei*, bold, large, blue-gray-green leaves, hardy zone 6. |
| Lily-of-the-Valley Shrub/<br>Japanese Andromeda<br>*Pieris japonica*<br>Photo page 95. | Zones 6-9. N, E.<br>Protect from wind and winter sun.<br>Well-drained, acid soil with iron, moisture and mulch. Subject to mites and lacebugs.<br>Slow. 6 to 8 feet.<br>Specimen, shady border, natural planting. | Evergreen. Dark-green, glossy leaves, new growth bronze-pink. Drooping panicles of tiny, urnlike flowers in spring. Many varieties with distinct foliage, flowers and growth habits. 'Variegata' has leaves marked creamy-white. Mountain pieris, *P. floribunda*, lower, dense and rounded, tolerates more alkalinity. |
| Longstalk Holly<br>*Ilex pedunculosa*<br>Photo page 95. | Zones 6-9. E, S.<br>Well-drained, slightly acid soil.<br>Fast. 10 feet and more.<br>Entrance or tub specimen plant. | Evergreen. Large, glossy, dark-green leaves with smooth margins, coppery in winter. Bright-red, drooping berries on female plants, need pollination. |

**Leatherleaf Mahonia**

**Twisted Juniper/Hollywood**

**Lily-of-the-Valley Shrub**

**Purple-leaf Sand Cherry**

**Longstalk Holly**

**Oregon Grape**

**Northern Bayberry**

95

# SMALL TREES—10 to 25 feet

Some are merely large shrubs trained into trees. Others will eventually grow more than 25 feet tall unless pruned. Well-suited to small yards, patios and confined spaces.

| Common Name<br>*Scientific Name* | Climate Zones/Culture<br>Growth Rate & Habit/Uses | Description/Remarks<br>Similar Varieties & Species |
|---|---|---|
| Shadblow/Serviceberry<br>*Amelanchier canadensis*<br>*(A. arborea)* | Zones 4-8.<br>Easy in any soil with some moisture.<br>Tolerates light shade.<br>Moderate. Upright. Can reach 50 feet with age,<br>but usually smaller.<br>Background, multitrunk specimen. | Deciduous. New leaves silver turning dark-green. Yellow to red fall color. Many white, nodding flowers in spring before leaves. Edible maroon berries attract birds. Light-gray bark. Apple serviceberry, *A. grandiflora*, smaller, spreading, with larger flowers. Allegheny serviceberry, *A. laevis*, young leaves purplish-green, larger flowers, fruit dark-blue. Both not as hardy, zone 5. |
| Japanese Tree Lilac<br>*Syringa reticulata*<br>*(S. amurensis japonica)*<br>Photo below. | Zones 4-8.<br>Neutral or slightly alkaline, well-drained soil.<br>Full sun best. Subject to scale, borers and mildew.<br>Moderate. Open pyramidal, often multitrunk.<br>Patio tree, flowering accent. | Deciduous. Large, heart-shaped, hairy, blue-green leaves. Showy, creamy-white flower clusters in early summer, not fragrant. Cherry-like bark on old trees. |

**Eastern Redbud**

**Japanese Tree Lilac**

| Common Name<br>*Scientific Name* | Climate Zones/Best Exposure<br>Culture/Growth Rate & Habit/Uses | Description/Remarks<br>Similar Varieties & Species |
|---|---|---|
| Cockspur Thorn<br>*Crataegus crus-galli*<br>Photo page 18 and below. | Zones 4-9.<br>Well-drained, dry soil. Subject to aphids and fireblight. Resists cedar rust better than other hawthorns.<br>Plant B&B in spring.<br>Slow-moderate. Round or flat-headed with dense, horizontal branches.<br>Hedge, barrier, background, screen. | Deciduous. Dark-green, shiny leaves, orange-red fall color. White flowers in clusters late spring. Orange-red berries into winter. Many large thorns. Use thornless variety, *C. c.* 'Inermis' where a hazard. Carriere hawthorne, C. *lavallei*, bronze-red fall color, white flowers with red markings, striking orange-red fruit through winter. Washington hawthorn *C. phaenopyrum*, faster, taller, shiny leaves with orange-red fall color. White flowers early summer, orange-red fruit fall and winter, dense, rounded top, often multitrunk, OK in lawn. |
| Fringe Tree<br>*Chionanthus virginicus*<br>Photo page 83 and below. | Zones 4-9.<br>Partial shade best. Well-drained, acid soil with moisture.<br>Slow. Upright, rounded, low-branching.<br>Background, flowering accent, specimen. | Deciduous. Large, coarse leaves, late to leaf out, yellow fall color. Airy, greenish-white, fragrant flowers cover tree in late spring. Dark-blue fruit on pistillate plants only. Chinese fringe tree, *C. retusus*, smaller leaves, shrubby, less-showy flowers. |
| Flowering Crabapple<br>*Malus* hybrids | Zones 4-8.<br>OK in lawn if well-drained soil. Salt sensitive. Protect tender bark from sun scald and mice. Apple scab, mildew, fire blight and cedar-apple rust can be serious problems. Choose resistant varieties where disease is prevalent.<br>Most slow-moderate. Various growth habits, some can be espaliered.<br>Flowering accent, specimen. | Deciduous. Medium leaves, deep-green, some with purplish cast. White, pink, red flowers in spring. Yellow to red fruit in fall attracts birds. Reasonably disease-resistant species: M. baccata, dense foliage, white flowers, red and yellow fruit. Carmine, *M. atrosan guinea*, shiny leaves, rose-purple flowers, yellow fruit, resists apple scab. Japanese, *M. floribunda*, many fragrant rose-red flowers late spring, fading to white, red and yellow fruit, dense, rounded, disease resistant. Sargent, *M. sargenti*, small, pink to white fragrant flowers, small dark-red fruit. Wide and shrublike to 8 feet. |
| Eastern Redbud<br>*Cercis canadensis*<br>Photo page 96. | Zones 5-9.<br>Prefers partial shade. Rich, well-drained soil with moisture best, but adaptable. Subject to borers. Transplant with care in spring.<br>Moderate. Irregular, low branching.<br>Flowering accent, lawn specimen. | Deciduous. Rich-green, heart-shaped leaves with yellow fall color. Small, rose-purple flowers along the branches in early spring before leaves. Attractive, dark-brown bark and brown pea pods. 'Alba' has white flowers. 'Forest Pansy' has maroon foliage all season. Chinese redbud, *C. chinensis*, more flowers, hardy zone 6. |

Fringe Tree

Cockspur Thorn

| Common Name<br>*Scientific Name* | Climate Zones/Best Exposure<br>Culture/Growth Rate & Habit/Uses | Description/Remarks<br>Similar Varieties & Species |
|---|---|---|
| Smoke Tree<br>*Cotinus coggygria* | Zones 5-9.<br>Well-drained, poor soil. New trees need water, then infrequently.<br>Slow. Broad, irregular, shrublike.<br>Background, accent. | Deciduous. Rounded, blue-green leaves, yellow to orange-red fall color. Purplish flower clusters in summer, fade to smoky effect.<br>*C. c.* 'Purpureus' has purple leaves. |
| Oriental Flowering Cherry<br>*Prunus serrulata*<br>varieties<br>Photo pages 85 and 99. | Zones 5-8.<br>Needs good, well-drained soil and regular watering.<br>Relatively short-lived, especially in wet soils.<br>Subject to scale.<br>Slow to moderate. Various growth habits.<br>Spring-flowering accent, bouquets. | Deciduous. Medium, pointed, green leaves. White to pink, single or double, fragrant flowers in late spring before leaves. 'Kwansan' large, double, deep-pink flowers, upright vase-shape, widely grown. Weeping Higan, *P. subhirtella,* 'Pendula' single, pale flowers, blue-black fruit, long-lived. Sargent, *P. sargentii,* deep-pink flowers, red fall color, purple fruit, upright to 40 feet, few problems. Amur chokeberry, *P. maackii,* has striking bronzy, flaking bark, hardy zone 2. |

**Purple-leaf Plum**

| Common Name<br>*Scientific Name* | Climate Zones/Best Exposure<br>Culture/Growth Rate & Habit/Uses | Description/Remarks<br>Similar Varieties & Species |
|---|---|---|
| Purpleleaf Plum<br>*Prunus cerasifera*<br>'Atropurpurea'<br>*(P.* 'Pissardii')<br>Photo page 98. | Zones 5-10.<br>Widely adapted. OK in lawn if well-drained.<br>Subject to borers.<br>Moderate. Upright vase.<br>Spring flowering, foliage contrast. | Deciduous. Medium, dark-purple leaves.<br>White flowers in spring before leaves. Small,<br>red plums late summer a nuisance on paving.<br>'Thundercloud' whitish-pink flowers, dark,<br>coppery leaves. 'Newport' pink flowers, purplish-red leaves, hardiest<br>to zone 4. *P. blireiana,* fragrant, pink flowers, greenish-bronze leaves. |
| Flowering Dogwood<br>*Cornus florida*<br>Photo pages 18 and 164. | Zones 5-9.<br>Partial shade preferred, protect from hot winds.<br>Well-drained, acid soil with moisture. OK in<br>lawn. Sensitive to salt. Subject to borers,<br>fungus and canker. Limit pruning to a minimum.<br>Wrap tender bark. Difficult to transplant.<br>Slow. Flat top, spreading.<br>Specimen, wooded background. | Deciduous. Large, deeply veined leaves, red fall color. Large, white<br>flower bracts in spring before leaves. Shiny, red berries into winter.<br>'Cloud 9' profuse white bracts. *Rubra,* rose-pink bracts. 'Cherokee<br>Chief' red bracts. 'Hohman's Golden' variegated leaves, shrubby<br>habit. Japanese dogwood, *C. kousa,* blooms later with pointed,<br>greenish-white bracts among leaves, large, red, raspberrylike fruit<br>late summer. Cornelian cherry, *C. mas,* tiny, yellow flowers early<br>spring. Edible, tart, red cherries. Tall shrub, pest and disease<br>resistant, hardy zone 4. Pagoda dogwood, *C. alternifolia,* small,<br>creamy-white flowers, clump or multitrunk, hardy zone 4. |
| Saucer Magnolia<br>*Magnolia soulangiana*<br>Photo page 97. | Zones 5-9.<br>Rich, well-drained, acid soil with moisture.<br>Plant B&B in spring with extra care. Subject<br>to scale.<br>Slow. Upright, multistemmed.<br>Lawn specimen, flowering accent. | Deciduous. Large, green leaves. White to purple cup-shaped flowers to<br>6'' across, before leaves in late spring. Smooth, gray bark. 'Lennei'<br>has purple flowers. *M. liliflora,* 'Nigra' dark, reddish-purple<br>flowers. Star magnolia, *M. stellata,* is shrublike, has fragrant, white<br>flowers with narrow petals. Early blooms subject to frost damage. |
| Japanese Maple<br>*Acer palmatum*<br>Photo page 165. | Zones 6-9.<br>Prefers deep, rich soil, partial shade with<br>moisture. Protect from hot, dry winds.<br>Slow. Dense, rounded, well-behaved.<br>Specimen, accent, large container. | Deciduous. Bright-green, lobed leaves, red fall color. Purple and cut-<br>leaf selections popular. |

**Oriental Flowering Cherry**

# MEDIUM TREES—25 to 40 feet

In time, most of the following will grow taller than 40 feet in a favorable climate. However, they can serve in a normal-sized yard for many years without taking over if properly pruned. Keep 15 feet or more away from house walls.

| Common Name *Scientific Name* | Climate Zones/Culture Growth Rate & Habit/Uses | Description/Remarks Similar Varieties & Species |
|---|---|---|
| River/Red Birch *Betula nigra* Photo pages 85, 101 and 113. | Zones 2-9. Best with acid soil and high water table or frequent watering. OK in lawn. Tolerates heat and cold. Resistant to borers. Prune in August to prevent bleeding. Rapid. Upright vase, multitrunk. Natural groupings, accents. | Deciduous. Diamond-shaped, dark-green leaves, gray-green undersides. Attractive pinkish-brown, flaking bark. 'Heritage' whitish-pink bark. European white birch, *B. pendula (B. verrucosa)* and Canoe/Paper birch, *B. papyrifera,* have striking white bark, both subject to borers, short-lived. Gray birch, *B. populifolia,* smaller, tolerates dry, sandy soil. Monarch birch, *B. maximowicziana,* large and fast. Both appear resistant to borers. |
| Red Horsechestnut *Aesculus carnea* Photo page 83. | Zones 3-9. Tough, but prefers fertile, moist soil. Slow. Dense, rounded. Shade, background. | Deciduous. Large, coarse, dark-green, toothed leaflets. Upright plumes of pink-red flowers in late spring. Ruby Red, 'Briotii' has darker red flowers. Ohio Buckeye, *A. glabra,* yellow-green flowers, yellow-orange fall color, grows rapidly. Horsechestnut, *A. hippocastanum,* creamy-white flowers, grows larger. Subject to leaf blotch and leaf scorch, fruit can be a nuisance. 'Albo-plena' double, white flowers, no fruit. |
| Littleleaf Linden *Tilia cordata* Photo page 101. | Zones 3-8. Needs moisture, OK in lawn. Protect tender bark from sun. Aphids are a seasonal problem. Subject to Japanese beetles and flowers attract bees. Slow. Dense pyramidal. Shade, large natural or clipped screen. | Deciduous. Medium, dark-green leaves, silvery undersides. Small, fragrant, yellow flowers in summer. 'Greenspire' and 'Glenhaven' have straight trunks. Basswood, *T. americana,* is larger, heart-shaped leaves, grows faster and taller, hardy zone 2. 'Redmond' has red-tipped branches in winter. |
| American Yellow-wood *Cladrastis lutea* | Zones 3-8. Rich, well-drained, moist soil. Tolerates alkalinity, OK in lawn. Full sun best, but wrap bark to protect in winter. Moderate. Broad, rounded form, low branching. Specimen, natural planting. | Deciduous. Large, bright-green leaves, yellow fall color. Hanging clusters of fragrant white flowers in summer, not consistent. Brown, flat seed pods in fall. Smooth, gray bark. |
| Amur Corktree *Phellodendron amurense* Photo pages 85 and 101. | Zones 4-8. Tolerates heat and drought. OK in lawn. Pest and disease resistant. Fast. Low-branching, sculptural. Accent, specimen, feature tree. | Deciduous. Large, bright-green leaves. Yellow fall color. Black fruit in fall. Beautifully patterned bark. |
| Katsura Tree *Cercidiphyllum japonicum* Photo page 101. | Zones 4-8. Best in rich, moist soil. OK in lawn. Protect from hot winds. Pest and disease resistant. Prune when young to direct form. Moderate-fast. Upward growth, often multitrunk. Shade or accent. | Deciduous. Blue-green, heart-shaped leaves. Outstanding yellow to red fall color. |
| Goldenrain Tree *Koelreuteria paniculata* Photo page 101. | Zones 5-10. Withstands heat, drought, alkaline soil, salt, air pollution. OK in lawn or dry. Pest and disease resistant. Slow-moderate. Open, rounded. Shade, patio, multitrunk specimen. | Deciduous. Green, toothed leaflets. Twelve inch long, upright clusters of yellow flowers in summer. Tan pods persist into winter. |
| Japanese Pagoda Tree *Sophora japonica* | Zones 5-9. Tolerates poor and salty soil, heat and dryness, but protect from hot winds. OK in lawn. Pest and disease resistant. Moderate-fast to 30 feet, slowly thereafter. Round, spreading. Shade, background. | Deciduous. Divided, dark-green leaflets. Fragrant, cream-colored, pealike flowers in summer. Interesting yellow-green, bumpy pods. |
| Sweetbay Magnolia *Magnolia virginiana* | Zones 5-9. Moist to wet, acid soil. Protect from hot, dry winds. Transplant carefully in spring only. Moderate. Upright. Shade, lawn specimen, background. | Deciduous large shrub north, semievergreen zone 7 southward. Shiny, bluish-green leaves, whitish undersides. 3-inch, very fragrant, creamy-white flowers in summer. Red fruit pods in fall. Merrill magnolia, *M. loebneri,* low-branched, vigorous with petaled, fragrant, white flowers in spring. Cucumber tree, *M. acuminata,* is faster, larger, hardy to zone 4, flowers not showy, but has attractive fruit. |
| Silk Tree/Mimosa *Albizia julibrissin* Photo page 83. | Zones 6-9. Widely adapted. Tolerates poor, gravelly soil and dryness, but also OK in lawn. Protect from strong winds. Subject to mimosa webworm and wilt. Best planted small B&B or container. Slow to start, then fast. Low, flat, spreading with horizontal branching. Shade, multitrunk specimen. | Deciduous. Delicate, ferny foliage, casts light shade. Light-pink, fragrant, flowers in late summer. Long, flat, brown pods. 'Rosea' has deep-pink flowers, is slightly hardier. Drops leaves, flowers and pods. Suffers from wind and ice-storm damage. Usually not long-lived. |
| Japanese Black Pine *Pinus thunbergiana* Photo pages 82 and 101. | Zones 6-10. Top kill from freezes in zones 5 and 6. Widely adapted. Tolerates sandy soil and coastal conditions. Moderate. Irregular or pyramidal. Picturesque silhouette, Oriental effect, large container. | Evergreen. Rich, dark-green needles. Can be kept to small size by pruning out new growth in spring. Japanese red pine, *P. densiflora,* flat-topped, reddish-brown bark. Lacebark pine, *P. bungeana,* slow, tall, upright, multitrunk with striking bark that peels in creamy patches. Swiss stone pine, *P. cembra,* slow, smaller, dense pyramidal. All three hardy to zone 4. |

**Japanese Black Pine**

**Katsura Tree**

**Amur Corktree**

**Littleleaf Linden**

**River/Red Birch**

**Goldenrain Tree**

# LARGE TREES—40 feet and over

Use these trees with caution. They require considerable room, cast a lot of shade and can drop enormous quantities of leaves when mature. Plant 20 feet or more away from house walls.

| Common Name<br>*Scientific Name* | Climate Zones/Culture<br>Growth Rate & Habit/Uses | Description/Remarks<br>Similar Varieties & Species |
|---|---|---|
| Green Ash<br>*Fraxinus pennsylvanica*<br>*lanceolata*<br>*(F. p. subintegerrima)* | Zones 3-8.<br>Widely adapted. Tolerates wind, some dryness, OK in lawn. Minor pest and disease problems.<br>Fast. Broad, upright, dense. To 50 feet.<br>Shade tree. | Deciduous. Bright-green leaves. Yellow fall color. Winged seeds litter and sprout. 'Marshall Seedless' pyramidal, seedless, shiny, dark-green leaves. 'Summit' more upright, produces seeds. White ash, *F. americana,* taller to 100 feet, yellow to purple fall color, especially 'Rose Hill'. |
| Sugar Maple<br>*Acer saccharum*<br>Photo pages 103 and 164.<br>Red Maple<br>Photo page 105. | Zones 3-8.<br>Prefers well-drained, neutral soil with moisture. OK in lawn. Salt sensitive, subject to wilt.<br>Wrap young trees to protect trunk.<br>Slow to start. Upright, dense with arching branches. To 80 feet.<br>Shade tree, fall color. | Deciduous. Large, bright-green leaves, whitish undersides. Number 1 fall color tree, bright-yellow to red, mixed with green. 'Newton Sentry' and 'Temple's Upright' are columnar forms. Red maple, *A. rubrum,* is faster and smaller with reddish flowers in spring, bright, red-orange fall color, tolerates wet soils. |
| Norway Maple<br>*Acer platanoides*<br>Photo page 104. | Zones 3-8.<br>Widely adapted. Best in rich, well-drained, lime soil with moisture. Salt tolerant.<br>Wrap young tree trunks. Subject to wilt.<br>Moderate. Dense, round headed. To 60 feet.<br>Shade tree, too dense for lawn under.<br>Purple forms for foliage accents. | Deciduous. Large, dark-green leaves, yellow fall color. Small but showy yellow flowers before leaves in spring. Large clusters of 2-winged samaras. 'Cleveland' rich, dark-green. 'Crimson King' and 'Schwedleri' are red-purple leaf varieties. 'Columnare' is narrow form. Silver maple, *A. saccharinum,* attractive leaves have white undersides, very fast but brittle and relatively short-lived. |

**Eastern White Pine**

| Common Name<br>*Scientific Name* | Climate Zones/Best Exposure<br>Culture/Growth Rate & Habit/Uses | Description/Remarks<br>Similar Varieties & Species |
|---|---|---|
| Hackberry<br>*Celtis occidentalis* | Zones 3-8.<br>Widely adapted. Tolerates alkaline soil, dryness, but OK in lawn. Subject to leaf gall and witches broom.<br>Moderate. Sturdy vase. 50 feet and up.<br>Shade tree. | Deciduous. Light-green, elmlike leaves. Yellowish fall color. Small, purple fruit late summer. Light-gray, warty bark. |
| Red Oak<br>*Quercus rubra*<br>*(Q. borealis)*<br>Photo page 105. | Zones 3-8.<br>Fertile soil with moisture. OK in lawn. Salt tolerant. Relatively easy to transplant. Very subject to oak wilt.<br>Moderate. Broad, round-headed. 60 feet and up.<br>Shade tree, specimen. | Deciduous. Large, glossy, pointed, lobed leaves. Red-orange fall color. Scarlet oak, *Q. coccinea,* bright-red fall color, fast, very subject to oak wilt, hardy zone 5. Shumard oak, *Q. shumardii,* smaller, tolerates alkalinity, zone 5. |
| Eastern White Pine<br>*Pinus strobus*<br>Photo page 102.<br>Austrian Pine<br>Photo page 105. | Zones 3-8.<br>Widely adapted. Best in well-drained soil with moisture. Salt sensitive. Tolerates part shade. Subject to pine blister rust.<br>Slow to start, then fast. Pyramidal.<br>100 feet and up.<br>Screen, windbreak. | Evergreen. Soft, light-green needles with whitish stripe. Dwarf, upright and weeping forms available. Austrian, *P. nigra,* stiff, dark-green needles, fast, tolerates salt, alkalinity and wind. Scots, *P. sylvestris,* twisted, bluish-green needles, reddish-orange bark, fast and tolerates dryness. Both hardy to zone 4. |

**Sugar Maple**

**Northern Catalpa**

**Thornless Honey Locust**

| Common Name<br>*Scientific Name* | Climate Zones/Best Exposure<br>Culture/Growth Rate & Habit/Uses | Description/Remarks<br>Similar Varieties & Species |
|---|---|---|
| Kentucky Coffeetree<br>*Gymnocladus dioica*<br>Photo page 18 and below. | Zones 4-9.<br>Widely adapted. Tolerates poor soil, heat and dryness, but best in rich, moist soil. OK in lawn. Protect from hot winds. B&B or container plants best. Pest and disease resistant.<br>Slow. Upright, narrow growth in youth, broadens with age. 50 feet and up.<br>Shade tree, winter silhouette. | Deciduous. Handsome, dark-green leaves. Yellow fall color. 6-inch long, brown pods on female trees persist into winter. Picturesque branch structure. |
| Thornless Honey Locust<br>*Gleditsia triacanthos inermis*<br>Photo pages 103 and 165. | Zones 4-9.<br>Widely adapted. Tolerates heat, salt, dryness or moisture. Subject to wind damage, borers, webworm. Wrap young trunks.<br>Fast. Upright, open, spreading. To 50 feet.<br>Shade tree, patio, lawn. | Deciduous. Small, lacy leaves. Yellow fall color. Wide, long pods on female trees. Casts light shade, lawn grows well under. 'Moraine' resists webworm. 'Rubylace' smaller, slower, has deep-red new growth 'Sunburst' has yellow foliage, moderate growth rate. 'Skyline' narrower. 'Imperial' more compact. |
| White Oak<br>*Quercus alba* | Zones 4-8.<br>Fertile, well-drained soil with moisture. Salt tolerant. Resists wilt. Plant small in spring.<br>Slow. Massive, wide-spreading. 60 feet and up.<br>Specimen. | Deciduous. Large, bright-green leaves with rounded lobes. Purplish-red fall color hangs on tree through winter. Fallen acorns a minor nuisance. Magnificent when mature, slow growth main drawback. Bur oak, *Q. macrocarpa,* similar, very slow to start, then moderately fast. OK in lawn. No fall color. English oak, *Q. robur,* moderately fast, smaller, transplants easily. Willow oak, *Q. phellos,* narrow leaves, upright. |
| European Beech<br>*Fagus sylvatica* | Zones 4-8.<br>Well-drained soil with moisture. OK in lawn, but old trees cast dense shade. Sensitive to salt. Protect tender bark, prune in early spring.<br>Slow. Broad pyramidal with low, sweeping branches. To 80 feet.<br>Specimen. Colored and weeping forms for accents. | Deciduous. Large, dark-green, toothed leaves. Red-brown fall color persists into winter. Edible nuts on old trees. Massive trunks with smooth, gray bark. Copper beech, 'Atropunicea' bronzy-purplish leaves. Dawyck, 'Fastigiata' narrow, upright. Weeping, 'Pendula' branches recurve to ground. American beech, *F. grandiflora,* yellow-bronze fall color, difficult to transplant, hardy to zone 5. |

**Kentucky Coffeetree**

**Redleaf Norway Maple**

| Common Name<br>*Scientific Name* | Climate Zones/Best Exposure<br>Culture/Growth Rate & Habit/Uses | Description/Remarks<br>Similar Varieties & Species |
|---|---|---|
| Weeping Willow<br>*Salix babylonica*<br>Photo page 131. | Zones 4-9.<br>Moist or wet soils. Subject to borers, canker, aphids and caterpillars. Litters leaves and branches. Short-lived. Requires annual pruning.<br>Fast. Pendulous, round. To 40 feet.<br>Waterside accent. | Deciduous. Long, narrow, green leaves, grayish undersides. Yellow fall color. Wisconsin willow, *S. blanda,* bluish-green leaves, not as weeping, resistant to blight. White, *S. alba,* larger, upright. Golden, *S. a. tristis,* weeping with striking yellow branches. Corkscrew, *S. matsudana,* 'Tortuosa' unique, twisted, multiple trunks, hardy to zone 5. |
| Sawleaf/Japanese Zelkova<br>*Zelkova serrata* | Zones 5-9.<br>Widely adapted. Tolerates alkaline soil. OK in lawn. Pest and disease resistant.<br>Moderate-fast. Upright-vase shaped.<br>50 feet and up.<br>Shade tree. Similar to, and good substitute for, American elm. | Deciduous. Medium leaves with toothed margins. Rusty-red fall color. Smooth, gray bark. 'Village Green' is faster, hardy to zone 4. |
| Northern Catalpa<br>*Catalpa speciosa*<br>Photo page 101. | Zones 5-9.<br>Widely adapted. Tolerates poor drainage, OK in lawn. Foliage better away from strong winds.<br>Moderate-fast. Irregular form, eventually quite large.<br>Shade, foliage contrast. | Deciduous. Very large, heart-shaped, yellow-green leaves. Upright clusters of white flowers in summer. Twelve inch long, brown pods into winter. Coarse texture, not refined. |
| London Plane Tree<br>*Platanus acerifolia*<br>Photo pages 85 and 172. | Zones 6-9.<br>Widely adapted. Tolerates city conditions. Appreciates water, OK in lawn. Subject to mites, anthracnose blight.<br>Fast. Broad, upright. 60 feet and up.<br>Shade tree, formal row. | Deciduous. Large, yellowish-green, maplelike leaves. Hanging, ball-like fruit. Attractive, peeling bark with creamy patches. Can be pollarded for formal effect. 'Bloodgood' is blight resistant. American sycamore, *P. occidentalis,* narrower, taller with whitish bark, poor fall foliage, very subject to anthracnose blight, hardy to zone 5. |

**Red Maple**

**Austrian Pine**

**Red Oak**

# UPRIGHT TREES—for narrow spaces

Although some of these get quite tall, they can be used in most gardens because of their relatively narrow spread. Planting in groups or groves 10 to 20 feet apart will further limit lateral growth. Also see Hedges, Screens and Windbreaks, page 70.

| Common Name / *Scientific Name* | Climate Zones/Culture / Growth Rate & Habit/Uses | Description/Remarks / Similar Varieties & Species |
|---|---|---|
| Norway Spruce / *Picea abies* / Photo page 107. / Colorado Blue Spruce / Photo page 107. | Zones 3-8. / Moist, well-drained soil. Wind resistant. Salt sensitive. Subject to aphids and mites. / Fast. Pyramidal, pendulous branches. / 60 feet and up. / Specimen, background, windbreak. | Evergreen. Deep-green needles. Long, hanging, attractive cones. White spruce, *P. glauca,* slower with gray-green needles. Black Hills, *P. g. densata,* bluish-green, dense and compact, good hedge. Colorado spruce, *P. pungens,* very slow, symmetrical, has sharp, bluish-green needles. 'Glauca', 'Hoopsii' and 'Koster' are striking silvery-blue. Lower branches often lost to canker in older trees. |
| European Mountain Ash / *Sorbus aucuparia* / Photo page 107. | Zones 3-8. / Widely adapted. OK in lawn, salt sensitive. Subject to borers and fire blight. Wrap trunk for protection. / Slow. Oval, to 30 feet. / Accent, specimen. | Deciduous. Divided, fernlike, green leaves. Reddish fall color. Clusters of white flowers in summer. Outstanding orange-red orange-red berries in fall. |
| White Fir / *Abies concolor* | Zones 4-8. / Withstands city conditions, wind, heat and drought, but best with moisture. / Slow. Pyramidal. 60 feet and up. / Specimen, windbreak. | Evergreen. Long, soft, bluish-green needles. Large, erect, grayish-purple cones. Douglas fir, *Pseudotsuga menziesii,* short, flat needles with two whitish bands on undersides, large, hanging, egg-shaped cones. Rapid to 100 feet or more. 'Glauca' is narrower with blue foliage, similar to Colorado blue spruce. 'Pendula' is weeping form. |
| Bradford Pear / *Pyrus calleryana* / 'Bradford' / Photo page 156. | Zones 4-9. / Widely adapted. Tolerates wind, OK in lawn. Pest and disease resistant. / Moderate. Oval pyramid. 25 to 35 feet. / Flowering accent, patio, formal row. | Deciduous. Shiny, dark-green, oval leaves. Yellow to red fall color. Covered with white flowers in spring. Tiny, pearl like fruit. 'Aristocrat' is rounder form. |
| Lombardy Poplar / *Populus nigra* / 'Italica' / Photo page 107. | Zones 4-9. / Widely adapted. Wind and salt tolerant. Appreciates moisture. Subject to borers, poplar canker. Suckers, invasive roots, short-lived. / Fast. Narrow-columnar. 60 feet and up. / Roadside, skyline silhouette, windbreak. | Deciduous. Triangular, light-green leaves. Yellow fall color. Bolleana, *P. alba* 'Pyramidalis' and Simon, *P. simoni* 'Fastigiata' are longer-lived substitutes. Cottonwood, *P. deltoides* and Balm-of-Gilead, *P. candicans,* larger and broader. Quaking aspen, *P. tremuloides,* quivering leaves, grayish-white bark, picturesque. |
| Ginkgo/Maidenhair Tree / *Ginkgo biloba* / Photo pages 20 and 164. | Zones 4-9. / Widely adapted. OK in lawn. Pest and disease resistant. / Slow. Narrow in youth, broadens with age. 50 feet and up. / Accent, specimen, light shade. | Deciduous. Odd, fan-shaped, light-green leaves. Yellow fall color. 'Autumn Gold' most reliable. Plant male selections only to avoid foul-smelling fruit. 'Fastigiata' and 'Sentry' are narrower. |
| Pin Oak / *Quercus palustris* / Photo page 107. | Zones 4-8. / Acid soil and moisture, OK in lawn. *Must* have iron. Protect from hot, dry winds. Subject to wilt. Easiest oak to transplant. Moderate-fast. Broad pyramidal with horizontal branches. 50 feet and up. Lawn specimen. | Deciduous. Shiny, light-green, deeply cut oak leaves. Red-crimson fall color. Upright English oak, *Q. robur,* 'Fastigiata' deeply lobed leaves, narrow, columnar habit. |
| Tupelo/Pepperidge/ Black Gum / *Nyssa sylvatica* / Photo page 164. | Zones 5-9. / Tolerates wet soils, OK in lawn. Transplant with care. / Slow. Pyramidal with drooping branches. 30 to 50 feet. / Fall color accent, wet areas. | Deciduous. Glossy, dark-green leaves. Glowing, red fall color. |
| Tulip Tree / *Liriodendron tulipifera* / Photo page 107. | Zones 5-9. / Moist, acid soil. OK in lawn. Protect trunk from sunscald. Transplant carefully in spring from B&B or container. / Fast. Broad, oval. 60 to 100 feet. / Shade, lawn tree. | Deciduous. Large, odd-shaped, light-green leaves. Yellow fall color. Greenish-yellow flowers in late spring pretty but difficult to see high up on old trees. |
| American Sweet Gum / *Liquidambar styraciflua* / Photo pages 18 and 107. | Zones 5-10. / Acid soil with iron and moisture. OK in lawn. B&B or container with care. / Moderate. Narrow pyramidal. 50 feet and up / Group, lawn specimen, fall color accent. | Deciduous. Dark-green, maplelike leaves. Variable yellow, orange, red purple fall color. Round, spiny fruit through winter can be a nuisance. Furrowed, corky bark. 'Palo Alto' orange-red and 'Burgundy' deep purple, have reliable fall color. |
| Dawn Redwood / *Metasequoia glyptostroboides* | Zones 5-9. / Best in well-drained soil with moisture. OK in lawn. / Fast. Narrow pyramidal. To 60 feet. / Natural grove, background. | Deciduous. Bright-green, feathery, needlelike leaves. Bronze fall color. European larch, *Larix decidua,* somewhat similar with light-green foliage. |
| Bald Cypress / *Taxodium distichum* | Zones 5-10. / Acid soil with iron and ample water best, but withstands both swampy and dry conditions. / Moderate. Broad pyramidal. 60 feet and up. / Group, accent specimen. | Deciduous. Lacy foliage, new growth light-green. Bronzy fall color. Weeping form available. |

**American Sweet Gum**

**Tulip Tree**

**Norway Spruce**

**Pin Oak**

**Colorado Blue Spruce**

**Lombardy Poplar**

**European Mountain Ash**

# GROUND COVERS

Consider these plants for slopes, narrow strips, rocky soils and shady areas instead of lawn. Purchase in peat pots or small containers, as rooted cuttings 50 to 100 per flat, or in bundles of divisions.

| Common Name<br>*Scientific Name* | Climate Zones/Best Exposure<br>Culture/Growth Rate/Height & Spacing | Description/Remarks/Uses<br>Similar Varieties & Species |
|---|---|---|
| Moss Pink/Creeping Phlox<br>*Phlox subulata* | Zones 3-9.  S, W.<br>Foliage browns in cold winters. Well-drained soil.<br>Tolerates dryness. Fast.<br>Height: 6 inches.<br>Spacing: 1 to 1-1/2 feet. | Evergreen. Small, olive-green, needlelike leaves. Showy white, blue pink, red or rose flowers in spring and summer. Cut back after flowering. Rock gardens, sunny beds and slopes. |
| Ground Ivy/<br>Creeping Charlie<br>*Glechoma hederacea*<br>Photo page 110. | Zones 3-9.  E, N, S.<br>Widely adapted. Moist soils best.<br>Fast, roots as it goes.<br>Height: to 3 inches.<br>Spacing: 1 to 1-1/2 feet. | Dies back in cold. Fragrant, roundish leaves in pairs. Small, purple-blue flowers in spring and summer. Can become invasive in shade. 'Variegata' has green and yellow leaves. |
| Crown Vetch<br>*Coronilla varia*<br>Photo page 126. | Zones 3-9.  E, S, W.<br>Widely adapted. Tolerates dryness.<br>Pest and disease resistant. Slow to start, then fast.<br>Height: 1 to 1-1/2 feet.<br>Spacing: 1-1/2 to 2 feet. | Dies back in cold. Small, bright-green leaflets. Pink, cloverlike flowers in summer to frost. Cut back old foliage in spring. Plant from divisions or sow inoculated seed. Hydroseed best for slopes and large areas. 'Penngift' is common. |

**Japanese Spurge**

**Goldmoss Sedum**

**Purpleleaf Winter Creeper**

**Thorndale Ivy**

| Common Name<br>*Scientific Name* | Climate Zones/Best Exposure<br>Culture/Growth Rate & Habit/Uses | Description/Remarks<br>Similar Varieties & Species |
|---|---|---|
| Creeping Thyme/<br>Mother-of-Thyme<br>*Thymus praecox arcticus*<br>*(T. serpyllum)*<br>Photo pages 60 and 182. | Zones 3-9.  S, W.<br>Best with good drainage on dry side.<br>Tolerates poor soils and drought. Pest and disease resistant. Fast and spreading, matlike.<br>Height: to 3 inches. Spacing: 1 to 1-1/2 feet. | Evergreen. Tiny, aromatic, dark-green leaves. Many white to rose flowers in midsummer. Rock garden, between stepping stones, lawn substitute. Wooly thyme, *T. pseudolanuginosus,* similar with gray, fuzzy leaves, not many flowers. |
| Lily-of-the-Valley<br>*Convallaria majalis*<br>Photo page 110. | Zones 3-9.  N, E.<br>Rich, acid soil with moisture best, but not fussy.<br>Subject to slugs and snails.<br>Slow to start, then spreads rapidly.<br>Height: 6 to 12 inches.<br>Spacing: 1 to 1-1/2 feet. | Dies back in winter. Bright-green, wide, upright leaves, yellowing in late summer. Spikes of fragrant, bell-like, white flowers late followed by orange fruit. All parts poisonous. |
| Goldmoss Sedum/Stonecrop<br>*Sedum acre*<br>Photo page 108. | Zones 4-9.  S, W, E.<br>Well-drained, sandy soil. Tolerates heat and drought. Moderate to fast.<br>Height: 3 inches.<br>Spacing: 6 to 12 inches. | Evergreen. Winter dieback in severe climates. Tiny, succulent, light-green leaves. Yellow flowers in late spring. Rock gardens, between stepping stones, small areas. *S. album,* similar to 6 inches, white flowers, red winter foliage. Dragon's blood, *S. spurium,* 6 inches, semievergreen, dark-red flowers summer, rosette leaves bronze in fall and winter. *S. sieboldi,* roundish leaves, 12 inches high, pink flowers in fall, red fall color. |
| Creeping Lilyturf<br>*Liriope spicata*<br>Photo pages 111 and 150. | Zones 4-9.  E, N, S.<br>Widely adapted, tolerates heat, dryness and salt.<br>Subject to slugs and snails. Fast, spreads underground.<br>Height: 8 to 12 inches.<br>Spacing: 1 to 1-1/2 feet. | Semievergreen. Dark-green, grasslike, arching leaves, 1/4 inch wide, turn yellow in severe cold. Pale, purple-whitish flowers in summer. Mow or cut back in spring before new growth. Big Blue Lilyturf, *L. muscari,* taller with wider leaves, blue to white flowers, clumping, hardy zone 6, good variegated forms. Mondo grass, *Ophiopogon japonicus,* similar, narrow, dark-green leaves, lower, better with moisture, zone 6. |

**Periwinkle**

| Common Name<br>*Scientific Name* | Climate Zones/Best Exposure<br>Culture/Growth Rate & Habit/Uses | Description/Remarks<br>Similar Varieties & Species |
|---|---|---|
| Japanese Spurge<br>*Pachysandra terminalis*<br>Photo page 108. | Zones 4-8.  N, E.<br>Needs snowcover zone 4. Difficult in heat. Well-drained, acid soil with moisture. Subject to fungus and scale.<br>Moderate growth.<br>Height: 6 to 12 inches.<br>Spacing: 9 to 12 inches. | Evergreen. Shiny, light- to dark-green leaves with serrated edges. Occasional, fragrant, white flowers in early summer. Neat-appearing with beautiful, uniform texture. Good under trees. Easy to divide for more plants. Variegated forms are weak-growing. |
| Periwinkle/Myrtle<br>*Vinca minor*<br>Photo page 109. | Zones 4-8.  N, E.<br>Needs mulch or snowcover zone 4. More sun OK where cool. Widely adapted. Well-drained, slightly acid soil with moisture best. Subject to twig blight in some areas. Slow to moderate growth.<br>Height: 3 to 9 inches.<br>Spacing: 9 to 12 inches. | Evergreen. Small, oval, shiny, dark-green leaves on trailing stems. Blue, purple or white flowers in spring and summer. Can be interplanted with bulbs. 'Bowles' clumping to 12 inches high. 'Variegata' cream and white leaves. |
| Carpet Bugle<br>*Ajuga reptans*<br>Photo below. | Zones 4-9.  E, N, S.<br>Well-drained soil with moisture, especially in sun. Subject to crown rot and nematodes. Fast.<br>Height: 3 to 6 inches.<br>Spacing: 6 to 12 inches. | Evergreen. Dormant in winter in severe climates. Crinkly, shiny, dark-green leaves. Upright blue-purple flowers late spring and early summer. Mow in early spring to renew. Lawn substitute, will tolerate some traffic. 'Purpurea' bronze leaves. *A. genevensis* slightly larger, not as spreading. |

**Carpet Bugle**

**Ground Ivy**

**Lily-of-the-Valley**

| Common Name<br>*Scientific Name* | Climate Zones/Best Exposure<br>Culture/Growth Rate & Habit/Uses | Description/Remarks<br>Similar Varieties & Species |
|---|---|---|
| Hall's Honeysuckle<br>*Lonicera japonica*<br>'Halliana'<br>Photo page 64. | Zones 4-10.   S, E, W.<br>Widely adapted. Tolerates poor soil, drought and heat. Very fast. Pest and disease resistant.<br>Height: 1-1/2 to 2-1/2 feet.<br>Spacing: 1-1/2 to 2-1/2 feet. | Evergreen. Deciduous in severe climates. Dark-green leaves. Fragrant, white, tubular flowers, late spring through summer, change to golden-yellow. Vigorous and invasive. Needs cutting back to prevent climbing over shrubs and trees. Best for slopes and large areas. Also grown as a vine. *L. j. chinensis* is easier to control, has purplish leaves. |
| Silveredge Goutweed<br>*Aegopodium podagraria*<br>'Variegatum'<br>Photo below. | Zones 4-8.   N, E.<br>Tolerates poor, dry soils. Fast.<br>Height: 6 to 12 inches.<br>Spacing: 1 to 1-1/2 feet. | Deciduous. Attractive, white-edged leaves. White flowers in spring not attractive, cut off to prevent seeding. Vigorous, can be invasive, needs frequent trimming to control. Good to brighten up dark, shady area. |
| English Ivy<br>*Hedera helix*<br>Photo pages 64 and 126.<br>'Thorndale'<br>Photo page 108. | Zones 5-9.<br>More sun OK where cool. Needs winter shade protection in severe climates. Widely adapted.<br>Moist, rich soil best.<br>Slow to moderate growth.<br>Height: 1 to 1-1/2 feet.<br>Spacing: 1 to 1-1/2 feet. | Evergreen. Dark-green, lobed leaves. Light-green growth of new runners gives distinctive texture. Slopes or flat areas. Also a good clinging vine. 'Baltica', 'Thorndale' and 'Bulgarian' have smaller leaves, hardiest. |
| Winter Creeper<br>*Euonymus fortunei*<br>varieties<br>Photo page 108. | Zones 5-9.   S, E, N.<br>Needs part shade and snow cover in severe climates.<br>Widely adapted. Tolerates heat and dryness.<br>Subject to scale. Moderate growth.<br>Height: 1 to 1-1/2 feet.<br>Spacing: 1 to 1-1/2 feet. | Evergreen. Dark-green, shiny leaves, variable shapes. Many varieties. Purple-leaf, 'Colorata' fast, purple foliage in fall, slopes and large areas. 'Radicans' trailing or climbing. 'Minima' and 'Kewensis' tiny leaves, low and slow, good for small areas. 'Gracilis' green and white leaves, not rampant. |

**Creeping Lilyturf**

**Silveredge Goutweed**

# SHRUB COVERS—12 inches to 3 feet

Similar to ground covers except woodier and usually slower to fill-in. More likely to discourage traffic. Makes an interesting transition between flat areas and taller shrubs. Usually planted from 1-gallon cans or small B&B.

| Common Name<br>*Scientific Name* | Climate Zones/Best Exposure<br>Culture/Growth Rate/Height & Spacing | Description/Remarks/Uses<br>Similar Varieties & Species |
|---|---|---|
| Bearberry<br>*Arctostaphylos uva-ursi*<br>Photo page 113. | Zones 3-9. E, S, W.<br>Well-drained, acid, sandy soil. Good on coast, wind tolerant. Transplant carefully. Slow to moderate growth.<br>Height: 3 to 6 inches.<br>Spacing: 1-1/2 to 2 feet. | Evergreen. Small, dark-green, pointed leaves, reddish in winter. Tiny, urnlike, pinkish flowers late spring. Long-lasting, brown-red berries in fall and winter. Branches root along stems, hold sandy soil in place. |
| Creeping/Prostrate Junipers<br>*Juniperus horizontalis varieties* | Zones 3-10. S, W, E.<br>Widely adapted. Well-drained soil. Tolerates heat and dryness. Subject to mites and twig blight. Slow to moderate growth.<br>Height: 6 inches to 2 feet.<br>Spacing: 3 to 5 feet. | Evergreen. Scalelike foliage. Good on rocky, dry slopes. 'Yukon Belle' silvery-blue, 6 inches high, hardy to zone 2. 'Blue Rug'/'Wilton' silvery-blue, 6 inches, draping, resists blight. 'Bar Harbor' steel-blue, 12 inches, fast open, purplish in winter. 'Douglas'/'Waukegan' blue-green, 12 inches, fast, purplish in winter. 'Andorra' feathery, gray-green, 18 inches, plum color in winter. |
| Dwarf Redleaf Barberry<br>*Berberis thunbergii*<br>'Crimson Pygmy'<br>Photo page 97. | Zones 4-9. S, E, W.<br>Tolerates poor soil and some dryness. Best well-drained with regular water. Slow and compact.<br>Height: 2 feet.<br>Spacing: 1-1/2 to 2 feet. | Deciduous. Small, spiny, red leaves, brightest in full sun. Can be clipped for low hedge or edging. 'Kobold' similar with bright-green leaves. |
| Japanese Garden Juniper<br>*Juniperus chinensis procumbens*<br>Photo page 113. | Zones 4-10. E, S.<br>Prefers cool location and well-drained soil. Subject to scale, mites and twig blight. Slow and compact.<br>Height: 1 to 1-1/2 feet.<br>Spacing: 3 to 4 feet. | Evergreen. Fine-textured, light-blue-green needles. 'Nana'/'Compacta Nana' slower and lower with very tight growth. Susceptible to twig blight in some areas. Sargent juniper, *J. c.* 'Sargentii' has short, upright growth to 18 inches, 'Glauca' blue-green, 'Viridis' rich-green. 'Arcadia' has lacy, bright-green foliage, semispreading to 18 inches. Sargent and Arcadia resist blight. |
| Cranberry Cotoneaster<br>*Cotoneaster apiculatus*<br>Photo page 113.<br>Rock Cotoneaster<br>Photo page 113. | Zones 4-9. S, E, W.<br>Well-drained soil best. Tolerates dryness. Subject to aphids, mites. Resists fire blight better than others.<br>Moderate to fast. Dense, irregular mounding habit.<br>Height: 3 to 4 feet. | Deciduous. Semievergreen in mild climates. Small, shiny, dark-green leaves. Red fall color. Small, whitish-pink flowers in late spring. Large, red berries into winter. Mass plantings and low hedge. Rock cotoneaster, *C. horizontalis,* slower, flat, layered growth to 3 feet, hardy zone 5, semievergreen where warm. Creeping cotoneaster, *C. adpressus praecox,* to 18 inches. Bearberry cotoneaster, *C. dammeri,* evergreen with long, creeping branches to 12 inches, hardy zone 6. 'Lowfast' similar, more vigorous. Willowleaf cotoneaster, *C. salicifolius,* 'Repens' semievergreen. Fast, trailing, rooting branches to 12 inches, hardy zone 6. |
| Silvermound Artemisia<br>*Artemisia schmidtiana*<br>Photo page 182. | Zones 4-9. S, W.<br>Sandy, well-drained soil. Tolerates dryness. Pest and disease resistant. Fast, compact mound.<br>Height: 12 inches.<br>Spacing: 1-1/2 to 2 feet. | Evergreen. Feathery, aromatic, silvery foliage. Striking foliage accent. 'Silver King' and 'Silver Queen', *A. albula* varieties more open, 2 to 3 feet tall, hardy zone 6. |
| Memorial Rose<br>*Rosa wichuraiana* | Zones 5-9. S, W, E.<br>Any soil. Tolerates pure sand. Fast, low spreading.<br>Height: 12 inches.<br>Spacing: 3 to 4 feet. | Semievergreen. Shiny, rose leaves. Small, single, scented, white flowers in summer. Red fruit in fall. Good on slopes and coastal dunes. Rugosa hybrid, 'Max Graf' similar with large, single, pink flowers. |
| Scotch Heather<br>*Calluna vulgaris*<br>Photo page 113. | Zones 5-9. S, W, E.<br>Moist, sandy, well-drained, acid soil. Fast, compact.<br>Height: 1 to 1-1/2 feet.<br>Spacing: 1 to 1-1/2 feet. | Evergreen. Tiny, thickly set leaves. Small, nodding flowers, rose-pink, red, purple or white, midsummer to fall. Heaths, *Erica carnea, E. cinerea, E. darleyensis,* similar, tolerant of alkaline soils, hardy zone 6. |
| Spreading English Yew<br>*Taxus baccata*<br>'Repandens' | Zones 6-9. N, E.<br>Well-drained, neutral soil. Protect from winter sun and wind in severe climates. Subject to vine weevils, scale, mites. Slow, wide-spreading and drooping.<br>Height: 3 to 4 feet.<br>Spacing: 4 to 5 feet. | Evergreen. Typical, dark-green yew leaves. Tips of new growth yellow-green. Scarlet berries on female plants. Leaves and berries of all yews poisonous. Best unclipped. Similar yews: Anglo Japanese, *T. media,* 'Chadwickii' zone 5, withstands heavy snow. Spreading Japanese, *T. cuspidata,* 'Densiformis' faster, zone 5. Dwarf Canadian, *T. canadensis,* 'Stricta' more upright, hardy to zone 3. |
| Blue Leadwort<br>*Ceratostigma plumbaginoides*<br>Photo page 113. | Zones 6-10. S, E.<br>Tolerant of most conditions, best with moisture. Fast growth starts in late spring, spreads underground.<br>Height: 6 to 12 inches.<br>Spacing: 1-1/2 to 2 feet. | Dies back in cold winters. Foliage tinged with bronze, especially in fall. Bright-blue flowers late summer. Can be interplanted with English ivy, periwinkle or wintercreeper for added color interest. |
| Sweet Box<br>*Sarcococca hookerana*<br>Photo page 113. | Zones 6-9. E, N.<br>Needs good soil with moisture. Slow, spreading underground to 8 feet wide.<br>Height: 1 to 1-1/2 feet.<br>Spacing: 2 to 3 feet. | Evergreen. Glossy, dark-green, pointed leaves. Aromatic, tiny, whitish flowers in early spring. Followed by shiny, black fruit. Refined appearance. Valuable for shady areas. |

**Japanese Garden Juniper**

**Blue Leadwort**

**Sweet Box**

**Rock Cotoneaster**

**Cranberry Cotoneaster**

**Scotch Heather**

**Bearberry**

# VINES

Perhaps the most difficult of all types of plants to use correctly—and they can be the most striking. Provide adequate support to suit the specific method of climbing, and allow time for training. Also see Large Shrubs, page 90, for those suitable for training as espaliers.

| Common Name<br>*Scientific Name* | Climate Zones/Best Exposure<br>Culture/Height | Description/Remarks<br>Similar Varieties & Species |
|---|---|---|
| American Bittersweet<br>*Celastrus scandens* | Zones 2-8.  E, N.<br>Widely adapted. Tolerates dryness.<br>Pest and disease resistant. Start with small plants.<br>Moderate, twining growth.<br>Height: 20 to 30 feet. | Deciduous. Large, light-green, variable oblong leaves. Yellow fall color. Poisonous yellow-orange fruit open to show red seeds on female plants, lasting through winter. Can overrun shrubs and trees. Oriental bittersweet, *C. orbiculatus*, roundish leaves, more vigorous, similar fruit, hardy zone 4. |
| Grape<br>*Vitis labrusca*<br>Photo page 163. | Zones 3-10.  S, W.<br>Well-drained soil. Allow to dry out between waterings. Subject to mildew and Japanese beetles. Fast, climbing by tendrils.<br>Height: 20 feet. | Deciduous. Large, lobed leaves. Summer fruit attracts ants and bees. Select, prune and train according to variety. 'Concord' and 'Niagara' are consistent and widely grown. Large arbor or chain-link fence. Gloryvine, *V. coignetiae*, fast with red fall color, non-edible fruit, hardy zone 5. |
| Common Trumpet Creeper<br>*Campsis radicans* | Zones 4-10.  S, W.<br>Widely adapted. Well-drained soil with moisture best. Rapid, climbing by aerial rootlets and twining stems.<br>Height: 40 feet. | Deciduous. Divided leaflets. Large, orange-red trumpet flowers in summer. Rampant grower, needs large space. *C. tagliabuana*, 'Madame Galen' has larger, salmon-pink flowers, is better behaved. Not for wood houses. |
| Boston Ivy<br>*Parthenocissus tricuspidata*<br>Photo page 115.<br>Virginia Creeper<br>Photo page 115. | Zones 4-9.  E, N, S.<br>Widely adapted, appreciates water.<br>Fast, tight-clinging and dense.<br>Height: 30 to 50 feet. | Deciduous to semievergreen. Glossy, 3-lobed leaves, orange-red-purple fall color. Blue-black berries in fall. Excellent on masonry walls. Not for wood houses. 'Lowii' and 'Veitchii' have smaller leaves, deeper fall color, are less aggressive. Virginia creeper, *P. quinquefolia*, has sawtooth leaflets in fives, reddish-yellow fall color. Can be used as deep ground cover for natural effect. Growth more open than Boston ivy. 'Engelmannii' has small leaflets, is denser. |
| Climbing Hydrangea<br>*Hydrangea anomala petiolaris* | Zones 4-8.  S, E.<br>Rich, moist soil. Pest and disease resistant.<br>Slow at first, then fast.<br>Clinging.<br>Height: to 50 feet. | Deciduous. Large, heart-shaped leaves. Flat clusters of creamy flowers in summer. Red bark is winter feature. |
| Hybrid Clematis<br>*Clematis jackmanii* varieties<br>Photo pages 115 and 131. | Zones 4-9.  E, S.<br>Well-drained, rich soil with moisture.<br>Not too acid, but subject to iron chlorosis if too alkaline. Best with roots in shade, top in sun with heavy mulch. Plant with main stem 2 inches deep. Moderate to rapid growth, climbing by twining leaf stalks.<br>Height: 10 to 20 feet. | Deciduous. Dark-green leaflets. Spectacular flowers in white, pink, purple, red and mixed colors up to 8 inches across in spring and summer. Post, fence or trellis, also large tubs. Pruning methods vary with specific type. Pink Anemone clematis, *C. montana rubens*, bronzy-green leaves, deep-pink flowers in summer. Sweetautumn clematis, *C. paniculata*, has masses of fragrant flowers in late summer and fall, vigorous to 30 feet. |
| Scarlet/Trumpet Honeysuckle<br>*Lonicera sempervirens*<br>Photo page 115. | Zones 4-10.  E, S.<br>Widely adapted. Pest and disease resistant. Slow to moderate twining growth.<br>Shrubby without support.<br>Height: 20 feet. | Deciduous. Semievergreen where warm. Oval, bluish-green leaves. Long, tubular, coral-with-yellow flowers in summer, attracts hummingbirds, but not fragrant. Orange-red fruit in fall. Well-behaved, OK for small areas. Improved selections include 'Magnifica', 'Superba', 'Sulphurea' and 'Dropmore Scarlet'. Goldflame/Everblooming honeysuckle, *L. heckrottii*, red flowers, gold inside, fragrant. |
| Dutchman's-Pipe<br>*Aristolochia macrophylla* | Zones 4-9.  E, S.<br>Well-drained soil with regular water.<br>Fast, twining growth.<br>Height: 15 to 20 feet. | Deciduous. Very large, heart-shaped leaves. Interesting, yellow-brown flowers in summer. Dense growth for screening. |
| Silver-lace/Chinese Fleece Vine<br>*Polygonum aubertii*<br>Photo page 114. | Zones 4-9.  S, W.<br>Widely adapted. Tolerates dryness.<br>Fast. Climbs by twining and tendrils.<br>Height: 20 to 30 feet. | Deciduous. Narrow, reddish-green leaves, Covered with cloudy clusters of fragrant, small, whitish flowers in late summer, attracts bees. Good on chain-link fence. *P. reynoutria* similar, has pink flowers, can be used as ground cover. |
| Large-flowered Climbing Rose<br>Photo pages 63 and 64.<br>Lady Bank's Rose<br>Photo page 115. | Zones 4-9.  S, E.<br>Provide winter protection zone 6 northward. Well-drained soil with ample water, mulch and fertilizer. Aphids, mildew and black spot are the most common problems. Moderate to rapid growth, needs support.<br>Height: 10 to 20 feet. | Deciduous. Foliage varies with numerous selections available. America, Blaze Improved, Golden Showers and White Dawn have a long period of bloom and are more cold hardy than climbing hybrid tea sports. Ramblers such as 'Evangeline' 'Chevy Chase' and 'Sander's White' are vigorous growers, best for large arbors. Lady Bank's Rose with double, white or yellow flowers and glossy foliage is virtually trouble-free. |
| Big-leaf Wintercreeper<br>*Euonymus fortunei* 'Vegeta'<br>Photo page 115. | Zones 4-9.  N, E.<br>Widely adapted. Prefers rich, moist soil.<br>Subject to euonymus scale.<br>Needs winter shade zone 5 northward.<br>Aerial rootlets.<br>Height: 15 to 20 feet. | Evergreen. Glossy, dark-green, leathery leaves. New spring growth chartreuse. Orange berries fall and winter. Variable growth, can be used as shrub, espalier, vine or slope cover. Good on masonry walls. |
| Chinese Wisteria<br>*Wisteria sinensis*<br>Photo page 115. | Zones 5-10.  E, S, W.<br>Well-drained, slightly acid soil with iron and moisture. To induce flowering on old plants, prune severely in summer, withhold nitrogen, root prune and keep on dry side. Rapid and vigorous. Twining habit.<br>Height: 30 to 40 feet. | Deciduous. Long leaflets. Hanging clusters of fragrant, violet or white flowers in late spring. Develops sturdy, twisted trunks with age, needs sturdy arbor or wall support. Often trained as large shrub or small tree. Japanese wisteria, *W. floribunda*, has longer flower clusters to 18 inches, blooms later. |

**Virginia Creeper**

**Lady Bank's Rose**

**Boston Ivy**

**Hybrid Clematis**

**Scarlet Honeysuckle**

**Chinese Wisteria**

**Big-leaf Wintercreeper**

# ACCENTS

To liven up an entrance, break the monotony of a ground cover and add a little sparkle where it is needed. Almost any plant that has a striking form, contrasting texture, brightly colored foliage or outstanding flowers can serve as an accent. Use with discretion or they may overwhelm the landscape and appear out of place.

| Common Name<br>*Scientific Name* | Climate Zones/Best Exposure<br>Culture/Height | Description/Remarks/Uses<br>Similar Varieties & Species |
|---|---|---|
| Bearded Iris<br>*Iris* hybrids<br>Photo below. | Zones 3-10.  E, S, W.<br>Needs snow cover or winter mulch in severe climates.<br>Well-drained soil, do not overwater. Subject to<br>borers, bacterial rot, summer leaf spot, snails.<br>Divide every 3 or 4 years in later summer, plant<br>rhizomes shallow, avoid manures.<br>Height: 1 to 3 feet. | Herbaceous perennial, dies back in winter. Stiff, sword-shaped leaves.<br>Orchidlike, fragrant flowers in wide color range, spring and summer.<br>Groups, flower border, in low ground cover. Siberian, *I. sibirica,* tall,<br>white, blue or yellow flowers, moist soils, low maintenance. Dwarf Iris,<br>*I. pumila* and *I. cristata,* grow to 6 inches, can be used as ground cover.<br>Japanese, *I. kaempferi,* needs acid soil and moisture, often planted<br>at water edge. |
| Dutch Bulbs<br>*Tulipa, Hyacinthus,* etc.<br>Photo pages 116 and 117. | Zones 3-9.  S, W, E.<br>Rich, well-drained soil with regular water. Subject<br>to squirrel and gopher damage. Plant bulbs in fall,<br>at a depth approximately 3 times diameter of bulb.<br>Height: 1 to 2 feet. | Herbaceous bulbs, die back in winter. Foliage and flowers vary with<br>type. In order of bloom: crocus, snowdrop, narcissus, hyacinth,<br>tulip and autumn crocus are most popular. Flower border, color mass,<br>containers, cut flowers. Countless varieties, all sizes and color. |
| Peony<br>*Paeonia* hybrids<br>Photo below. | Zones 3-8.  S, W.<br>Rich, well-drained soil. Subject to fungus, control<br>ants to limit spread. Stake tall flowers. Plant<br>in fall from divisions. Cut to ground in fall.<br>Height: 2 to 4 feet. | Herbaceous perennial, dies back in winter. Handsome, divided<br>leaflets, some bronzy-green. Large, white, pink or red, single,<br>semidouble or double flowers in June. Flower border, cut flowers.<br>Tree peonies are woodier, used more as deciduous shrub. Japanese<br>tree peony flowers freely and has wide range of colors. |
| Plantainlily/Hosta<br>*Hosta* hybrids<br>*(Funkia)*<br>Photo page 117. | Zones 4-9.  N, E.<br>Needs organic soil and summer moisture. Subject to<br>slugs and snails. Long-lived and reliable.<br>Height: 1 to 1-1/2 feet. | Herbaceous perennial, dies back in winter. Handsome leaves, 6 to 12<br>inches long, green, blue-green or variegated, some with ribs and<br>wavy margins. White, blue or lavender, bell-shaped flowers on tall<br>stems in summer. Shady border or plant 12 inches apart for ground<br>cover. |
| Bleeding Heart<br>*Dicentra spectabilis*<br>Photo below. | Zones 4-9.  E, S.<br>Well-drained, loam soil. Pest and disease<br>resistant. Plant divisions in fall.<br>Height: 1-1/2 to 3 feet. | Herbaceous, starts to die back late summer. Attractive, fernlike foliage.<br>White or pink, hanging, bell-like flowers in late spring. Fringed<br>bleeding heart, *D. eximia,* 'Bountiful' and 'Luxuriant' have cherry-<br>red flowers summer until frost, more compact to 18 inches. |

**Autumn Crocus**

**Bearded Iris**

**Japanese Tree Peony**

**Bleeding Heart**

| Common Name<br>*Scientific Name* | Climate Zones/Best Exposure<br>Culture/Growth Rate & Habit/Uses | Description/Remarks<br>Similar Varieties & Species |
|---|---|---|
| Chrysanthemum<br>*Chrysanthemum*<br>*morifolium*<br>Photo pages 147 and 155. | Zones 4-9. S, W, E.<br>Dig and store plants in severe climates, or replant new each spring. Widely adapted. Well-drained, sandy loam with mulch best. Soak deeply, keep water off foliage. Subject to aphids, leaf miner, mites, mildew, wilt and leaf spot. Pinch back several times in early summer for bushiness. Support tall plants.<br>Height: 1 to 3 feet. | Herbaceous perennial, dies back in winter. Aromatic, lobed leaves. White, yellow, gold, pink, red and purple flowers cover plant in late summer to fall. Small pompons to giant, flat, decorative and spoon shapes. Excellent fall flower border, cut flowers, containers, and hanging baskets. |
| Shasta Daisy<br>*Chrysanthemum superbum*<br>(*C. maximum*) | Zones 4-10. S, W, E.<br>Needs winter protection in cold climates. Well-drained, loam soil with regular water best, but fairly easy. Subject to crown gall, slugs, snails. Seed in spring or divisions in fall.<br>Height: 1 to 2 feet. | Herbaceous perennial, dies back in winter. Large, shiny, leathery leaves. White with yellow center, single or double flowers June through summer. Some selections light-yellow. Flower border, cut flowers. |
| Daylily<br>*Hemerocallis* hybrids<br>Photo page 164 and below. | Zones 4-10. E, S, W.<br>Widely adapted. Best in well-draine soil withd water during blooming season. Pest and disease resistant. Easily divided in fall.<br>Height: 1-1/2 to 3 feet. | Herbaceous perennial, dies back in winter. Light-green, arching, strap-shaped leaves. Large flowers on tall stalks. White, yellow, orange, red, pink and blends, early summer to fall. Flower border, plant 18 inches apart for ground-cover effect. |
| Adams-Needle<br>*Yucca filamentosa* | Zones 4-10. S, W, E.<br>Well-drained soil. Tolerates dryness, do not overwater. Slow growth.<br>Height: To 4 feet. | Evergreen. perennial. Rosette clump of rigid, swordlike leaves, bending at ends. 4 foot spikes of creamy-white flowers in late summer. 'Ivory Tower' light-green leaves. 'Golden Sword' yellow leaves with green margins. |
| Ornamental Grasses<br>*Miscanthus, Phalaris,*<br>etc.<br>Photo below. | Zones 4-10. S, W, E.<br>Most do best in not too rich, well-drained soil. Cut to ground in early spring to renew. Generally pest and disease resistant.<br>Height: 6 inches to 10 feet. | Mostly evergreen, some die back in cold. Narrow, grasslike leaves, some with airy flowers. Background, foliage contrast, dry arrangements. Eulalia grass, *Miscanthus sinensis*, several varieties with green and variegated foliage. White, yellowish, pink or reddish flowers in fall. To 10 feet. Ribbon grass, *Phalaris arundinacea*, 'Picta' has white-pinkish striped leaves, white-pink flowers in summer. Tolerates wet soil. To 4 feet. Sedges, *Carex* species, narrow leaves, often striped white. Tolerates shade and moisture, 6 inches to 2 feet, water edge and ground cover. Sweet flag, *Acorus* species, similar to *Carex.* |
| Ferns<br>*Adiantum, Osmunda,* etc. | Zones 3-10. E, N.<br>Rich, organic soil with moisture. Generally pest and disease resistant.<br>Height: 1 to 4 feet. | Evergreen or herbaceous. Fronds vary from coarse to fine. Wooded area, shady border. Reliable types include: Cinnamon, *Osmunda cinnamonea*, arching fronds to 3 feet. Maidenhair, *Adiantum pedatum*, delicate, lacy foliage with black stems to 2 feet. Ostrich, *Pteretis nodulosa*, upright, feathery fronds to 4 feet. Christmas, *Polystichum acrostichodes*, evergreen, dark-green, to 3 feet. |

**Eulaliagrass/Zebragrass**

**Daylily**

**Hosta**

**Tulips**

# HEDGES, SCREENS AND WINDBREAKS

Listed in order of height. Indicated size assumes some pruning or clipping.

| Common Name *Scientific Name* | Climate Zones/Best Exposure/Culture Growth Rate & Habit/Height & Spacing | Description/Remarks/Uses/Climate Similar Varieties & Species |
|---|---|---|
| Korean Littleleaf Box *Buxus microphylla koreana* Photo pages 69 and 147. English Boxwood Photo page 68. | Zones 5-9. E, N, S. Well-drained, slightly acid soil best. Withstands heat and average soil better than English boxwood. Needs shade in north to limit winter discoloring. Slow-moderate, compact growth. Height: 1-1/2 to 2 feet x 1 foot wide. Spacing: 1 foot. | Evergreen. Small, shiny leaves, bronzy to brown in winter cold. 'Wintergreen' retains color best. Usually clipped hedge or edging, but can be left unclipped, also for topiary. Japanese boxwood, *B. m. japonica,* taller, hardy zone 6. English boxwood, *B. sempervirens,* best on East coast in cool, acid soil, eventually to 10 feet, hardy zone 6. 'Suffruticosa' very dwarf to 12 inches. |
| Alpine Currant *Ribes alpinum* Photo page 69. | Zones 3-8. E, S, N. Widely adapted. Subject to leaf spot in late summer. Slow, compact. Height: 2 to 3 feet x 2 feet wide. Spacing: 1 to 1-1/2 feet. | Deciduous. Dark-green, lobed leaves. Small yellow flowers followed by small, red fruit, neither significant. Clipped hedge or shrub Dwarf ninebark, *Physocarpus opulifolius* 'Nanus' similar, often confused with Alpine currant. Golden ninebark, *P. o.* 'Aurea'/'Luteus' is taller, has striking yellow foliage. |
| Blue Arctic Willow *Salix purpurea* 'Nana' *(S. p.* 'Gracilis') Photo page 71. | Zones 3-8. S, E, W. Tolerates wet, clay soil. Subject to scale and borers. Fast, arching. Height: 3 to 4 feet x 3 feet wide. Spacing: 1-1/2 to 2 feet. | Deciduous. Striking silvery, blue-green, narrow leaves. Purple twigs in winter. Best when clipped. Color contrast for wet soils. Purple osier willow, *S. purpurea,* to 10 feet, wild, natural screen, same culture. |
| Clavey's Dwarf Honeysuckle *Lonicera xylosteoides* 'Clavey's Dwarf' Photo page 71. | Zones 4-8. S, E, W. Widely adapted. Occasional mites. Slow-moderate. Compact and dense. Height: 3 to 5 feet x 3 feet wide. Spacing: 2 to 3 feet. | Deciduous. Gray-green leaves. Small, light-yellow flowers in late spring. Red berries in summer. Needs little clipping, rounded form best. 'Emerald Mound' has bright-green leaves, more compact. |
| Japanese Barberry *Berberis thunbergii* Photo pages 19 and 71. | Zones 4-9. S, W, E. Tolerates poor soil and some dryness. Well-drained soil with regular water best. Moderate. Upright. Height: 3 to 5 feet x 3 feet wide. Spacing: 1 to 2 feet. | Deciduous. Small, spiny leaves. Red-orange fall color. Thorny twigs. Red berries in fall-winter. Clipped hedge or natural barrier. 'Atropurpurea' similar with red foliage. Truehedge columnberry *B. t.* 'Erecta' narrower. Korean, *B. koreana,* lush, green foliage, taller, suckers. Mentor, *B. mentorensis,* semievergreen, upright, zone 6. |

**Russian Olive**

**Privet**

**Siberian Pea Tree**

| Common Name<br>*Scientific Name* | Climate Zones/Best Exposure<br>Culture/Growth Rate & Habit/Uses | Description/Remarks<br>Similar Varieties & Species |
|---|---|---|
| Flowering Quince<br>*Chaenomeles* hybrids<br>Photo page 120. | Zones 5-9.  S, E, W.<br>Widely adapted. Well-drained, slightly acid soil best. Subject to scale, aphids, fire blight.<br>Moderate-fast. Spreading.<br>Height: 2 to 6 feet x 4 feet, depending on variety.<br>Spacing: 2 to 3 feet. | Deciduous. New growth dark-red, turning green. Bronzy fall color. Large flowers early spring before leaves, white to light-pink to scarlet. Yellow, applelike fruit late summer. Spiny branches. Clipped or natural hedge, screen or barrier. Also trainable as espalier. 'Alpina' orange, no fruit, 18 inches. 'Texas Scarlet' red, few thorns, 3 feet. 'Pink Beauty' pink, upright, 6 feet. 'Nivalis' white, 6 feet. 'Apple Blossom' whitish-pink, 6 feet. |
| Vanhoutte Spirea<br>*Spirea vanhouttei*<br>Photo page 68. | Zones 4-9.  S, W, E.<br>Widely adapted. Responds to good soil.<br>Fast. Graceful, arching form.<br>Height: 4 to 6 feet x 6 feet wide.<br>Spacing: 3 to 4 feet. | Deciduous. Blue-green, toothed leaves. Covered with clusters of white flowers in late spring. Prune after flowering. Unclipped hedge or screen. Bridal-wreath, *S. prunifolia*, 'Plena' is smaller, dantier, orange fall color, buttonlike, white flowers midspring. Billiard spirea, *S. billiardii*, upright with bright-pink, pointed flower clusters in later summer. Thunberg, *S. thunbergii*, fine-textured, white flower midspring. |
| Hedge Cotoneaster<br>*Cotoneaster lucidus*<br>Photo page 120. | Zones 4-8.  E, S, W.<br>Tolerates wind and poor, dry soil. Subject to fireblight, mites, scale. Slow-moderate.<br>Dense, upright.<br>Height: 5 to 6 feet x 5 feet.<br>Spacing: 1-1/2 to 2 feet. | Deciduous. Large, glossy, green leaves. Orange-red fall color. Very small, pinkish-white flowers in spring. Black berries summer and fall. Clipped hedge or natural screen. Peking cotoneaster, *C. acutifolia*, similar but leaves not glossy, often sold as hedge cotoneaster. Spreading cotoneaster, *C. divaricata*, semievergreen with small leaves, red berries. Arching habit, can be clipped or left natural, hardy zone 5. |
| Rose<br>*Rosa* species<br>Hugo Rose<br>Photo below. | Zones 4-9.  S, W, E.<br>Widely adapted. Well-drained soil with ample water and fertilizer best. These types are less subject to insects and disease than garden hybrids.<br>Moderate.<br>Arching, tangled.<br>Height: 4 to 8 feet x 4 to 8 feet wide.<br>Spacing: 2 to 4 feet. | Deciduous. Medium, dark-green leaves. Thorny branches. Single or double flowers in spring, some through summer, all typical rose colors. Natural barrier, casual effect, not refined, attracts birds. *R. rugosa* hardy to zone 3, 5 feet high, tolerates sea spray and wind. *R. moschata*, 'Robin Hood' zone 4, to 6 feet. *R. multiflora* zone 5, to 8 feet. Hugo Rose, *R. hugonis* hardy zone 5. Single flowers, to 6 feet. |
| Privet<br>*Ligustrum* species<br>Photo page 118. | Zones 3-10.  S, W, E.<br>Widely adapted. Wind tolerant. Withstands clipping well. Subject to borers.<br>Moderate-fast. Most upright.<br>Height: 4 to 10 feet x 2 to 4 feet wide.<br>Spacing: 1 to 2 feet. | Deciduous. Medium leaves, color varies with type. Whitish flowers, clusters of black berries. Amur, *L. amurense*, olive-green to 10 feet, zone 3. Ibolium, *L. ibolium*, glossy, green to 8 feet, zone 4. Regel, *L. obtusifolium regelianum*, graceful, arching branches to 6 feet, zone 3. Golden Vicary, *L. vicaryi*, yellow leaves to 6 feet, zone 5. Lodense, *L. vulgare nanum*, to 3 feet, zone 4. Cheyenne, *L. v.* 'Cheyenne' 10 feet, hardy zone 3. |

**Amur Maple**

**Hugo Rose**

**Winged Burning Bush**

119

| Common Name<br>*Scientific Name* | Climate Zones/Best Exposure<br>Culture/Growth Rate & Habit/Uses | Description/Remarks<br>Similar Varieties & Species |
|---|---|---|
| American Arborvitae<br>*Thuja occidentalis*<br>Photo page 70. | Zones 3-8.  E, S.<br>Foliage brown in severe winters. Best in cool location with moist, fertile soil. Shear for compactness or tie branches to prevent snow breakage. Subject to mites. Slow-moderate. Compact, pyramidal form.<br>Height: 4 to 20 feet x 3 to 8 feet wide.<br>Spacing: 2 to 5 feet. | Evergreen. Dark-green, fanlike leaves. Clipped hedge, natural screen, windbreak, accent specimen. 'Woodwardii' globe to 4 feet. 'Wareana' broad pyramidal, 10 feet and up. 'Techny'/'Mission' good winter color, wide pyramidal, 10 feet and up. 'Pyramidalis' bright-green, narrow pyramid, 15 feet and up. 'Nigra' good winter color, upright pyramidal, 20 feet and up. |
| Siberian Pea Tree<br>*Caragana arborescens*<br>Photo pages 118 and 182. | Zones 2-9.  S, W.<br>Tough. Wind and drought tolerant. Pest and disease resistant. Fast. Broad, upright.<br>Height: 10 feet x 6 feet wide.<br>Spacing: 3 to 4 feet. | Deciduous. Small, yellow-green leaflets. Yellow fall color. Yellow, pealike flowers in spring. Windbreak or screen. Needs some clipping to keep neat. *C. a. pygmaea* similar to 3 feet. *C. frutex*, 'Globosa' slow, rounded, to 3 feet, very hardy. |
| Tatarian Honeysuckle<br>*Lonicera tatarica*<br>Photo page 70. | Zones 4-8.  S, E, W.<br>Widely adapted. Tolerates dryness. Generally pest and disease resistant, occasional canker. Fast. Upright, arching habit.<br>Height: 10 feet x 6 feet wide.<br>Spacing: 2 to 3 feet. | Deciduous. Bluish-green leaves. Small, fragrant, white, pink or rose flowers in late spring. Bright-red fruit summer and fall, attracts birds. Background, windbreak. Needs regular pruning to prevent legginess. 'Nana' white flowers to 5 feet. Morrow, *L. morrowi*, smaller and wider with whitish-yellow flowers. Zabel, *L Korolkowii* 'Zabelii' more ornamental white flowers. Amur, *L. maakii*, white flowers, larger, rank grower, needs room, hardy zone 3. Winter, *L. fragrantissima*, semievergreen, fragrant, creamy-white flowers, zone 5. |
| Buckthorn<br>*Rhamnus frangula*<br>'Tallhedge'<br>Photo page 69. | Zones 2-8.  S, W, E.<br>Moist, well-drained soil. Generally pest and disease resistant, but individual plants sometimes die out. Fast. Narrow, upright, dense, minimum trimming required.<br>Height: 10 feet x 4 feet wide.<br>Spacing: 2 to 3 feet. | Deciduous. Shiny, dark-green leaves. Red berries. Narrow hedge, windbreak. Best with facer, lower branches tend to thin out. Common Buckthorn, *R. cathartica*, wider, tolerant of poor soil, shade. Natural background. Spreads by seedlings and can be invasive. |

**Hedge Cotoneaster**

**Hicks Yew**

**Flowering Quince**

| Common Name<br>*Scientific Name* | Climate Zones/Best Exposure<br>Culture/Growth Rate & Habit/Uses | Description/Remarks<br>Similar Varieties & Species |
|---|---|---|
| Russian Olive<br>*Elaeagnus angustifolia*<br>Photo page 118. | Zones 3-8.  S, W, E.<br>Tolerates poor soil, salt, heat, wind and dryness.<br>Subject to wilt in some areas. Fast. Angular,<br>sprawling.<br>Height: 15 to 20 feet x 6 to 10 feet wide.<br>Spacing: 4 to 5 feet. | Deciduous. Small, silvery-gray leaves. Dark-brown, thorny branches.<br>Fragrant, small, greenish-yellow flowers in early summer. Greenish<br>berries. Clipped or unclipped natural screen or windbreak, small,<br>feature tree. Cardinal olive, *E. umbellata cardinalis,* smaller and<br>thornless with red berries that attract birds, hardy zone 4. |
| Upright Yews<br>*Taxus* species<br>Hicks Yew<br>Photo page 120. | Zones 4-8.  N, E.<br>Protect from winter sun in cold climates. Prefers<br>well-drained, organic soil. Suffers from hot,<br>dry winds. Subject to black vine weevil, scale<br>and mites. Slow. Upright. Can be formally sheared.<br>Tie tops together to prevent opening.<br>Height: 10 feet x 4 feet wide.<br>Spacing: 2 to 3 feet. | Evergreen. Thick, shiny, dark-green, needlelike leaves. Red berries<br>on female plants. Berries and leaves poisonous. Anglojap, *T. media,*<br>zone 4. 'Hicksii' narrow, fast, to 10 feet. 'Hatfieldii' slow, broad,<br>conical, to 20 feet. Irish, *T. baccata,* 'Stricta' zone 6, slow, very<br>narrow, to 20 feet. Upright Japanese, *T. cuspidata,* zone 4, slow, to<br>20 feet. Canadian, *T. canadensis,* 'Stricta' zone 3, slow, 3 to 5 feet. |
| Winged Burning Bush<br>*Euonymus alatus*<br>Photo pages 119 and 164. | Zones 4-9.  S, W.<br>Park shade OK, but lessens fall color. Well-<br>drained soil. Subject to euonymus scale and<br>aphids. Slow. Rounded, dense.<br>Height: 10 feet x 10 feet wide.<br>Spacing: 3 to 4 feet. | Deciduous. Small, toothed leaves, turn pink-red in fall, Small, red<br>berries. Name derives from interesting corky wings on branches.<br>Dwarf Burning Bush, *E. a.* 'Compactus' more common, fiery-red fall<br>color, needs little clipping to keep 5 x 5 feet. |
| Canada Hemlock<br>*Tsuga canadensis*<br>Photo below. | Zones 3-8.  E, S.<br>Moist, well-drained, acid soil. Salt sensitive.<br>Prefers coolness, OK in lawn. Rapid. Dense<br>growth.<br>Height: 10 feet and up x 5 to 10 feet wide.<br>Spacing: 3 to 5 feet. | Evergreen. Short, dark-green needles, new spring growth. Yellow-<br>green. Small, hanging cones. Natural or clipped hedge, windbreak.<br>Also large, pyramidal tree to 90 feet with graceful, low-sweeping<br>branches, usually multitrunk. Dwarf, weeping forms available.<br>Carolina hemlock, *T. caroliniana,* similar, hardy zone 4. |
| Amur Maple<br>*Acer ginnala*<br>Photo page 119. | Zones 2-8.  S, E, W.<br>Widely adapted. Tolerates exposed situations,<br>dryness, but appreciates regular water.<br>Moderate. Thick and low branching.<br>Height: 20 feet x 10 feet wide. Can be kept<br>smaller.<br>Spacing: 2 to 4 feet. | Deciduous. Dark-green, 3-lobed leaves. Orange-red fall color. Small,<br>yellowish, fragrant flowers in spring. Attractive, red-winged fruit<br>in summer. Clipped hedge, windbreak, small, multitrunk tree. Compact<br>form available. Tatarian maple, *A. tataricum,* similar. Hedge maple,<br>*A. campestre,* larger with yellow fall color, hardy zone 5. Paper-bark<br>maple, *A. griseum,* more open with striking, reddish-brown, peeling<br>bark. Needs moisture and wind protection, hardy zone 5. |

**Canada Hemlock**

## PLANTS FOR SCREENS

*Additional plants often used as hedges, screens and wind- breaks. Listed in approximate order of height. See plant lists beginning on page 86, for descriptions.*

Dwarf Japanese Holly
Crimson Pygmy Barberry
Slender Deutzia
Cinquefoil
Northern Bayberry
Sarcoxie Euonymus
Weeping Forsythia
Glossy Abelia
Pfitzer Juniper
Blue Holly
Winterberry
Pyracantha
Rose-of-Sharon
Upright Juniper
Virginia Cedar
Viburnum
Lilac
American Holly
Cockspur Thorn
White Fir
Norway Spruce
Lombardy Poplar

# Foolproof Planting

Selecting plants from the *Plant Lists,* beginning on page 86, is not the end of your job. After you develop a planting plan similar to those on pages 132 through 135, you must provide a proper environment for the plants.

## PLANTING SEASON

The best time to plant depends on many factors. It is influenced by the plants you choose, how they are grown and how severe the climate is that you live in.

The best time to install balled-and-burlapped, called *B&B,* and container-grown plants is usually fall, before the ground freezes. Roots become established before winter sets in, and new growth appears the next spring. This means starting as early as August and September for Zones 3 and 4, and progressively later through Zones 5, 6 and 7. Timing for deciduous plants is less crucial than for evergreens. Evergreens can be damaged if planted too late in the fall or too early in the spring.

Plants of borderline hardiness are best planted in the spring after danger of frost has passed. This allows them to become well-established before winter. Many nurseries limit B&B digging of delicate plants, such as dogwood, red maple, birches, hawthorn, plum, pear and oaks, to spring only.

Fall and spring plantings benefit from cooler temperatures and more reliable rainfall than plantings during summer months. Install container-grown plants any time during the growing season. Water them carefully and protect them from sun and wind until well established.

Normally, the bareroot season is before new growth starts in early spring. Deciduous shade, fruit and nut trees, shrubs, roses, berries, perennial flowers and vegetables are available bareroot. Precise timing depends on how severe the climate is.

Some nurseries have bareroot stock available as early as March in warmer zones. The ground may not be workable, and leafing-out may not begin until April or May in the upper north. Some of the hardiest bareroot plants are available in the fall and can be planted at that time.

Mail-order catalogs come out in winter and allow time for selecting and placing an order. Bareroot plants are dug when the weather begins to warm up and are shipped in time for spring planting. I prefer to select bareroot, or any plant material, at the local nursery where I can see it before I buy it. But there is a thrill of anticipation when ordering by mail. I've had many satisfactory results from reputable firms. Catalog ordering is convenient and gives access to many plants not readily available. Check a plant's hardiness to cold and suitability to your specific climate.

**Your nurseryman can help you select the best soil amendment for your specific situation.**

No matter when you plant, it's advisable to avoid hot, windy days. If you don't have that choice, wait until it starts to cool off in late afternoon; then water plants immediately. For exposed locations, provide a temporary sun and wind shelter, or spray the foliage with an antitranspirant, sold as Wilt-Pruf and Cloud Cover. This reduces water loss until new root growth can supply the plant's needs.

## SOIL PREPARATION

It would be great if topsoil were always stockpiled at the start of construction, then replaced when the house is finished. Many sites are stripped bare, and you end up with poor soil. Or soil may have been poor to begin with. In some extreme cases, it may be advisable to bring in good-quality topsoil. Usually, adding organic material and fertilizer to existing soil is less expensive. The problems of imported weeds and diseases and a drastic change in soil texture, or *interface,* are also avoided. When topsoil is brought in, blend it with the native soil by deep spading or rototilling instead of just laying it on top.

Weeds are a good indicator of soil quality. If you have a lush crop of various types of weeds, desirable plants should grow as well. If the neighbors' yards are thriving, yours should too. Ask neighbors if they had to make extensive modifications to get everything to grow.

In the absence of weeds and nearby landscapes, it's difficult to tell what your soil is like by looking at it. The safest thing to do is to have the Cooperative Extension Service or a private lab do a soil test. Along with the test, you get recommendations about what to add to your soil before planting. It's fun to do your own testing with a home kit, but results are not as accurate. You have to figure out what to add yourself.

Soil texture *can* be visually

**Left: Good planting practices and proper plant selection pay off in results like this. Synnestvedt Nursery Co., Glenview, Illinois.**

determined. Take a handful of moist soil, and squeeze it into a ball. Sandy soil crumbles at the slightest touch. Clay soil sticks together. Loam soil holds the shape but can easily be broken apart. If you're fortunate enough to have a natural loam, only minimum soil preparation is necessary. To grow lawn, ground covers, flowers and vegetables in sandy or clay soils, use the following mixture.

For each 1,000 square feet, mix 3 or 4 cubic yards of organic material, 50 to 250 pounds of processed sewage sludge—the amount varies with the manufacturer—and 35 pounds of balanced fertilizer, 8-8-8 or similar. Rototill or dig the mix by hand 6 inches deep. For poor soils, such as subsoil or pure sand, increase the amount of organic material.

At a cost of about 15 to 20 cents per square foot for all materials, this treatment loosens clay soils, increases the water-holding capacity of sandy soils and provides humus, nitrogen, phosphorus and potassium, along with some micronutrients.

Adding sand to clay soils is not effective unless a large amount is used and mixed in thoroughly. Extra organic material is better, unless you have an inexpensive source of salt-free sand.

Organic material should have nitrogen fertilizer added to replace nitrogen lost during decomposition. Composted sawdust and shavings, ground pine bark and sphagnum peat moss are excellent organic materials. Be sure the material is low in salt content and free of weed seeds, insects and diseases.

Where available, mushroom compost and composted cow manure cost less. These materials may have a fairly high salt content that could be a problem in poorly draining soils. Limit applications to 3 cubic yards per 1,000 square feet. Mix it thoroughly with the soil, and water before planting. Be sure manure is composted for a year before using. Fresh manure can damage tender plant roots, and the odor may be overwhelming.

Buy organic material by the truckload for quantities of more than 5 cubic yards. If you can find a bulk source, you can save 50% or more over the sack price.

## ACIDITY AND ALKALINITY

Determine whether the soil is acid or alkaline. This is expressed on a pH scale from 1 to 14. Neutral is 7.0. Anything higher is *alkaline;* anything lower is *acid.* Most plants, including lawns, prefer a slightly acid soil close to 6.5. However, many soils, especially in the Northeast, are below 6.0. This can be too acid for best growth of many plants and lawn grasses. These soils need to be "sweetened" by the addition of ground limestone.

Use dolomitic limestone for acid soils deficient in calcium and magnesium. Treat soil that is high in magnesium with calcite limestone. Wood ashes are alkaline and supply potassium. They are a good addition to acid soils. Acid-loving plants, such as azaleas, rhododendrons, pieris, holly, leucothoe and mountain laurel, thrive with a pH between 5.0 and 5.5. Liming is inadvisable, except in extremely acid soils.

In the Midwest and other areas, naturally alkaline alluvial or limestone soils occur frequently. Soil may also become alkaline from irrigation water or excess application of lime. When pH is above 7.0, it should be lowered for many plants. You can do this by adding soil sulphur, iron sulphate, aluminum sulphate or magnesium sulphate. Or avoid acid-lovers, and concentrate on plants that tolerate a high pH.

Technical chemical relationships are complicated. Unless you want to become a soil expert, it's easiest to follow the recommendations of a soil test. You can also choose to follow proven local practices. Rough quantities often used are 50 to 100 pounds of dolomitic limestone per 1,000 square feet for moderately acid soil. Increase the amount for highly acidic and clay soils. Use 10 to 20 pounds of soil sulphur per 1,000 square feet for alkaline soil. Include 200 pounds of agricultural gypsum per 1,000 square feet for tightly compacted, alkaline clay soil where a high-sodium content is indicated by a soil test. This improves drainage without altering the pH. Gypsum is of little value in sandy and low-sodium soils.

## COMPOST AND COVER CROPS

**Composing**—The ideal way to get organic material is to produce it yourself by *composting.* This is not usually possible for a new garden, but once established, you can make compost of leaves and trimmings instead of burning or hauling them away. Compost is excellent for vegetable gardens and mulching. Some cities have community leaf mulching and wood-chip programs. Check first before you buy more expensive materials.

One precaution: *Avoid infected material.* The temperature inside the pile may not get high enough to destroy some insects and diseases.

**Cover Crops**—These are often used by farmers for nitrogen and green manure. An area is planted in a nitrogen-fixing legume, such as alfalfa, clovers, lupines and vetches. You can use rye and other grasses, but nitrogen is not produced.

If you anticipate at least a year before planting your landscape or vegetable garden, a temporary cover crop sown in the spring looks better than bare ground. It can be rototilled under in the fall or following spring to enrich soil before installing permanent planting.

If soil depth is limited by an impermeable layer, such as rock or hardpan, break through it by drilling or excavating to permit root penetration. A minimum of 12 inches of soil is desirable for lawn and ground cover, 24 to 36 inches for shrubs, and 36 to 60 inches for trees. Use raised planting beds and containers when it is impractical to provide minimum depths.

Ground covers on steep banks and shrubs and trees are normally treated individually by incorporating materials directly in the planting hole rather than in the entire area. Don't worry

**Overgrown variegated holly in a 1-gallon can is a real bargain. Loosen roots prior to planting.**

about having a minimum depth of soil over the entire yard. You need it only at each individual planting hole.

## PLANTING

There are many formulas for planting. The American Indians used "fish-with-the-corn-seed." It was successful, but considering the cost of fish, it is impractical today. Experienced gardeners have mysterious ingredients they insist are essential for proper growth. In fact, nearly everyone has a favorite planting method, and most of them work.

Even though every variety of plant has specific individual needs, these needs are not always critical. Most plants do well if basic requirements are met. Planting directions in this section have proven to be satisfactory for almost all plants. The directions are simple, economical and almost foolproof.

The key to success is to blend original soil on the site with added organic material. Roots grow more easily into the blended soil. Drainage is better through capillary action when existing soil and backfill around the new plant are similar. Otherwise, an *underground pot* is created, and roots and water stay confined within the planting hole.

Drainage is the crucial factor. To check drainage, try this simple test. Dig the plant hole, and fill it with water. Be sure the soil isn't thoroughly wet when you dig the hole. If water is still there several hours later, additional measures for drainage are needed.

Use a post-hole auger or large drill to dig two or more *chimneys* several feet deep in the bottom of the hole. *Don't* fill them with sand or gravel. This impedes water flow because of the change in soil texture. Fill the chimneys with the prepared backfill, as shown at right.

With proper watering techniques, drainage should be adequate unless excess water accumulates when it rains or when sprinklers run. In this case, choose tolerant plants, and raise them higher than the surrounding grade. Try to correct the overall drainage situation with better surface flow and by installing underground drain lines. Few plants thrive in a swamp.

The size of the plant at the time of planting is closely related to the problem of growth rate and spacing. If your budget permits, use relatively large plants, and space them properly. Choose large slower-growing plants so you don't have to wait years for their development. Many budgets don't allow for this. Large individual plants cost more and so does the labor for planting them.

There is much to be said for plants in smaller sizes. Many plants transplant better when they're young. The price chart above shows sizes and costs of various classes of plants.

Most nurseries sell container-grown and B&B plants. Usually B&B prices are slightly lower than a comparable plant grown in a container. Sometimes B&B costs more or about the same. It doesn't matter whether a plant is B&B or container-grown, as long as the plant is healthy and well-rooted.

Many deciduous plants are available bareroot during the dormant season at a lower price than B&B or containers. In addition to greater choice and lower cost, bareroot plants are lighter and easier to handle. There is no prob-

| Plant Prices | | | |
|---|---|---|---|
| Class of Plant | Usual Container Size & Height | Approximate Price Retail | Installed |
| Perennial | 1 quart/6 inches | $ 1.50 | $ 2.00 |
| Most shrubs & vines | 1 gallon/12-18 in. | $ 3.50 | $ 5.50 |
| Special shrubs | 5 gallon/18-24 in. | $ 12.00 | $ 16.00 |
| Ground cover | peat pot | $ .50 | $ .75 |
| Most trees | 5 gallon/5-6 feet | $ 12.50 | $ 25.00 |
| Special trees | 15 gallon/6-8 feet | $ 50.00 | $ 75.00 |
| Specimen trees | 24-inch box/2-1/2 in. caliper/10 to 12 feet | $200.00 | $250.00 |

## HOW TO PLANT A SHRUB

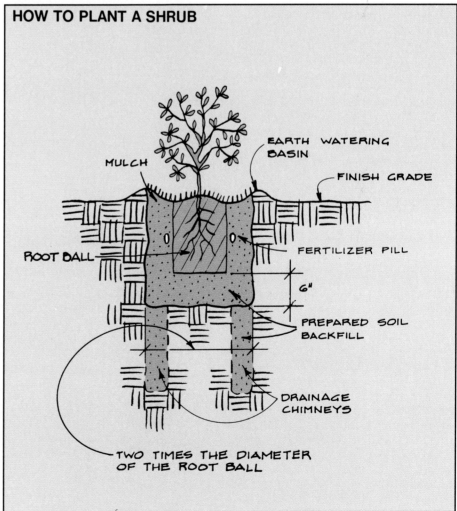

lem of incompatible-soil types that can occur when B&B and container plants are planted in a different native soil.

It's fun to shop for bargains, but when purchasing plants at markets and discount-house nurseries, the advice and reliability of an experienced nurseryman may be lost. Beware of overgrown specials with root problems. Avoid undersize plants in large containers. To avoid mix-ups in identification, be sure of the plant you want, or look for the wholesaler's tag. If you know what you want, a $1.99 special may be as good as the same plant at the regular price of $4.95.

But how do you know what you're after? A good plant appears healthy, young and vigorous. As you examine more plants, you begin to notice differences in color and form that indicate health and vigor. Look for shrubs with a nice shape and trees with a stout trunk and sturdy framework.

For container plants, stick your finger down into the soil. See if there are roots circling directly around the main stem or trunk. Sometimes when a seedling is transferred to a new pot, its roots are directed in a circle. This can seriously limit growth. It could eventually choke the plant, which is more important than if the plant appears to be root-bound or too big for its container. Actually, most plants are okay if the root ball is full of roots, as long as roots are not kinked, circling or girdling.

## STEPS IN PLANTING

1. Modify the soil pH as necessary. This was described under *Soil Preparation,* page 123.
2. Dig the hole for the plant about twice the diameter of the plant's root ball or spread, and 6 to 12 inches deeper.
3. Check the drainage as described on page 125. If drainage is poor, dig chimneys.
4. Make a mixture for backfill of 1/3 organic material and 2/3 soil excavated from the plant pit, plus some processed sewage sludge, according to manufacturer's directions. A 1/2 cup of super phosphate per cubic foot of backfill helps stimulate root growth without burning. Recent research indicates that in *very good* soil, growth is as good without special backfill.
5. Backfill the bottom of the hole so

the plant is at the same level as it was grown. Tamp the backfill firmly to prevent settling. In soggy soils and for sensitive plants, such as azaleas and rhododendrons, add a little more backfill so the plant is slightly above the surrounding grade.
6. Remove container-grown plants from their containers. Be careful not to break the root ball. Slice the sides vertically in 3 or 4 places to stimulate root growth and interrupt a circular pattern. Spread the roots out when setting them in the hole. Even though pressed fiber pots deteriorate, remove them or break them away after the plant is set.
7. For B&B plants, loosen the twine or wire, and open the burlap at the top of the root ball. Roll it back so it is below

Jute mesh is held in place with special oversized staples. Ground cover is then planted in small openings.

Hydroseeding large slopes is much easier than planting individual plants by hand. Crown vetch, pictured above, or grasses and wildflowers can be successfully planted by this method.

the finished soil surface. Do not remove the burlap unless it is treated *not* to deteriorate. Remove plastic wrappings entirely.
8. Make a cone of soil from mixed soil in the bottom of the hole for bareroot plants. Spread the roots over the cone. Roots should be plump and fresh. If they are dry, soak them overnight in water before planting. Cut off broken or frayed ends.
9. After the plant is set in position, check again to make sure it's at the proper level. Fill the pit with soil mixture, and tamp soil firmly around the root ball. Place time-release granules, such as Osmocote, or slow-release fertilizer pills, such as Nitroform, next to the roots, according to manufacturer's directions. Avoid chemical fertilizers or fresh manure that can injure tender new roots.
10. Add vitamin B-1 or a transplanting product, such as Hormex or Superthrive, to reduce transplanting shock and stimulate root growth. Researchers don't agree as to how effective it is, but it can't do any harm to try.
11. If the plant has a large amount of foliage in proportion to the size of the root ball, reduce the leaf surface by thinning out and pruning back. Spray with an antitranspirant.
12. In exposed locations, construct a temporary shield to protect tender plants from sun and wind until they adapt.
13. Build a temporary earth watering basin at the outside edge of the plant pit. Install a mulch of organic material, bark chunks or stone, 2 to 4 inches thick.

English ivy is an excellent permanent slope cover. Main limitations are intolerance to extreme cold and at least one full season to establish.

14. Soak the plant by filling the basin several times. Don't allow roots to dry out. Unless there is ample rainfall, supplementary watering is necessary until roots have spread into the surrounding soil. Be careful not to overwater dormant plants, especially bareroot. Their need for water is when new growth begins in the spring.

**Planting Trees**—Follow the above directions. Remove existing stakes, then restake, guy, prune and wrap the trunk, as described in the next column and on page 128.

## GROUND COVER AND SLOPE PLANTING

For gentle slopes that are easy to mow, lawn is usually the best choice. Steep slopes, along with narrow areas, rocky soil and heavy shade, are prime candidates for a ground cover or shrub cover.

Plants spread and fill in faster if soil-preparation materials are tilled into the entire area without creating an erosion problem. Or dig small, individual pockets, similar to those needed for shrubs and trees.

Treat flats or bundles of ground-cover plants with care. Don't let them dry out after you bring them home from the nursery. Plant them in slightly moist soil, then water immediately. If rainfall is insufficient, supplementary irrigation is necessary until plants are well-established. Light applications of liquid or pelletized fertilizer at monthly intervals speeds growth.

Consider *hydroseeding* application instead of conventional ground cover for large banks. The cost is about 10 cents per square foot for a minimum area of 5,000 square feet. Mixes containing grasses, clover, crown vetch and various wildflowers can be attractive and naturalize under favorable conditions.

## PLANTING TREES

Follow the planting steps on page 126 and the illustrations on page 128. In addition, staking is an important part of tree planting. It is often overlooked until windstorms break branches or blow trees over. Ideally, a nursery tree has a stout trunk, called *heavy caliper,* that will require only temporary support until roots become established.

Low-branching and pyramidal trees, such as sweet gum, birch, ginkgo and many conifers, often get by with one short stake or none at all. Trees with *small caliper,* flexible trunks and a heavy head of foliage are usually grown with a stake at the nursery. These trees cannot stand without help. Large trees may have to be anchored with guy wires to keep them from tipping over.

Remove the nursery stake, and tie the trunk loosely between two sturdy stakes. Allow the trunk to flex with the wind and gain strength. This is like exercise for the tree. Rigid constraint keeps the tree dependent on the stakes. When a big wind comes, the entire head of the tree can snap off if it cannot bend. Thinning the foliage allows wind to pass through, reducing the "sail" effect.

Use rubber or plastic ties so bark isn't chafed or the trunk cut by thin wires. When guy wires are used, attach them to the trunk or heavy branches in three places. Run the wires at a 45° angle to sturdy stakes driven into firm ground. Enclose wires in sections of hose where they touch the bark. Mark the wires with plastic flags so people don't trip on them.

Remove about 1/3 of the potential leaves of bareroot trees by trimming side branches. Remove damaged, weak or crossing branches. Do not cut back the central leader or small twigs.

To protect against sun scald, wrap trunks of tender-bark trees, such as dogwood, maple, linden, crabapple and honey locust. Use tree-wrap paper, burlap or a plastic commercial product sold as Spiral Wrap or Tree GARD.

Start from the base of the tree, and wrap up to the lower branches. Remove wrappings when foliage shades the trunk. In severe winter climates, protection may be advisable even on mature trees, as described on page 186. If there are rabbits and mice nearby, guard trunks with 1/4-inch wire mesh from below the ground to 2 feet above the anticipated snow level.

As the tree develops, enlarge its watering basin. Keep the area next to

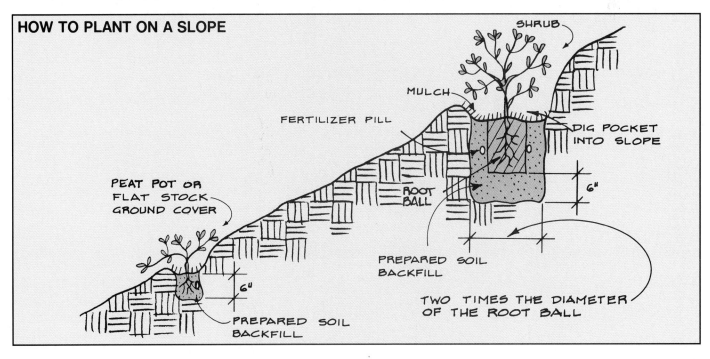

HOW TO PLANT ON A SLOPE

# HOW TO PLANT A TREE

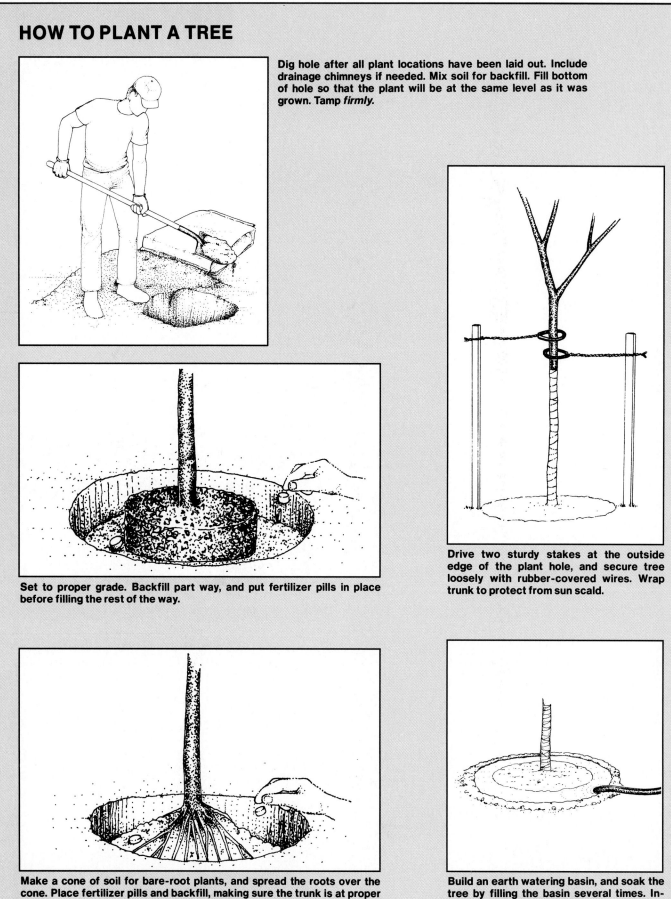

Dig hole after all plant locations have been laid out. Include drainage chimneys if needed. Mix soil for backfill. Fill bottom of hole so that the plant will be at the same level as it was grown. Tamp *firmly*.

Set to proper grade. Backfill part way, and put fertilizer pills in place before filling the rest of the way.

Drive two sturdy stakes at the outside edge of the plant hole, and secure tree loosely with rubber-covered wires. Wrap trunk to protect from sun scald.

Make a cone of soil for bare-root plants, and spread the roots over the cone. Place fertilizer pills and backfill, making sure the trunk is at proper level.

Build an earth watering basin, and soak the tree by filling the basin several times. Install a mulch 4-inches thick.

**Tender trunk is securely wrapped and tree basin mulched to prepare for winter.**

the trunk relatively dry to prevent disease. Make the outside diameter of the basin at least as wide as the *drip line* of the tree—the point where most rain rolls off the tree's leaves.

Enlarge the basin beyond the drip line to encourage root growth. Deep watering does the same thing. Roots only grow where there is moisture. Too-small a basin inhibits growth, and shallow watering produces shallow roots. In either case, the tree won't grow as strong as it should. When the tree is established, remove the earth basin entirely, except in low-rainfall areas where too much water is not a problem.

## WEED CONTROL

The best time to control weeds is *before* planting. This is important in ground cover and lawn areas. Existing weeds, and those germinated when the soil is soaked, are easy to eliminate. Keep the area moist for several weeks for a good crop.

Most broad-leafed weeds and grasses can be rototilled into the soil or hoed off. Spray perennial, broad-leafed weeds with a 2,4-D mix or Round-up or Kleen-up. Spray quackgrass, bentgrass, bermuda and other perennial grasses with Dowpon, Round-up or Kleen-up several weeks before cultivating. Two applications may be necessary.

Eliminating existing weeds is only part of the problem. Most soils still contain many weed seeds. For extreme situations, use a temporary soil sterilant to kill weed seeds without affecting future planting.

Vapam is applied at the rate of 2-1/2 gallons per 1,000 square feet in a water solution. Allow ground to dry out for 3 weeks before planting. Cost is about 2 cents per square foot. Vapam also provides some control of nematodes and soil diseases. Apply it after completing all other soil preparation. Keep it outside the root area of existing trees and shrubs.

This weed control is most effective in warm weather and is often disappointing in extremely cold or hot weather. *Read labels carefully and follow manufacturer's directions when applying any chemicals.* Plant treated

areas as soon as the waiting period is over. This avoids reinfestation.

## NEMATODES AND SOIL DISEASES

When nematodes and soil diseases are a serious problem, drastic measures may be necessary. In areas where there are no existing trees and shrubs, use methyl bromide or a nematocide before any planting is done. These chemicals are hazardous to handle. They should be applied only by licensed personnel on the recommendation of a Cooperative Extension Agent or landscape professional.

## USING PLANTING PLANS

Planting plans beginning on page 132, give you some ideas for plant selection. They are based on the lot plans beginning on page 24. Plans give you some ideas for plant selection. Follow the steps below, and use the *Plant Lists,* beginning on page 86, to select the best plants for you.

Think about the purpose you want a plant to serve. Decide on the general category, size and placement of each plant. Determine if the plant is adapted to your climate and whether it will have proper exposure.

Focus on use and function. If a large tree is needed for quick shade, a red maple is a better choice than a slower-growing, more-upright little-leaf linden. If you want a large shrub that won't get too wide, an upright juniper is better than a mock orange.

In many situations, choice is not critical. You may be able to use any plant suited to your climate and exposure. You can combine plants for a pleasing composition of color, form and texture. Perhaps you can add seasonal interest with something occurring throughout the year. If you're interested in fragrance, consider lilac, mock orange, honeysuckle, pines and roses. Group plants together according to their watering needs.

Don't sacrifice utility for the sake of color. There's no need for every plant in your garden to be a heavy bloomer. However, many plants on the foolproof lists are reliable *and* flowering. If you want more color, use annuals, bulbs and perennials in addition to basic plantings.

Planting design is challenging. Possibilities are unlimited, and rewards are tremendous.

# NURSERY CONTAINER SIZES

Nursery plants are sold in many different sizes—from 1-quart perennials and bedding plants to large trees in boxes or barrels. Most containers are made of plastic or metal. Some nurseries sell plants *balled and burlapped* (B&B). See pages 126 to 128 for tips on planting various types.

1-gallon fern and 1-quart chrysanthemum.

Balled-and-burlapped (B&B) Mugo pine.

Left: Root balls of 6- to 8-foot-tall trees securely wrapped in burlap.

More nurseries are growing at least part of their stock in containers. This is a 15-gallon Japanese black pine.

Left: There can be a considerable size difference between 1-gallon and B&B shrubs.

# STYLING YOUR LANDSCAPE

Plants help set the tone or style of your landscape. Carefully placed trees and accents add interesting color, contrast and texture to the scene. Plants help establish mood and feeling. The well-planned landscapes on this page may give you some good ideas.

If you have water-front property, weeping willows can help set the appropriate mood.

A welcoming lamp post with hybrid clematis entwined makes guests feel warm and comfortable even before they get to the front door.

Neighborhood planting of white and pink flowering dogwoods adds beauty to the individual homes and the entire street as well.

Landscape designer Robert E. Morrell used restraint, simplicity and strong organization to give this garden a neat, orderly feeling. Landscape contractor: Mavroff Inc., Brookfield, Wisconsin.

Boston ivy lends dignity and a feeling of age to this home in Hartford, Connecticut.

Well-placed common snowball reflects the crisp white trim of the house.

# PLANTING PLAN—Interior Lot

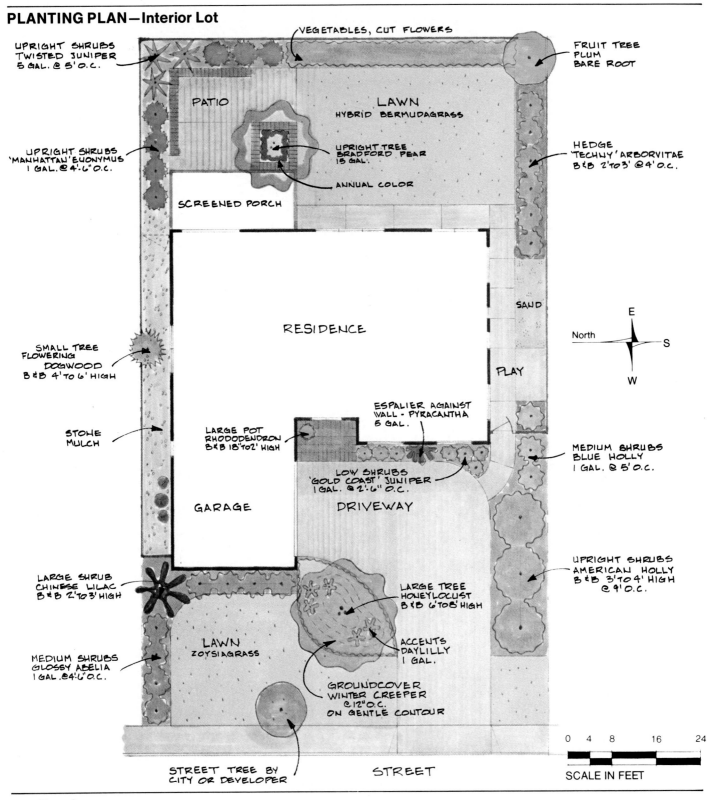

**UPRIGHT SHRUBS**
TWISTED JUNIPER
5 GAL. @ 5' O.C.

VEGETABLES, CUT FLOWERS

**FRUIT TREE**
PLUM
BARE ROOT

PATIO

**LAWN**
HYBRID BERMUDAGRASS

**UPRIGHT SHRUBS**
'MANHATTAN' EUONYMUS
1 GAL. @ 4'-6" O.C.

UPRIGHT TREE
BRADFORD PEAR
15 GAL.

**HEDGE**
'TECHNY' ARBORVITAE
B & B 2' TO 3' @ 4' O.C.

ANNUAL COLOR

SCREENED PORCH

SAND

RESIDENCE

E
North
W
S

**SMALL TREE**
FLOWERING
DOGWOOD
B & B 4' TO 6' HIGH

PLAY

ESPALIER AGAINST
WALL - PYRACANTHA
5 GAL.

**STONE**
MULCH

LARGE POT
RHODODENDRON
B & B 18" TO 2' HIGH

**MEDIUM SHRUBS**
BLUE HOLLY
1 GAL. @ 5' O.C.

LOW SHRUBS
'GOLD COAST' JUNIPER
1 GAL. @ 2'-6" O.C.

GARAGE

DRIVEWAY

**UPRIGHT SHRUBS**
AMERICAN HOLLY
B & B 3' TO 4' HIGH
@ 9' O.C.

**LARGE SHRUB**
CHINESE LILAC
B & B 2' TO 3' HIGH

LARGE TREE
HONEYLOCUST
B & B 6' TO 8' HIGH

**MEDIUM SHRUBS**
GLOSSY ABELIA
1 GAL. @ 4'-6" O.C.

**LAWN**
ZOYSIAGRASS

ACCENTS
DAYLILLY
1 GAL.

GROUNDCOVER
WINTER CREEPER
@ 12" O.C.
ON GENTLE CONTOUR

STREET TREE BY
CITY OR DEVELOPER

STREET

0   4   8      16      24

**SCALE IN FEET**

## Zone 6

- Approximate average annual minimum temperature -10F to 0F (-24C to -18C).
- Generally good growing conditions for ornamental plants.
- A wide range of plants can be grown if placed in the proper location and given reasonable care.

### Planting Considerations

- Relatively mild climate allows use of broad-leafed evergreen and coniferous shrubs for year-round foliage.
- Simple, orderly plant placement could be termed a *Combination* style.
- Small plant sizes are used to stay within a modest budget.
- Hybrid bermudagrass provides a rugged back yard play area. Zoysiagrass will be a low-maintenance front lawn once established.

## PLANTING PLAN—Corner Lot

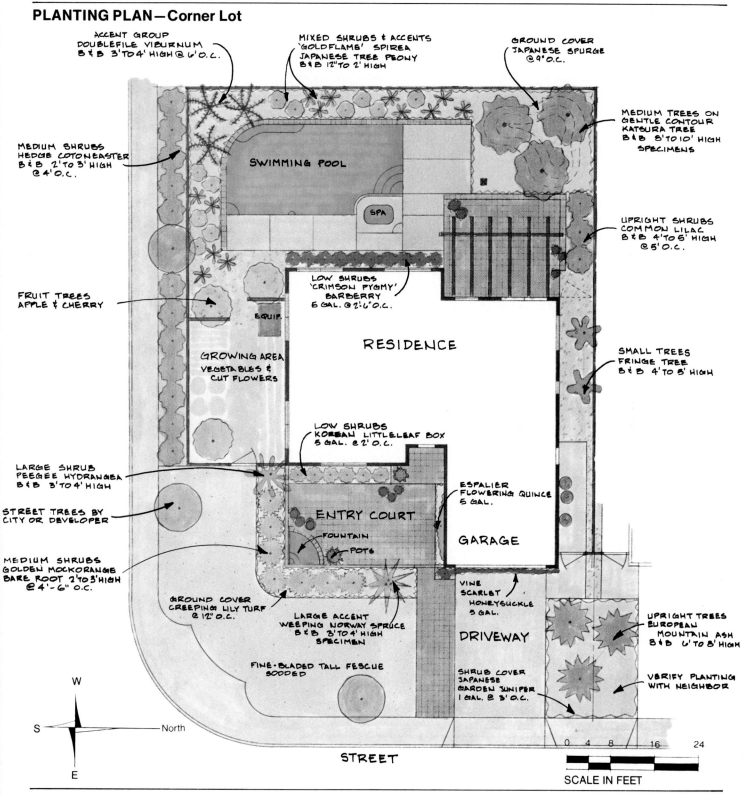

ACCENT GROUP
DOUBLEFILE VIBURNUM
B&B 3'TO 4' HIGH @ 6' O.C.

MIXED SHRUBS & ACCENTS
'GOLDFLAME' SPIREA
JAPANESE TREE PEONY
B&B 12" TO 2' HIGH

GROUND COVER
JAPANESE SPURGE
@ 9" O.C.

MEDIUM TREES ON
GENTLE CONTOUR
KATSURA TREE
B&B 8'TO 10' HIGH
SPECIMENS

MEDIUM SHRUBS
HEDGE COTONEASTER
B&B 2'TO 3' HIGH
@ 4' O.C.

SWIMMING POOL

SPA

UPRIGHT SHRUBS
COMMON LILAC
B&B 4' TO 5' HIGH
@ 5' O.C.

FRUIT TREES
APPLE & CHERRY

EQUIP.

LOW SHRUBS
'CRIMSON PYGMY'
BARBERRY
5 GAL. @ 2'-6" O.C.

RESIDENCE

GROWING AREA
VEGETABLES &
CUT FLOWERS

SMALL TREES
FRINGE TREE
B&B 4' TO 5' HIGH

LOW SHRUBS
KOREAN LITTLELEAF BOX
5 GAL. @ 2' O.C.

LARGE SHRUB
PEEGEE HYDRANGEA
B&B 3'TO 4' HIGH

ESPALIER
FLOWERING QUINCE
5 GAL.

STREET TREES BY
CITY OR DEVELOPER

ENTRY COURT

GARAGE

FOUNTAIN

POTS

MEDIUM SHRUBS
GOLDEN MOCKORANGE
BARE ROOT 2'TO 3' HIGH
@ 4'-6" O.C.

VINE
SCARLET
HONEYSUCKLE
5 GAL.

GROUND COVER
CREEPING LILY TURF
@ 12" O.C.

LARGE ACCENT
WEEPING NORWAY SPRUCE
B&B 3'TO 4' HIGH
SPECIMEN

DRIVEWAY

UPRIGHT TREES
EUROPEAN
MOUNTAIN ASH
B&B 6'TO 8' HIGH

FINE-BLADED TALL FESCUE
SODDED

SHRUB COVER
JAPANESE
GARDEN JUNIPER
1 GAL. @ 3' O.C.

VERIFY PLANTING
WITH NEIGHBOR

W
S — North
E

STREET

0  4  8    16    24

SCALE IN FEET

### Zone 5

- Approximate average annual minimum temperature −20F to −10F (−29C to −24C).
- Summer heat and winter cold.
- Occasional summer droughts.
- Plants of borderline hardiness worth a try in southern portion of zone.

### Planting Consideration

- *Contemporary* theme is carried out by colored foliage, flowering plants and striking forms.
- Ample budget allows for large shrubs and several specimen trees.
- Pots add seasonal color for outdoor entertaining.
- Fine-bladed tall fescue sod lawn gives immediate effect and survives dry spells well.

# PLANTING PLAN—Cul-de-sac Lot

## Zone 4

- Approximate average minimum temperature -30F to -20F (-35C to -29C).
- Summer heat and winter cold.
- Both high and low humidity.
- Strong winter winds.

### Planting Considerations

- Plants hardy to cold are emphasized.
- Most plants have a casual quality and are placed in clumps and groups for a *Natural* feeling.
- Modest-size plants fit in with the average budget.
- Bluegrass/rye mix lawn will withstand considerable wear.

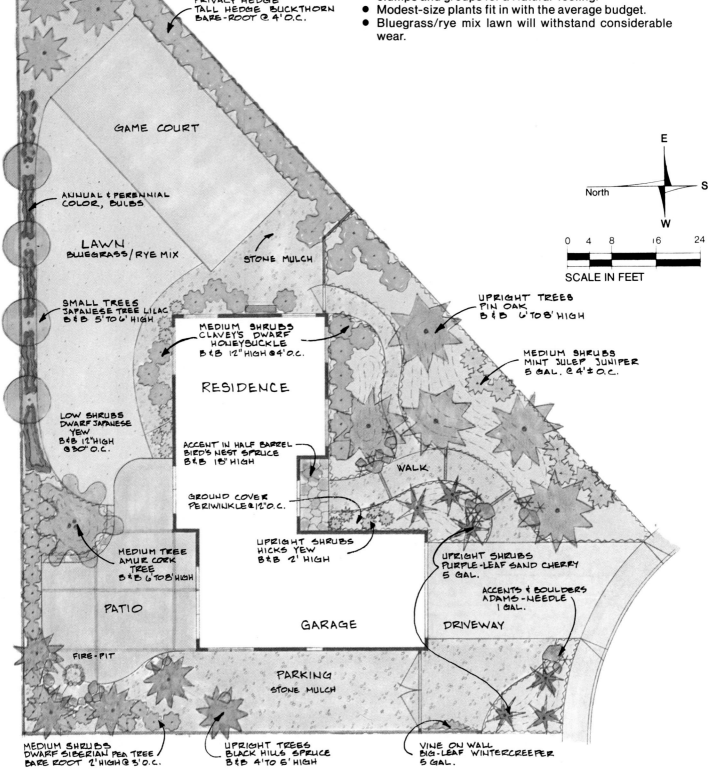

UPRIGHT TREES
BLACK HILLS SPRUCE
B&B 4' TO 5' HIGH

PRIVACY HEDGE
TALL HEDGE BUCKTHORN
BARE-ROOT @ 4' O.C.

GAME COURT

ANNUAL & PERENNIAL
COLOR, BULBS

LAWN
BLUEGRASS/RYE MIX

STONE MULCH

SMALL TREES
JAPANESE TREE LILAC
B&B 5' TO 6' HIGH

MEDIUM SHRUBS
CLAVEY'S DWARF
HONEYSUCKLE
B&B 12" HIGH @ 4' O.C.

RESIDENCE

UPRIGHT TREES
PIN OAK
B&B 6' TO 8' HIGH

MEDIUM SHRUBS
MINT JULEP JUNIPER
5 GAL. @ 4'± O.C.

LOW SHRUBS
DWARF JAPANESE
YEW
B&B 12" HIGH
@ 30" O.C.

ACCENT IN HALF BARREL
BIRD'S NEST SPRUCE
B&B 18" HIGH

WALK

GROUND COVER
PERIWINKLE @ 12" O.C.

UPRIGHT SHRUBS
HICKS YEW
B&B 2' HIGH

MEDIUM TREE
AMUR CORK
TREE
B&B 6' TO 8' HIGH

UPRIGHT SHRUBS
PURPLE-LEAF SAND CHERRY
5 GAL.

ACCENTS & BOULDERS
ADAMS-NEEDLE
1 GAL.

PATIO

GARAGE

DRIVEWAY

FIRE-PIT

PARKING
STONE MULCH

MEDIUM SHRUBS
DWARF SIBERIAN PEA TREE
BARE ROOT 2' HIGH @ 3' O.C.

UPRIGHT TREES
BLACK HILLS SPRUCE
B&B 4' TO 5' HIGH

VINE ON WALL
BIG-LEAF WINTERCREEPER
5 GAL.

E
North S
W

0  4  8  16  24
SCALE IN FEET

## PLANTING PLANT—Condo Lot

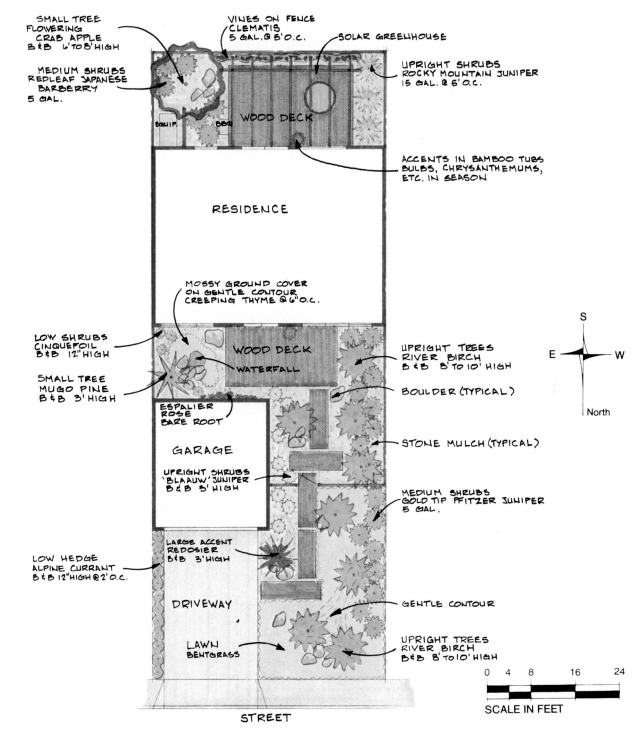

SMALL TREE
FLOWERING
CRAB APPLE
B & B 6' TO 8' HIGH

VINES ON FENCE
CLEMATIS
5 GAL. @ 5' O.C.

SOLAR GREENHOUSE

UPRIGHT SHRUBS
ROCKY MOUNTAIN JUNIPER
15 GAL. @ 5' O.C.

MEDIUM SHRUBS
REDLEAF JAPANESE
BARBERRY
5 GAL.

WOOD DECK

EQUIP.   BBQ

RESIDENCE

ACCENTS IN BAMBOO TUBS
BULBS, CHRYSANTHEMUMS,
ETC. IN SEASON

MOSSY GROUND COVER
ON GENTLE CONTOUR
CREEPING THYME @ 6" O.C.

LOW SHRUBS
CINQUEFOIL
B & B 12" HIGH

WOOD DECK

WATERFALL

UPRIGHT TREES
RIVER BIRCH
B & B 8' TO 10' HIGH

BOULDER (TYPICAL)

SMALL TREE
MUGO PINE
B & B 3' HIGH

ESPALIER
ROSE
BARE ROOT

STONE MULCH (TYPICAL)

GARAGE

UPRIGHT SHRUBS
'BLAAUW' JUNIPER
B & B 3' HIGH

MEDIUM SHRUBS
GOLD TIP PFITZER JUNIPER
5 GAL.

LARGE ACCENT
REDOSIER
B & B 3' HIGH

LOW HEDGE
ALPINE CURRANT
B & B 12" HIGH @ 2' O.C.

GENTLE CONTOUR

DRIVEWAY

LAWN
BENTGRASS

UPRIGHT TREES
RIVER BIRCH
B & B 8' TO 10' HIGH

STREET

S
E — W
North

| 0 | 4 | 8 | 16 | 24 |

SCALE IN FEET

---

### Zone 3

- Approximate average annual minimum temperature -40F to -30F (-40C to -35C).
- Late spring frosts and early fall frosts can damage non-hardy plants.
- Strong winter winds.
- Usual snow cover protects low plants.

**Planting Considerations**

- Hardiest plants from the top of the lists are used.

- Conifers, irregular forms, mossy ground cover, bentgrass lawn, boulders and contours enhance an *Oriental* motif.
- Feature plants are of specimen size in accordance with ample budget.
- Low maintenance achieved with rugged plants, stone mulch and limited lawn area.

It's hard to imagine what neighborhoods would look like without lawns. Lawns provide the continuity that links individual landscapes in a harmonious whole. Grass is a wonderful surface to play on. It also helps control erosion and dust, reduces noise and glare and has an overall cooling effect. A lawn of some type is usually the best landscape treatment for large, open, level areas.

How much care a lawn needs and how much it costs depends on the soil, climate, type of grass and whether you want a casual meadow or a manicured carpet. There are many choices. In general, cool-season types— bluegrass, fescue, bentgrass and ryegrass—are best for the cooler areas of Zone 7 and north. You might be able to use the hardiest warm-season grasses, zoysia and bermudagrass, in Zone 7 and the warmest areas of Zone 6.

All zone designations are approximations. See what grows well locally, and select the type that best suits your needs. Seeds, sprigs, stolons, plugs and sod that are *certified* guarantee purity and are worth the slight additional cost. Question cheap blends containing grasses that could be undesirable in the long run.

## COOL-SEASON GRASSES

Best planting time for these grasses is fall and spring.

**Kentucky Bluegrass**—*Poa pratensis.* This is the standard lawn grass for most of Zone 6, up into Canada. It can also be grown in Zone 7 and south but doesn't perform as well. There are better choices available.

There are many varieties of this grass, and new ones are being developed all the time. It's confusing for the professional—unfathomable for most homeowners. Common blue-

**Verdant expanse of bluegrass-mix lawn explains its popularity.**

grass and varieties such as 'Arboretum', 'Park' and 'Kenblue', are good for low-maintenance situations where there is maximum sun. Cut grass at least 2 inches high, and keep water and fertilizer to a minimum.

'Adelphi', 'Baron', 'Birka', 'Fylking' and 'Sydsport' are a few improved turf-type varieties that perform well when given regular watering and proper maintenance. 'Glade', 'Bensun (A-34)', 'Bristol', 'Eclipse' and 'Touchdown' are considered shade tolerant but do better in the sun. Rough bluegrass, *Poa trivialis,* is valuable for moist, shady areas. 'Sabre' is a variety worth searching for.

When not to use a lawn? Steep slopes are difficult to mow. No grass thrives under trees with heavy shade and root competition. Rocky soils may cost too much to improve enough to support a lawn. Small, narrow strips are difficult to mow and edge. In these cases, a ground cover or shrub cover would most likely be a better choice.

Where rainfall is low, periodic droughts common and irrigation water limited, lawn areas should be reserved for use and viewing adjacent to the house. Fringe areas can be covered with bark chips, pine needles, gravel or similar materials. Drought-tolerant plants can be added where desired. If there is native vegetation, consider cleaning it up a bit. Enjoy a woodsy effect instead of tearing it out to install a high-maintenance lawn.

A blend of three to five varieties is best, with no less than 20% of any one kind. A mixture of 50% fine-bladed fescue and 50% shade-tolerant bluegrass or rough bluegrass is often used for a shady mix. To increase wearability, add 20% fine-bladed perennial rye to the bluegrass blend.

Uniformity, fine texture, ability to withstand normal wear and rich, green color explains the popularity of bluegrass. It grows in full sun or light shade. For best performance, it requires good soil, slightly on the acid side, supplemental watering during dry spells, regular fertilization and a

**Left: In many situations, there's just no substitute for a beautiful lawn.**

program of weed, insect and disease control.

Sow seed at 2 to 3 pounds per 1,000 square feet. Mowing height is about 2 inches, higher for shaded areas. Some varieties withstand shorter mowing. Main drawbacks are susceptibility to fungus diseases and the high water requirement.

**Tall Fescue**—*Festuca arundinacea.* This grass is tough and deep-rooted. It tolerates heat, drought, more shade than bluegrass, and has a wide pH range, from 5 to 8. Tall fescue establishes quickly, doesn't build up much thatch, is not often troubled by insects and diseases, grows in almost any soil—including wet and salty ones—doesn't require much fertilizer and seldom has a weed problem.

Sounds like the perfect grass. Some objections are that it gets bunchy if not sown thickly. It's not as cold hardy as bluegrass—Zones 6 and 7 are best—and it needs frequent mowing.

The main reason it hasn't been planted more is the coarseness of wide-bladed 'Alta', 'K-31' and other varieties that were the only ones available. Now there are several fine-bladed selections available that appear to retain all the advantages, along with a more-appealing texture. 'Olympic', 'Rebel', 'Houndog', 'Falcon' and 'Marathon' look good. They may supplant bluegrass in hot summer areas and where water supplies are limited.

Tall fescues are best sown alone or as a mix of two or more varieties at 8 to 10 pounds per 1,000 square feet. Because of the rapid germination rate and growth, plant it any time during the growing season in all but the hottest areas. Cover seed with mulch, and water it carefully. Mowing height is 2 to 3 inches.

**Meadow Fescue**—*Festuca elatior.* This is often used as a fast-germinating nurse crop in service-type mixes. Texture is coarse, and it tends to bunch. This type persists rather than dying out after more-desirable grasses are established. Fine-bladed perennial ryegrasses are now favored in a bluegrass blend rather than meadow fescue.

**Fine Fescues**—*Festuca rubra, F. r. commutata, F. longifolia.* These fine-textured grasses are best suited to cool, dry, partially shaded areas in Zone 6 and north. These grasses do not do well in extreme heat, in salty

Kentucky bluegrass will withstand dappled shade for part of the day. Landscape architect: CR3 Inc., Avon, Connecticut.

or poorly drained clay soils or when overfertilized.

Commonly available varieties are 'Pennlawn', 'Fortress', 'Banner', 'Dawson', 'Golfrood', 'Biljart' and 'Jamestown'. Each variety has certain characteristics that might be advantageous for specific situations. 'Biljart' and 'Fortress' have better heat tolerance. 'Jamestown' and 'Banner' can be mowed low. 'Golfrood' and 'Dawson' are salt tolerant, and 'Pennlawn' combines well with other grasses.

Fine fescues are usually blended with bluegrass and fine-bladed perennial ryegrass for shade and drought tolerance. Rate of sowing and mowing height is determined by other grasses in the mix. 'Pennlawn' and other *F. rubra* types can be sown at 5 to 6 pounds per 1,000 square feet as an unmowed slope or ground cover for a casual, natural effect. Use creeping red fescue to overseed dormant warm-season grasses in the fall.

**Ryegrasses**—*Lolium* species. There are two basic types of ryegrass. Annual ryegrass, *L. multiflorum,* is used for winter overseeding of warm-season grasses and as a fast-growing nurse crop constituting up to 10% of a mix.

The other type is perennial ryegrass, *Lolium perenne.* This makes a coarse, bunchy, hard-to-mow, infe-

Fine-bladed tall fescue is just a little coarser than bluegrass/rye mix.

rior lawn. Along with annual ryegrass, it has been replaced with turf-type, fine-bladed varieties, such as 'Citation', 'Derby', 'Diplomat', 'Manhattan', 'Pennfine' and 'Yorktown II'. These grasses have a texture and color similar to bluegrass. Growth is somewhat slower, and the softer leaves mow better. They also have a greater heat and cold tolerance, although the best climate is in mildest

Landscape architect John Clayton Thomas, ASLA, used gently sloping bluegrass to emphasize the front entry.

Marathon fine-bladed tall fescue withstands periods of drought well.

winter areas of Zone 5 and warmer, and where summers are cool and moist.

Turf-type perennial ryegrass is not often used alone. It is usually blended 20% with bluegrasses and fine fescues for fast germination, erosion control, moderate shade tolerance and wearability. Other good uses are to sow 3 to 5 pounds per 1,000 square feet after verticutting an existing lawn that has seen better days or to over-seed warm-season grasses in the fall.

Ryegrasses do best in well-drained sandy soils but also tolerate clay and some wetness. The 2-inch mowing height is compatible with bluegrass.

**Bentgrasses**—*Agrostis* species. Unless you want a specialized putting green, lawn-bowling surface or meticulous carpet, there is little reason to plant a bentgrass lawn. It is a high-maintenance lawn and requires lots of water, fertilizer, mowing and regular fungus and insect control. Creeping bentgrass must be mowed very low and managed carefully to avoid thatch build-up. 'Colonial' bentgrass tends to take over when used as part of a mix. It is seldom included today. Best adaptation is in the Great Lakes and northern New England regions, where the grasses take to the cool climate and acidic soils.

Redtop, *Agrostis alba,* is a fast-germinating grass. It is sometimes used in small amounts—up to 3% in mixtures as a nurse crop—until slower grasses develop. It disappears in a few years after serving its purpose.

## WARM-SEASON GRASSES

Best planting time is late spring and early summer.

**Bermudagrass**—*Cynodon dactylon.* Zone 7 and south is bermudagrass country, but some varieties even survive winters in Zone 6. These rugged grasses are tolerant of heat, drought, poor soil, alkalinity, salt and heavy traffic. They look better with regular watering but can survive on very little water. Insect and disease resistance is generally good. They *do* require frequent mowing and nitrogen fertilization during the summer growing season. They build up considerable thatch and go dormant in winter.

Bermudagrasses can be overseeded with cool-season grasses or sprayed with a lawn dye if the brown color is objectionable. Shade tolerance is poor, so plant this grass in full sunlight. Adjacent planting beds are subject to invasion by bermudagrass. Mowing strips and weedicides are necessary.

Common bermudagrass makes a presentable, low-maintenance lawn when given reasonable care. Sow 1 to 2 pounds of seed per 1,000 square feet. Mow often to a 1-inch height to prevent formation of seed heads. Cold tolerance is poor.

Hybrid bermudagrasses are often used for high-quality lawns. They require more care but have a more-pleasing color and texture than common bermudagrass. 'Midway', 'Midiron' and 'Pee Dee' are among the most cold-tolerant varieties currently available. The hybrids set no viable seed, so they must be sodded or planted from sprigs or plugs spaced 6 to 12 inches apart. They can also be planted from stolons spread at the rate of three bushels per 1,000 square feet. Mow 1 inch high at least once a week during the growing season. Annual dethatching is advisable to prevent excessive build-up.

**Zoysiagrass**—*Zoysia* species. 'Meyer/Z-52' zoysia is the hardiest warm-season turfgrass. It grows fairly well in Zone 6 but does better south. Other species and varieties are adapted only to warmer climates. Choose this grass if you want a smooth, even-textured lawn that withstands wear, tolerates partial shade and is not fussy about soil. It requires only moderate fertilization, is thick enough to crowd out most weeds and doesn't need frequent mowing. This type of grass is subject to little insect and disease damage and doesn't have to be watered as often as bluegrass.

This meticulously maintained zoysiagrass lawn looks good even when dormant.

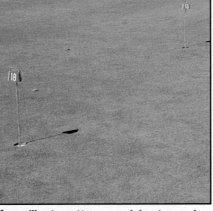

If you like to putter around, bentgrass has the finest texture of them all.

Common bermudagrass. The hybrids are finer-textured and don't spread by self-seeding.

There's nothing like a rolling lawn. This is hybrid bermudagrass. It requires first-class maintenance to look first class but will survive even if neglected. Landscape architect: Ken Smith, ASLA.

There are drawbacks to zoysiagrass. It establishes very slowly, and plugs may take several years to cover an area completely. Sprigs in rows at 6 inches apart take at least a full year to mature. Stolonizing at five bushels per 1,000 square feet may fill in a little faster under ideal conditions. This is a situation when sod may be worth the added expense, especially if a small area is involved. Be prepared for prices between 75¢ to $1 per square foot for the sod, plus soil preparation and laying. Seed, which is seldom available, produces a variable texture and coarser appearance.

Although somewhat cold tolerant, this grass turns brown in the fall and doesn't renew growth until late spring. Lawn dyes are effective, but overseeding is difficult because of its high density. This grass is not as rampant as bermudagrass, but it can invade adjacent planting beds. Pull it by hand or spray it. Thatch build-up occurs, and regular dethatching is necessary. A sharp, heavy-duty mower is needed for mowing to 1 inch.

**Buffalograss**—*Buchloe dactyloides.* This prairiegrass is the ultimate in low maintenance. It almost never needs water or fertilizer. Too much of either gives weeds the advantage. You can mow it to 2 inches, or let it grow naturally to 3 to 4 inches. It is cold hardy to Zone 5 and requires a dry climate. Best performance is in the prairie states, but it does grow on sunny, well-drained sites farther east if it is kept on the dry side.

Although fine textured, bluegrass it's not. The overall color is gray-green. It tends to be sparse and goes dormant in winter. This grass is best used in a casual, natural setting. It looks good with boulders, gently rolling contours and drifts of wildflowers.

Plant treated seed at 2 pounds per 1,000 square feet after the soil has warmed in early summer and through July for best establishment. A half inch is considered the optimum planting depth. Initial growth rate is slow, and it may take two seasons for a good stand to develop. Water seedlings early in the day so the soil can warm up before night. Thereafter, water deeply and infrequently. 'Sharps Improved' and 'Texoka' are varieties currently available, along with blends containing wheatgrass and blue grama. Plant plugs or sprigs, or lay sod when available.

## OTHER GRASSES

**Weeping Alkaligrass/Fults**—*Puccinellia distans.* There are some situations where traditional lawn grasses are unsatisfactory. An extremely saline condition is one of them, and 'Fults' is a choice worth considering. It is a dark green, coarse bunch grass. It is not a substitute for a manicured lawn but is a last resort where little else will grow. Try it along a roadway subject to salt spray from deicing, where irrigation water is highly salty or alkaline, on coastal beaches or in any other saline soil.

It withstands considerable traffic, germinates quickly and can be left unmowed to grow naturally to 12 to 18 inches, including seed stalks. It can also be mowed to 1 to 2 inches for a lawn effect. Seed is not easy to find, but your nurseryman can probably order it pure or in a salt-tolerant blend containing 'Dawson' red fescue, 'Park' Kentucky bluegrass and 'Pennfine' perennial ryegrass. 'Fults' is hardy to Zone 4 and can be planted in fall or spring, using normal planting techniques.

**Dutch White Clover**—*Trifolium repens.* White clover is not a grass. It used to be a common ingredient in lawn mixes as a fast-growing cover crop. Now it has fallen into disfavor and is more likely to be considered a

weed. The bright-green foliage stands out in patches in a bladed lawn. Flowers attract bees, and leaves can stain clothes. However, it does have advantages. It grows almost anywhere, dying back in winter in Zone 7 and north. Neutral or alkaline soil, coolness and moderate watering are best. Rich soil and too much water result in excessive growth that is susceptible to insects and disease. It greens up early in spring, doesn't need frequent mowing, manufactures its own nitrogen and establishes rapidly from seed sown at 5 pounds per 1,000 square feet.

Best use is as a temporary lawn to hold down dust, eliminate mud and control erosion until a permanent lawn or ground cover is installed. When you're ready to switch over, till the clover into the soil, but surviving pieces and seedlings need control. It can also be used as a permanent, casual lawn or as a ground cover for slopes. 'O'Connor's legume' from Australia and 'Birdsfoot trefoil' are similar in appearance and are included in hydroseed mixes for the same general uses as white clover.

## INSTALLING YOUR LAWN

Installing a lawn isn't as much fun as planting shrubs and trees. But it can be satisfying, and you can save money if it's done properly. Soil preparation, pH modification and weed control are the same whether the lawn is seeded, sprigged, stolonized, plugged or sodded. The pH level for most grasses is 6 to 7. Some grasses show micronutrient deficiencies above 7.5, especial-

ly iron. Below 5.5, high acidity can reduce root growth and toxic levels of certain elements can occur. When soil is ready and water piping or sprinklers are installed, you're ready to begin. Check pages 51 and 162 for grading and drainage information.

Many nurseries lend or rent mechanical seeders and rollers if you buy material from them. Cost and type of grass determine which method of installation is best. Don't forget to allow 15 to 20 cents per square foot for normal soil preparation. Add the following per square foot—seeded lawns 10 to 15 cents; sprigging 15 to 25 cents, depending on spacing; stolonizing 20 to 30 cents; and sodding 25 to 50 cents. Sod prices vary with type and locality. These are contractor prices—do it yourself and save about 50%.

### SEEDING

Drag the area with a 4-foot-long 2x4 with about 50 pounds of weight added on top. This helps avoid low spots. Soil should be moist but not muddy. Prepare the seed bed by raking lightly. Remove rocks over 1/2 inch in diameter.

Sow the seed at the rate prescribed on the package. Don't sow seed when the wind is blowing. Use a mechanical seeder for even distribution. Rake the seed in very lightly, so it isn't more than 1/4 inch deep. Include 30 pounds of 8-8-8 commercial fertilizer per 1,000 square feet if it wasn't previously applied.

Top-dress or cover the seed bed with organic material about 1/4 inch

deep. This equals 1/2 cubic yard per 1,000 square feet. Nitrolized sawdust, peat moss or commercial top dressings are good. Don't use material with high-salt content, such as some types manure.

Roll the area with a water-filled lawn roller. Water the area thoroughly to saturate the mulch, and keep it moist until seeds germinate. If rainfall is insufficient, water several times a day in hot weather for the first few weeks. If you have sprinklers, turn them on for short periods to avoid washing away seeds.

### HYDROSEEDING

Large lawn areas are often installed with a spray-on method called *hydroseeding*. Seed and fertilizer are combined with a wood fiber making a slurry similar to thin papier-mache. Advantages are built-in mulch for seed, good erosion control—especially when a binding additive is used—and lower cost than hand-seeding when sufficient area is involved.

### SPRIGGING

Some grasses cannot be sown as seed. It may also be advantageous to install some grasses by another method. Hybrid bermudagrass, zoysiagrass, buffalograss and bentgrass can be sprigged by inserting a living piece of grass into the soil with a portion extending above the ground. Firm the soil around the sprig. A light top dressing is advisable but is not as crucial as with seed.

The closer sprigs are planted together, the faster the coverage is. For fast-growing hybrid bermudagrass, plant 12 inches apart. Six inches is better for all grasses but is essential for slow-growing zoysiagrass. Use only fresh, moist sprigs, and don't allow them to dry out. Avoid overwatering, or sprigs may develop water-borne diseases. Coverage time varies from 30 days for bermudagrass under ideal conditions to 2 years for zoysiagrass and buffalograss.

### STOLONIZING

Stolonizing is similar to sprigging. *Stolons,* living pieces of grass, are distributed evenly over the surface and pressed into firm contact using a spe-

Sodding costs about twice as much as a seeded lawn but saves a lot of trouble. A light rolling levels the surface and firms the roots.

Hydroseeding is worth considering for large areas. Special binders minimize erosion, a problem with conventional seeding. The green dye shows areas already covered.

cial ridged roller. They can also be lightly covered with a thin layer of soil. Apply top dressing, and water immediately to prevent drying out.

Hybrid bermudagrass, zoysiagrass, buffalograss and bentgrass can be installed by stolonizing. The advantage over sprigging is that the time needed for coverage is reduced considerably, and a more-even surface is obtained.

## SODDING AND PLUGGING

The best way to avoid erosion and eliminate weeding, watering and care of tender seedlings is to install a ready-made carpet of *sod*. It looks good immediately and is ready for normal traffic after a few weeks. Lay pieces on slightly moist soil that has been properly prepared and leveled. Butt joints tightly, staggering ends in a bricklike manner. Roll lightly before watering thoroughly.

If you're doing a large area, or if it's a hot day, water small areas as they're laid. Don't wait until it's all finished. That way sod won't dry out. Top-dressing is not used. After the lawn is established, level minor unevenness with a thin layer of fine sand. Look for new sod-growing techniques where grass is grown in easy-to-handle mesh and mats. Some bunchgrasses, such as tall fescues, are now successfully being grown as sod where previously they were impractical.

**Plugs**—These are 2-inch squares of hybrid bermudagrass, zoysiagrass, buffalograss or bentgrass sod. They are planted 6 to 12 inches apart. Disadvantages are time needed for full coverage and a tendency to bumpiness. Zoysiagrass plugs are often used in existing lawns to take over less-desirable existing grasses.

Gentle slopes of lawn are easy to mow. In most cases, it is more serviceable than a ground cover.

European white birch thrives in a lawn. Light shade allows the lawn to also thrive.

it. Bermudagrass looks presentable during warm months and responds well to water and fertilizer.

• Select the desired seed. Sow it according to the directions on page 141.

• Another alternative is to spray the actively growing, unmowed lawn with Round-up or Kleen-up to eliminate all weeds and grasses, including bermudagrass. Wait a week, then remove thatch with a verticutter so about 25% bare soil is exposed. Replant as for a new lawn.

## INSECTS AND DISEASES

This book is not big enough to thoroughly discuss all insects and diseases that attack lawns. Depending on where you live and what kind of lawn you have, you may encounter chinch bugs, sod-web worms, army worms, grubs, brown patch, rust and dollar patch. With luck, you won't end up with all of them.

Some anticipatory chemical applications are advisable in many situations. This is discussed on pages 181 and 182. Diagnosis is often difficult, and products are constantly changing. If you have a lawn-care service, ask what treatments they use. If you do your own mowing, ask your nurseryman or Cooperative Extension Agent for advice and informational publications.

## HOW ABOUT TREES?

You may want to plant trees in a lawn for shade and appearance. Select a tree that tolerates lawn watering and won't cast dense shade or develop surface roots. Don't plant the tree in a low spot, and be sure it doesn't settle after planting. If soil drains poorly, select a tree adapted to wet soils or plant the tree on a gentle rise. Shallow watering encourages surface rooting. Use a root feeder or soil soaker occasionally to provide deep moisture.

Some trees that are compatible with lawns include purple-leaf plum, birch, sweet gum, tulip tree, dogwood, little-leaf linden, Japanese maple, katsura tree, pin oak, green ash, sugar maple and honey locust. See the *Plant Lists,* beginning on page 86, for additional information.

Sometimes it works, but usually the results are slow and irregular.

## IF YOU HAVE A LAWN

If your lawn is a collection of volunteer grasses and your garden is natural, consider living with it. Mow it high for a casual, meadow effect. If you have a shady area with poorly drained soil, covered with moss or ground ivy, think twice about going to the expense and effort to convert it to lawn. A little design ingenuity could turn it into an asset. If it's a typical run-down lawn that looks poor, but isn't bad enough to tear out and start over, here's what you can do to improve it.

• Mow it short, to about 1/2 inch. Rake deeply to expose some soil. If existing thatch is thick, *verticut* it with a rented machine, and remove debris.

• Soak thoroughly for several days.

• Aerate by removing cores of soil with a hand or power aerator.

• Remove any weeds that come up. If there are many broad-leafed weeds, apply a 2,4-D mixture of Trimec or Trex-San. Wait a week for it to do its job.

• If you live in a warm zone where common bermudagrass is a problem, consider joining it rather than fighting

# Instant Landscaping

There are several advantages to starting out with small plants. They're easier to install, cost less and often establish better than larger ones. After 5 years, the 98-cent special may be as big as if you'd started with a $27.50 specimen. But there are situations where an instant effect is worth paying more.

The average length of stay in a house is estimated to be less than 5 years. Most families move out about the time plants start to look nice. It is frustrating to see all your expense, hard work and loving care benefit the new owners rather than yourself. Even if you don't sell within 5 years, there is little use and enjoyment of an unshaded patio, a back yard with no privacy or a bleak, barren landscape.

Most homeowners do not have the budget to imitate the exterior decorating of model homes and commercial buildings. But we *can* borrow some techniques that transform a blank area into a beautiful full-grown garden overnight.

Don't rely entirely on plants. Use a solid fence instead of a hedge if immediate privacy is desirable. A shade trellis cools a patio the day it is finished—you don't have to wait years for a tree to grow. Planter boxes, low walls, benches and other landscape construction help make up for small plants.

## TREES

Large trees are the backbone of instant landscaping. Field-grown or container specimens are available in heights up to 10 feet. This is not a full-grown tree, but it's a step in the right direction. Cost and height vary with the type of tree. A slow-growing Kentucky coffeetree is smaller and more expensive than a rapid-growing silver maple. You can usually get a respectable-sized tree for $100 to $250, including planting.

Trees taller than 10 feet are often available in metropolitan areas—for a price. A 20-foot honey locust with a 4-inch caliper could cost $400 to $500. Don't plan on installing a large tree yourself. Even a 10-foot tree can weigh up to half a ton. It often requires a big truck with a winch to set in in place.

Another bargain is to buy large, bare-root deciduous trees, such as sycamore, birch, ash, pin oak, maple and honey locust. The timing must be right because the planting season is limited to the 2 or 3 months when trees are dormant. Only a few nurseries carry bare-root trees in extra-large sizes. Mail-order is not feasible. If you can find a source nearby, it's the least-expensive way to get good-sized trees the first season.

## SHRUBS

Rather than buy all shrubs in large sizes, just get a few of the most important ones. Larger plants near the front door or patio can help a lot. One $50 shrub in the right place can impart a lushness as soon as it is planted. Balance the budget by using small-sized shrubs for less-important areas. Like trees, bare-root, deciduous shrubs cost less than B&B and container-grown plants.

## GROUND COVERS

Most ground covers take one or more seasons before they actually cover the ground. They don't qualify for an instant effect. With some plants, such as Japanese spurge, periwinkle and English ivy, speed things up by planting as closely together as 9 inches. Be sure they get proper care. You can also cover the bare areas in between plants with a bark or stone mulch. This eliminates mud and dust, and it looks good immediately.

## RAPID GROWERS

Instead of buying larger sizes to begin with, select rapid-growing plants for a *delayed* instant effect. In one or two seasons, these plants will be ahead of the slow-growers. This is especially true for a shade tree, ground cover, privacy screen, hedge or windbreak. However, be aware that many fast growers are relatively short-lived. They are subject to storm damage and can soon outgrow their allotted space. Figure on periodic clip-

These balled-and-burlapped trees have sturdy trunks and well-developed root balls. They'll make a good showing as soon as they're planted.

Left: A well-designed shade trellis can turn a dull, blank wall into an inviting entranceway.

# THE ART OF INSTANT LANDSCAPING

Left: Monday morning: Bare dirt without even a weed.

Right: First, walkways were poured and sprinklers installed. Organic material was spread, and contractor John Rooney rototilled it into the soil.

Next, plant holes were dug. A heavy steel digging bar is helpful for hard soils.

It took two strong men to plant this specimen tree. It weighed more than 500 pounds.

Sod arrived in rolls like carpet.

Sod should be laid as quickly as possible so it can be watered before it starts to dry out. Edges must be trimmed to fit, so it takes several workers to get the job finished in time.

Friday afternoon: The finished yard after adding a few well-placed trees and shrubs. Bare ground was covered with bark chunks or stone mulch.

ping or pruning. Give them plenty of room and use them cautiously.

The following rapid-growing plants deserve your consideration: creeping charlie, variegated goutweed, blue leadwort, weigela, forsythia, spirea, peegee hydrangea, Hall's honeysuckle, Boston ivy, silver-lace vine, privet, Siberian pea tree, Russian olive, weeping willow, river birch, London plane tree, and white ash.

## SOD LAWNS

Installing a lawn from sod is a technique used when you want immediate results. It has a definite advantage over seeding. Within 6 months, a seeded lawn looks as good. However, sod eliminates the crucial germination period when frequent watering may be required between rains. It also reduces erosion and keeps weeds to a minimum. It can be walked on in a few weeks rather than several months as from seed.

The biggest reward of all is seeing bare dirt transformed into a green carpet in a few hours.

When you take into account the labor for watering, weeding, reseeding bare spots and cleaning nuisance erosion, sod doesn't cost much more than seed. Soil preparation and grading are identical for both. Contractor's price for seeding 1,000 square feet is $150 to $200. Laying sod is about $300 to $400. The extra cost is often worth it for a small lawn. The cost difference becomes more significant when covering large areas.

## OTHER TOUCHES

Boulders, driftwood, sculpture and similar features help dramatize a new landscape. Earth sculpture or contouring is another effective, low-cost method often employed in model-home landscaping. If you have excess soil, it might save money to use it for contours rather than having it hauled away.

Use container plants to put foliage in the right spot. Rhododendron, yew, big-leaf hydrangea, holly, dwarf fruit trees and dwarf conifers are good subjects for large pots or wood tubs. Bulbs, herbs, azaleas, geraniums, chrysanthemums, succulents and annuals are great for seasonal interest. Grow them in smaller containers.

Hanging baskets planted with sprenger asparagus, spider plant and creeping charlie are effective because you

**Balled-and-burlapped English boxwood plants are $15 apiece. This is expensive if you're planting a long hedge, but two or three in key locations may be within the average budget.**

**Don't overlook seasonal color, such as these chrysanthemums, available from the nursery in full bloom.**

**Pressure-treated timbers with *chamfered* tops are used in a sculptural manner to set off an entrance planting. Landscape architect: John Clayton Thomas, ASLA.**

**Bark mulch is a good way to cover bare ground until the shrubs grow.**

**Rather than haul them away, large rocks and boulders can be used as dramatic accents in both lawn and planting areas.**

can hang them at eye level or outside a window. An advantage of container plants is that tender types, which would perish in the ground, can be enjoyed during the warm months. Move them inside to a protected spot in winter.

## LIGHTING

Don't overlook nighttime viewing. This is when most entertaining occurs, and you want your landscaping to look special. A few well-placed lights to emphasize the biggest plants and outstanding features can make a newly planted yard look even better.

Garden lighting can be divided into two main classifications: practical lighting for use, safety and security, and ornamental lighting for beauty and interest. When possible, combine the two types so lighting is useful *and* beautiful.

The need for practical lighting is easy to determine. Steps, walks, house numbers, driveways, patios, swimming pools, game courts and other areas often used at night need illumination. Ornamental lighting is more open to personal preference or can be left out entirely.

**Up-lighting**—This is using light at ground level, shooting upward. It is effective at the base of the object to be featured. Usually the light is placed in front of the object. Sometimes light can be in back, such as with a specimen tree. This creates an interesting silhouette. The main problem is placing the light so it won't be seen directly and shines only on the object to be illuminated.

**Down-lighting**—This is lighting directed downward. It can be above, below or at eye level. The larger the area to be covered, the higher the light must be. The problem of glare is encountered as soon as eye level is reached. Solve this problem with careful placement, shields or filters.

Outdoor fixtures must be waterproof, except low-voltage types, and well-made. A hidden light source does not need to be a beautiful fixture. When the fixture is seen, it should be a size and design appropriate to the setting. Costs of fixtures range from $10 to over $150, depending on size, type and quality. Junction boxes, as required by code, are distracting. Hide them or replace them with an approved underground type.

Up-lighting is less obtrusive when the floodlight has a hood and grille to reduce glare.

Brick pilaster lights define entry drive and provide safety and security.

Home-made wood lamp uses plastic instead of glass because it costs less and is easier to cut. Light source is a low-voltage floodlight.

Low-voltage wood light by Sylvan Designs costs approximately $15.

A well-conceived lighting plan extends use of pool-side entertainment area into evening hours. Design: Beauté la terre Designs of Wichita, Kansas. Photo: Kala Busby.

An l8-watt, low-voltage floodlight highlights the shape of this tree and creates a tranquil mood.

An old-fashioned gas light adds charm to this garden. Landscape architect: Lambert's.

Waterproof 120-watt transformer is plugged into an exterior outlet. No permit or electrician is required.

to allow at least $50 per outlet, plus the actual fixture price. Add to the basic figure costs for long conduit runs, breaking through walls and difficult connections.

## LOW-VOLTAGE LIGHTING

Except where high wattage is needed, such as a game court or security floodlighting, low-voltage lighting has many advantages over 110-volt. It is probably the way to go. Eight 18-watt, low-voltage lights use less energy than one 150-watt floodlight. Because the candlepower is lower, the effect is more subtle. Low-voltage lighting is safe to handle and doesn't require a building permit.

No special tools or skills are required to install low-voltage lights. Wires can be buried a few inches deep, hung on a wall or fence or laid on the surface where they are not likely to be severed with a lawn edger or spade. Because they require no conduit, placement is easily changed for best effect. They can be added to existing plantings with a minimum of disturbance.

An existing circuit may often be used without danger of overloading. Install floodlights flush with the ground or partially buried. Allow an extra coil of wire about 2 feet long at each fixture to give flexibility when shifting the light around.

The cost is lower than 110-volt lighting. Kits consisting of six lights, a waterproof transformer and 100 feet of wire are priced under $100. A wide range of fixtures is available, such as hanging lights, path lights, underwater lights and wood lanterns.

It's handy to be able to switch on outdoor lights from inside the house. If you have an exterior outlet operated from inside, plug in the transformer, and you're all set. For an exterior outlet that is not switched, get a transformer with a built-in timer for about $10 more. Another way is to drill a hole through the garage wall, and install the transformer inside with a switch. Or plug it in when you want to turn on the lights.

The typical 120-watt transformer handles six 18-watt lights. If you want more than six, use two transformers. Also available are 200-watt and 300-watt transformers for 11 and 16 lights, respectively. Be sure the transformer is waterproof if used in an exposed location.

Place garden lighting at night, after construction and planting are complete. Some experts advise working with extension cords, shifting fixtures until the desired effect is achieved. The trouble with this method is that trenches for conduits must be dug through existing plantings. Some damage is likely to occur. One way to avoid this is to install waterproof outlets before planting, and use plug-in type fixtures on short cords. Another way is to use a low-voltage system that is easy to move around.

All electrical work, except low-voltage, requires a permit and inspection. Because of the danger involved and the tools and experience

necessary, have an electrical contractor install all but the low-voltage types. It is possible for you to dig trenches and do other unskilled labor. The contractor can do the electrical hookup. If you run 110-volt lines, include some waterproof outlets and stub-outs for future work.

Costs vary for installation of garden lighting and individual fixtures. Outlet boxes for 110-volt lighting cost about $25 each. Conduits cost at least $1.50 per linear foot, plus switches, fixtures and a connection charge. Trenching through an existing garden can increase the cost, especially if trenches must be dug by hand. Prices listed here assume work is done by a contractor. A rough way to estimate is

# Small Spaces

You can use the ideas and information in this book whether you have a rambling ranch, a normal-sized city lot or a condominium with a tiny plot of land. If you want to include as many amenities as possible and your outdoor space is limited to a small area, it takes careful planning.

When an area is very small, such as an atrium or enclosed court, the first decision is whether you want to look at it or use it. If you have two small areas, sometimes one can be devoted entirely to planting and the other to outdoor activities. If there's only one area, the major portion of it may have to be paved and planting space severely limited.

Container plants, espaliers, vines and hanging baskets are good ways to get the maximum amount of greenery in a small space. Low shrubs, such as dwarf Japanese yew, Kurume azalea, Korean boxwood and Emerald-n-Gold euonymus are particularly suited to small beds. Narrow, upright shrubs and trees are also good for a walled-in patio.

In an area enclosed by high walls, heat may be intensified. Sun and shade patterns can also change drastically with the seasons. North-facing areas may never receive direct sunlight. The southern exposure can be a problem. It may receive direct sunlight part of the year and full shade the rest of the year. Choose plants carefully or give them special protection to survive the changing conditions of the seasons. Move container plants around so they receive more or less sun as needed. Check the exposure column on the *Plant Lists*, beginning on page 86, so a shade-loving plant doesn't cook against a sunny wall.

Left: Enclosed atrium was planned as a pleasant scene, not an outdoor activity area. Design: Ken Smith, ASLA.

Right: Owner-builder Dan Paul followed landscape architect Edith Henderson's plan to create an intimate sitting area.

Usable outdoor space was gained by carefully adding this front-yard sitting terrace. Landscape architect: Landshapes Inc.

Left: This carefully scaled Japanese garden makes the most of a small area.

Varying width of flagstone patio makes the most of a long, narrow space. Design/build: Land Techniques, Delaware, Ohio.

Shade trellis not only provides a pleasant patio area but also adds privacy. Design/build: Landscape Services Inc.

Just because the front yard of this mobile home is only 6 feet wide doesn't mean it isn't important to the owner. Upright-growing twisted junipers are a good choice to shade the front windows and soften the look of the structure.

Window boxes and a pyracantha espalier highlight this charming Maryland townhouse.

An expanding brick pattern and airy wrought-iron furniture give a spacious feeling to this outdoor barbeque and dining area. Landscape architect: Peter Muller.

Balconies and small decks are the most restrictive. Limit planting to containers and hanging baskets. Pots that hang outside the railing save interior space. Built-in planter boxes may look better than a row of pots. Unless carefully constructed, planter boxes leak and warp, and they can be heavy. One way to avoid the problem is to build a simple sturdy box the right size for pots to fit inside. This also makes it easy to remove plants for washing, leaching and replacing if they fail.

## SETTING THE SCENE

Scale of design is an elusive, intriguing consideration. Some Japanese

Squint your eyes a little and this miniature scene appears to be a mountain stream. Design and installation by landscape contractor Jim Keener.

Water is recirculated to spew out of a bamboo pipe and make a splashing sound on the rocks.

Tiny, submersible recirculation pump is only 1/30 horsepower and uses little energy.

gardens suggest distant mountains and infinite space in a confined area. One method is to accentuate perspective by placing large-textured, bright-green plants near the viewer and fine-textured, gray-purple plants at the far wall. This assumes you'll always view it from the same spot. It could make the space appear smaller when seen from the other end.

Miniature versions of larger plants help achieve a spacious quality. Prune a small tree, such as a Japanese black pine or weeping Canadian hemlock, to emphasize an ancient, gnarled effect. It can appear larger than it is. Choose other plants with small leaves, such as yew, Kurume azalea or juniper, to maintain the mood. One coarse-foliage hydrangea or rhododendron would ruin the whole effect. Small boulders, 2x4 wood decking on edge, tiny pebbles and a mossy ground cover complete the scene.

## SPECIAL TOUCHES

Built-in seating and storage can make the most of limited space. Avoid heavy-frame wood furniture. Thin wrought iron is more appro-

Furniture selection is especially important in confined areas. These webbed chairs don't overpower this small patio.

priate. Even a glass tabletop helps the illusion. If there's a chance for a see-through fence panel without sacrificing privacy, this is the ideal place for it. Wrought-iron gates provide security and give an airy quality.

Water can be used in any garden but is especially appropriate in miniature ones. A recirculating fountain operating on a 1/30 horsepower submersible pump requires little power to operate. The sound of the water is more apt to be heard in an enclosed space, and the visual effect is appreciated at close range.

The same applies to works of art. Sculpture, mobiles, murals and bas-relief sculpture often fit better in a small area than out in the open. This doesn't mean large artwork has no place in a normal-size garden. Smaller pieces are more within the average budget and are better protected from vandalism, theft and elements in a secured space.

Driftwood, mineral rocks, artifacts and other items that have a special meaning to the owner are also fun to include in a minigarden.

In a tiny area good workmanship is crucial. Select plants carefully and pay

No room for a full-sized fountain? Here's a pleasant-sounding waterfall that extends only 2 inches from the wall.

My neighbor's fence is only 5 feet away, so I built a shelf outside our kitchen window for a constantly changing display of flowers.

Indian peers out of a miniature forest for a light touch. Landscape architect: CR3 Inc.

What to do with a tiny dining room atrium? Water sheets down the ceramic wall and glistens at night when illuminated by a hidden light.

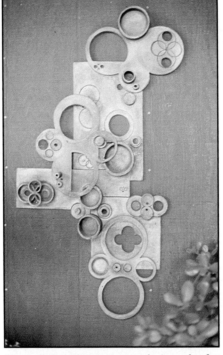

Bas-relief sculpture are made to order for garden walls. This one is an assembled clay piece by Nancy Smith.

This "natural creek" is actually tucked into a 15-foot space between house and property line.

attention to details. This is where the do-it-yourselfer can build a masterpiece without devoting a lot of time.

## CONTAINER PLANTS

Container plants are valuable for relieving expanses of paving. They introduce foliage and color when planting directly in the ground is impractical or impossible, such as patios, atriums, courts, porches and balconies. A few carefully selected, well-placed plants in containers can create

the feeling of a garden in a barren area.

Exotic plants often thrive within protected walls when they wouldn't last out in the open. Plant collections, such as bonsai, epiphyllums, cacti, succulents, herbs and pelargoniums, are best grown in containers. They can receive proper care and be appreciated at close range.

Almost any plant can be grown in a container, at least for a short period. Certain plants adapt better to this type of culture and are fairly permanent.

Some of the best plants include dwarf conifers, holly, rhododendrons and yews. Spider plant, creeping charlie and sprenger asparagus are excellent hanging-basket plants.

Another approach is to use the container as a holder. Set the plant inside it, leaving it in its nursery container. Use bulbs, annuals, perennials and flowering shrubs as a kind of living bouquet. Slip a 1-quart or 1-gallon plastic nursery container into a slightly larger ceramic pot or wood tub. Re-

A protected patio is a good spot for a hanging basket like this common spider plant. It overwinters fairly well indoors.

Custom-built wood tubs carry out weathered wood theme. Landscape architect: Paul H. Barton, ASLA.

Landscape architect Claire Bennett chose a pink geranium in a tan pot to subtly coordinate with the brick and slate colors.

Ninety-nine cent chrysanthemums are set inside pots for a temporary front door display. They'll be planted in the garden after blooming.

place the plant when it finishes blooming. Use 5-gallon-size shrubs and trees with seasonal features in a similar manner.

Ample root room in the container is critical for most plants. Bonsai, dwarf conifers, bamboo and most succulents are exceptions. A 16-inch size is sufficient if you start with a 5-gallon-sized plant. It isn't too heavy to move around. Larger shrubs and small trees in a 15-gallon size need a 24-inch or larger container. They're heavy, so you won't be able to shift them around very often.

Buy soil mix that is prepackaged or make it yourself from 50% organic material and 50% sandy loam with added nutrients and minerals. Commercial, lightweight mixes are fine for small plants. Larger shrubs and trees benefit from some sandy loam soil for better root anchoring.

Drainage holes are essential. Avoid pavement staining by *leaching* out the soil several times before moving the pot into place. Saucers are available for all but the largest pots. Cut a piece of heavy plastic to put under wood containers built with metal bands that can rust.

Choose the proper-sized container that is appropriate to the setting. For example, red clay looks good with a brick house, and wood tubs look good with wood siding and shake roofs. All containers don't have to be the same, but too many different types in a small area can be disturbing. A simple pot may show a plant to better advantage than one that attracts attention to itself.

Many containers are available, including clay, wood, concrete and plastic. Cost ranges from about $5 for small, mass-produced clay pots and redwood tubs, to $50 or more for larger, fancier ones. Some half

barrels, with a diameter of 24 inches, sell for $10 to $15. They can last for as long as 5 years.

## ESPALIERS

When you have a big, blank wall and only 12 inches of planting space, consider an espalier to alleviate bareness. The term *espalier* intimidates many people. Perhaps they picture a perfectly trained specimen in the classic European style. Actually, an espalier can be any plant flattened to grow against a wall or fence. Design considerations will dictate whether an espalier should be carefully trimmed or allowed to grow casually.

Pretrained plants on a trellis are available from many nurseries. The price is high—about $25 for a 5-gallon size. Develop your own by selecting a somewhat one-sided plant and doing a little pruning. Support is necessary for most plants. Use a trellis, plastic-coated wires, pegs or nails. When using a trellis, get one large enough or one that expands to allow for future growth. Set the plant about 6 inches away from the wall. This allows air circulate and lessens the possibility of damage from reflected heat.

In the box below are some of the best-suited plants for formal and informal espaliering. Plants that are most resistant to cold are listed first. Least resistant are listed at the end.

Try espaliering fruit trees to gain a tasty harvest in a small space. Many fruits are available in dwarf forms and require minimum clipping to espalier. Most vines can also be used in this manner. Refer to the *Plant Lists,* beginning on page 86, for climate, exposure and additional information.

## MAINTENANCE

Overall, more exacting maintenance is needed for container plants than for the same ones grown in the ground. Watering is critical. The water supply can be quickly exhausted during a hot day. When it's gone, there isn't any more available. Larger containers have more root room and more water reserves. Small clay pots and hanging baskets are the most demanding.

Setting one pot inside another and filling the space between with sphagnum peat moss reduces water loss considerably. A little garden soil in the mix described earlier also helps retain moisture better than a lightweight, fast-draining mix. Conversely, oversaturation easily occurs in pots without drainage. Periodic heavy watering is desirable because it assures saturation of the entire root ball and

Firethorn pyracantha is one of the best plants for espaliering. This is an especially interesting treatment.

English boxwoods flank a carefully trained Bradford-pear espalier. Landscape architect: Edith Henderson, FASLA.

leaches salt accumulated from fertilizers and water. Light, frequent fertilization is necessary to replace nutrients lost through leaching. Root pruning and repotting are also necessary when the plant outgrows its container.

## PLACING CONTAINER PLANTS

Selection and placement of container plants is tricky, but you don't have to do it perfectly the first time. Experiment a little. Containers can be easily moved, changed or even discarded.

The walled entry court of the corner lot on page 157 is ideal for container plants and is used here as an example. Red-clay pots were selected as appropriate for the brick house. Several 15-gallon or large B&B specimens were placed at the front door and by the fountain as focal points. The cluster of flowering plants was replaced when they were finished blooming to provide almost continuous color. Hanging baskets at the entry, on top of the wall, at the gate and in front of the windows added eye-level foliage.

---

**PLANTS FOR ESPALIERS**

*Plants in this list are arranged according to hardiness. The most cold-tolerant are at the top, and the most sensitive at the bottom.*

Apple
Pear
Rose
Cotoneasters
Flowering Quince
Bradford Pear
Twisted Juniper
Holly
Bigleaf Wintercreeper
Sarcoxie Euonymus
Yews
Pyracantha

---

You can purchase pretrained espaliered plants like this pyracantha if you don't want to attempt it yourself.

# CONTAINER PLANTS

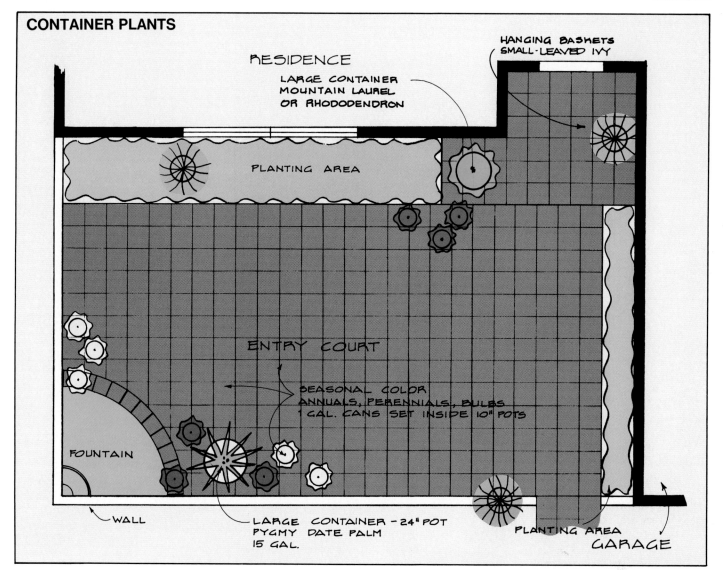

RESIDENCE

HANGING BASKETS
SMALL-LEAVED IVY

LARGE CONTAINER
MOUNTAIN LAUREL
OR RHODODENDRON

PLANTING AREA

ENTRY COURT

SEASONAL COLOR
ANNUALS, PERENNIALS, BULBS
1 GAL. CANS SET INSIDE 10" POTS

FOUNTAIN

WALL

LARGE CONTAINER — 24" POT
PYGMY DATE PALM
15 GAL.

PLANTING AREA
GARAGE

**Large pots of geraniums are in scale with the broad brick wall and large feature light. Design: Claire Bennett Associates, FASLA.**

# Growing Your Own

There are many reasons for including edible plants in your garden. Home-grown fruit and vegetables taste better than supermarket produce. You can even surpass roadside-stand quality by picking at the peak of flavor and ripeness. The ultimate in eating corn-on-the-cob is to start the water boiling first, then bring the ears in from the garden and cook them immediately. You can control what chemicals, if any, are applied. At least you know if the vegetables have been sprayed and with what.

Difficult-to-obtain, expensive and off-season items may be grown if you give them extra attention. Perk up salads with nasturtium leaves and flowers, Chinese parsley, arugala/roquette, yellow tomatoes and Jerusalem artichokes. Surprise guests by serving New Zealand spinach, yard-long beans, purple cauliflower and colbaga. These aren't standard items at the market.

Raising your own vegetables is a good way to introduce children to gardening. They may eat their "veggies" if they've had a hand in growing them. Increasingly precious water and fertilizer can be put to productive use. With food prices high, you can recover the cash outlay for seeds, plants, fertilizer, sprays and water. Think of the labor as recreation. I have some $1 carrots and $5 muskmelons—if I counted my time. Otherwise, they're a bargain.

Be prepared—gardening is hard work. If you haven't done it before, start slowly until you find out how much you can handle comfortably. Be aware that despite the hard work, growing vegetables can be addicting.

When surplus crops become a problem, trade extras with food-growing friends and neighbors. If you have too many tomatoes and cherries,

The vegetable gardens of Colonial Williamsburg represent an important part of our heritage.

**Left: A member of the sunflower family, Jerusalem artichoke puts on a nice display of flowers before dying back in the fall.**

Above: Some people cook the potatolike tuber, but a tastier use is raw as a crunchy substitute for water chestnuts.

**Left: Don't overlook flowers when you select *crops* to grow in your garden. Photo: William Aplin.**

Beck didn't care much for vegetables until he started helping his grandpa in the garden.

Bright-green and red-leafed lettuce can be sown in a flower bed or between shrubs for a quick and delicious display.

New Zealand spinach thrives in hot weather.

Clover cover crop adds organic matter and nitrogen to the vegetable garden.

Butternut, acorn and spaghetti are kinds of winter squash that can be stored for several months.

and there are extra squash and plums next door, trade. Everyone welcomes a little variety. Cold storage, freezing, drying and canning are ways to make best use of a bumper crop. HPBooks' *Canning* is an excellent reference for preserving foods. With vegetables, space planting times to avoid oversupply. After a few seasons, you'll know how much of what kind to plant.

If you have enough space, set aside a separate area for growing vegetables, preferably beyond the view of outdoor living areas. A tall wire fence will help keep out nibbling animals.

You can include vegetables in even the smallest plot. Rhubarb, flowering kale, New Zealand spinach, chard and Jerusalem artichoke look presentable most of the growing season. Some short-term effects can be achieved by sowing red-and-green leaf lettuce, beets and onions between ornamental shrubs. Carrots look like small ferns when tucked into a flower border. Look for compact varieties of squash, cucumber, muskmelon, corn, tomato and watermelon to make the most of a small plot.

There are several ways to increase production. Use *succession* planting by replacing an early harvested crop with a late season one. *Companion* planting combines two compatible crops in the same area at the same time. The *intensive* method uses shotgun sowing of a mixture of various types that results in very close spacing. I've grown an astonishing quantity of radishes, lettuce, onions and carrots in a 6x6' square. Pull new radishes and young lettuce when they're ready. This leaves room for others to mature.

## GROWING VEGETABLES

Most vegetables are easy to grow. Meet the requirements listed below and success is almost assured.

**Location**—Select a location that gets sun most of the day. A cool coastal or mountain garden needs more sun than a garden in a hot inland area. Corn, tomatoes, melons, okra, eggplant, cucumbers and other heat-lovers require lots of sun. Good crops of chard, beets, carrots, lettuce, radishes, turnips and other cool-season types can be grown if they get at least a half day of sun. If fungus disease is a problem in your area, good air movement and as much sun as possible are essential. Protection from strong winds is desirable. Plant away from large trees to avoid heavy shade and root competition.

**Soil**—Directions found on page 123 about soil preparation and pH modification for lawns and ground covers are also valid for vegetables. However, more organic material dug in at least 12 inches deep is desirable. Six cubic yards per 1,000 square feet, which is a layer 3 to 4 inches deep, is minimum for average soils. Heavy clay or poor sandy soils benefit from repeated applications every spring. Well-rotted manure and compost are especially good for vegetables. You may also want to consider a cover crop, as described on page 124. If drainage is poor, slightly sloping and raised beds help minimize adverse effects of overly wet soil.

**Selection**—Choose the right crop and variety for your specific climate, and plant during the proper season. Infor-

This small, wedge-shaped corner contains plum, pear, apricot and peach trees. Annual pruning keeps them from overgrowing the limited space.

Tomato transplants are easy to grow from seed. I've had good results with plant cubes and plastic nursery containers.

mation on the seed package tells you a little. You can get more specific information from your Cooperative Extension Agent or read HPBooks' *Vegetables: How to Select, Grow and Enjoy.*

**Watering**—Meet watering needs for each crop. Do not allow germinating seeds to dry out. Apply a thin layer of organic material, such as grass clippings, over the newly seeded crop. This *mulch* helps keep the top layer of soil moist and soft enough for the seeds to break through easily. Many vegetables become bitter or *bolt,* and go to seed if growth is slowed by lack of continuous moisture.

Conversely, too much water can result in lots of foliage and fewer, smaller edible portions. It's helpful to have a hose-bibb nearby so you can apply water when rainfall is insuffi-

cient. Drip systems apply water only where it's needed, without wasteful run-off. Mulching conserves moisture and often enables plants to go from rainfall-to-rainfall when they would otherwise dry out.

**Fertilizing**—A few weeks before planting, dig in 25 to 30 pounds per 1,000 square feet of a complete commercial fertilizer, such as 8-8-8 or 10-10-10. Apply liquid starter solution when setting out transplants. *Sidedress* with liquid or commercial fertilizer later in the season according to the plants' specific requirements. Stunted growth, pale-green foliage or loss of lower leaves may indicate the need for fertilizer if watering and other factors are normal. A healthy, green plant may be fine without additional feeding.

**Weed Control**—Apply chemicals *very* carefully, or avoid them entirely. Rely on shallow cultivation or hand-pulling when weeds are small, before they go to seed. Mulches of hay, lawn clippings, straw, compost or other similar material placed 2 inches thick smother out most weeds. Black plastic and newspaper are also effective weed-control measures.

**Insects and Diseases**—Watch for insects and diseases, and use proper controls immediately. Cutworms, aphids, cucumber beetles, cabbage worms and various diseases are common. Many diseases can be avoided by using resistant plant varieties. Pay a little more for high-quality seed or transplants—it's worth it. Don't overlook the importance of good air

circulation to minimize disease infections, especially in humid areas. The same insect-control principles discussed on page 181 apply to vegetables as well as ornamentals. You'll be eating the vegetables, so avoid materials with long-lasting residual effects.

When removing them in the fall, inspect the roots of tomatoes, okra, melons and other nematode-susceptible crops to determine if fumigation is necessary. Crop rotation is a good way to avoid soil insects and diseases. Don't plant the same vegetable year after year in the same location.

If eggplants, potatoes or tomatoes develop verticillium wilt, move them to another spot next season. Look for resistant varieties.

Mint makes an attractive ground cover in front of an apple espaliered on a fence.

Apples are a rewarding home-garden fruit when given proper care.

# SPACE SAVERS

Espaliered fruit trees save space and can be an attractive design element.

An 18-inch-tall container will be large enough for this dwarf peach for up to 5 years. Then it should be repotted.

Left: Attractive and edible celtuce, rhubarb chard and tomato grow happily in 5-gallon containers. They need watering almost every day in hot weather.

Below: Kale tastes good and has a fascinating texture. It grows well in a container.

## HERBS

Herbs can be valuable landscape subjects in addition to their culinary qualities. Many can be incorporated into the general design for dual use. Gray and silver-foliage lavender, artemisia, santolina, lamb's ears and sage are an interesting contrast to green shrubs. Creeping thyme is an excellent, drought-tolerant ground cover. Give mint plenty of water, and cut it back occasionally for an attractive filler. Upright and prostrate forms of rosemary are good permanent plants for mild winter areas. Grow them as annuals in below-zero temperature regions.

Less-attractive, but more seasonal, herbs are best grown in a separate area or formal garden. For small spaces, many herbs grow well in pots. Bring them indoors to a sunny window for winter protection. For serious herb gardeners, HPBooks' *Herbs: How to Select, Grow and Enjoy* is indispensable. Another book on herbs from HP-Books is the cookery book, *Herbs, Spices and Flavorings*. It provides valuable information and wonderful recipes for using many different herbs in cooking and meal preparation.

## FRUITS AND NUTS

Every garden can accommodate fruit trees of some kind. For maximum success, use specific varieties suited to your climate zone. Your

Nectarine flowers provide a spring bonus in the home orchard.

local nursery usually carries the types that have proven most reliable in your locality. When ordering by mail, verify that the information in the catalog is adequate and accurate. Don't forget to plant a pollenizer tree for those that require cross pollination. Your Cooperative Extension Service offers excellent information on selection and culture.

When there is plenty of room, standard-sized trees produce larger crops. They can also serve as shade or background. Apple, crabapple, pear and plum trees are good for a garden. Grow them outside the lawn area. Use a thick mulch, and water infrequently and deeply.

It's difficult to harvest fruit from big, old trees, and many gardens have space limitations. That's where smaller trees, such as peaches, nectarines, quince and apricot, may be easier to fit in. Apples are successful on semi-dwarfing rootstocks. In severe climates, these roots need a protective mulch because they may lack winter hardiness. Semidwarf pears, plums and cherries are also available but are not as reliable as apples.

When there isn't enough space for even a small tree, plant shrub-sized dwarf apples, peaches, nectarines and bush cherries. They can be grown in a large container, such as a half-barrel. Apple, quince and pear are trainable as espaliers against a wall or on a heavy wire trellis. They fit well into narrow areas.

Fruit trees do best in full sun on slightly sloping, well-drained soil. Avoid wind-swept locations. Good air circulation minimizes damage from late spring frosts and reduces fire blight and fungus diseases. Spraying is necessary, so keep plants away from the house to avoid discoloration of walls. Rabbits and mice like to chew bark, so protect trunks from animals and sun scald, as described on page 186. Netting is needed to protect some fruit, especially cherries, from birds.

Nut trees are more like shade trees that happen to bear an edible crop. Black walnut, butternut and hickory are hardy and tolerate the considerable cold of Zone 4. Carpathian walnut, Chinese chestnut, filbert and pecan are adapted to less severe winters. Of the trees listed, black walnut, hickory and pecan become large trees, so give them lots of room. The other trees are

Grapes can be used both ornamentally and for fruit production.

I couldn't resist planting some strawberries in the asparagus bed. So far, they're growing reasonably well together.

lower and more spreading. Filberts are the smallest.

## VINES AND BERRIES

Don't overlook food-bearing vines. You can have grapes *and* summer shade by planting them on an overhead structure. 'Concord' and 'Niagara' grapes are widely grown and adapted. Select those best suited to your tastes and specific climate. Vines need well-drained soil, with deep, infrequent watering and as much sun as possible. South-facing slopes are best. Regular pruning, spraying and protection from birds is necessary.

Freshly picked raspberries or blackberries for breakfast are a terrific way to start the day. Raspberries are the hardiest, and some can be grown in Zone 3. North of Zone 6, cover blackberries with soil or heavily mulch them every winter. You can pick berries from wild or neglected plants, but they soon become an impenetrable thicket, and insects and diseases prevail. Pruning is complicated and a chore—it's one of the few gardening jobs I dislike. Wear heavy gloves and long sleeves, or plant thornless varieties where they're hardy. Varietal selection, pruning and training methods are important. The best source of information is usually your Cooperative Extension Service.

Currants and gooseberries aren't for eating out-of-hand, but they're great for making jams, jellies, preserves and pies. They're even hardier than raspberries, and their bushy

growth is easier to handle. In a cool, moist, partially shaded location, they produce well with little care other than an annual spring pruning.

Strawberries are a rewarding crop. They do best in well-drained, sandy loam or organic soil with regular fertilization and lots of water. In cold climates, mulch them after frost in the fall before extremely low temperatures set in. Minimize damage from early spring frost by selecting a sloping site, applying straw mulch and lightly sprinkling them on cold nights. With good management, plants can last 2 years or more. Spring-bearing types have higher-quality fruit than everbearing types. However, if you want to extend the season, a patch of everbearers is worth considering.

And now my favorite—blueberries. Blueberries are exacting in their cultural requirements. They must have full sun most of the day and be kept constantly moist but with good drainage. They need very acid soil of pH 4.5 to 5.5. Except in natural peat soils, the best way to achieve this acidity is to incorporate as much as three parts sphagnum peat moss to two parts excavated soil with some aluminum sulphate and iron chelate thrown in. A heavy organic mulch conserves moisture and controls weeds. Highbush blueberries are not as hardy as native types and need snow cover or heavy mulch when temperatures drop below -20F (-29C). 'Blueray', 'Northland' and 'Bluecrop' are the hardiest varieties for the coldest zones. Insects and diseases are not a big problem,

**Tupelo/Black Gum**

**Japanese Dogwood**

## PLANTS WITH FALL FOLIAGE COLOR

*Arranged in approximate order of hardiness to cold. See Plant Lists, beginning on page 86, for description.*

Amur Maple
Sugar Maple
Red Maple
Andorra Juniper
Yellowwood
European Mountain Ash
Red Oak
Lombardy Poplar
Cottonwood
Amur Corktree
Ginkgo
Cranberry Cotoneaster
Bradford Pear
Winged Burning Bush
Viburnum
Pin Oak
Japanese Barberry
Eastern Redbud
Tulip Tree
Flowering Dogwood
Japanese Dogwood
Tupelo/Black Gum
American Sweet Gum
Smoke Tree
PJM Rhododendron
Flame Azalea
Japanese Barberry

**Winged Burning Bush**

**PJM Rhododendron**

**Sugar Maple**

**Ginkgo**

## PLANTS WITH COLORFUL FOLIAGE

*Arranged in approximate order of hardiness to cold. See Plant List, beginning on page 86, for descriptions.*

Wilton Juniper
Blue Arctic Willow
Redleaf Norway Maple
Wooly Thyme
Sunburst Honey Locust
Pathfinder Juniper
Purpleleaf Sand Cherry
Redleaf Japanese Barberry
Hosta
Golden Vicary Privet
Russian Olive
Copper Beech
Variegated Adams-needle
Gold Coast Juniper
Variegated Myrtle
Goldflame Spirea
Purple-leaf Honeysuckle
Bronze Ajuga
Hetz Juniper
Silveredge Goutweed
Blue Pfitzer Juniper
Silvermound Artemisia
Golden Mock Orange
Eulaliagrass
Skyrocket Virginia Cedar
Emerald 'N Gold Euonymus
Rainbow Leucothoe
Scotch Heather
Variegated Weigela
Variegated American Holly
Forest Pansy Redbud
Purple-leaf Plum
Hohman's Golden Dogwood
Redleaf Japanese Maple

but be prepared to fight the birds for each delicious morsel. Tightly closed netting installed at the red stage is mandatory.

## FLOWERS, BERRIES AND DECORATIVE FOLIAGE

Cut flowers are expensive, so the only way to have a fresh bouquet often is to grow it yourself. Possibilities are limited only by climate and the amount of time you want to devote to the plants.

I've had good success with roses, calla lilies, gladiolas, snapdragons, stocks, tulips, daffodils, poinsettias, chrysanthemums and marigolds. Plant some of these, and brighten up the house with flowers most of the year. Care is similar to that described for vegetables on page 160. There's no reason why you can't combine them in the same plot.

Don't overlook flowering trees and shrubs as flower sources. Spirea, forsythia, lilac, flowering crabapple, dogwood, fringe tree, pussy willow, flowering cherry, redbud and oriental magnolia can serve just as well as con-

ventional flowers. In some cases, flowers from these are available in greater quantity and last for a longer period than conventional cut flowers.

Some plants have such beautiful leaves they are considered a type of ornamental crop. Yew, holly, ginkgo, leucothoe, mountain laurel, smoke tree and various ferns are welcome additions to table arrangements. Various types of holly, cotoneaster, viburnum, snowberry, barberry and pyracantha are great for their highly ornamental berries, some of which coincide with the winter holidays.

Ornamental grasses are the basis of many dry arrangements. Most ornamental grasses are easy to grow—but grow them in the background. Quaking grasses, eulalia varieties, broom, side-oats grama, bridal veil, animated oats, ruby grass and silky bentgrass are common. Seeds of annual types are available from mail-order sources either separate or in mixtures. Some nurseries offer plants of perennial grasses, or you can take divisions from established clumps.

**Gold Coast Juniper**

**Redleaf Japanese Maple**

**Junipers**

**Redleaf Japanese Barberry, Cotoneaster and Daylily**

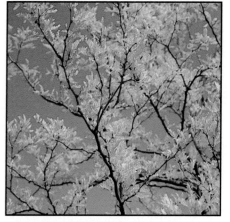
**Sunburst Honey Locust**

# Remodeling a Garden

Ask any landscape architect about remodeling and he will tell you it's easier to start with a new house and bare land than to redo an existing garden. If you've just moved, wait a few months before doing anything drastic. After you've lived there awhile, you'll have a better feeling of what the good and bad features are.

As with a new design, start with an overall assessment first. If the original garden was well-conceived and suits your requirements, only minor modifications may be involved. Otherwise, a master plan is called for incorporating existing items into the overall scheme.

After you decide whether major or minor changes are in order, the difficult decisions begin. You must decide what to save and what to tear out. Capitalize on any unique features that may exist.

An old stone wall, a stagnant fish pond or even scraggly bushes may be hidden treasures in disguise. The temptation is to raze everything, but this is not always the best way to go. Take it easy. Don't be afraid to tear out hopeless items, but avoid wanton destruction. It's best to take it step by step. Let's consider paving and construction first.

## UPGRADING PAVING

Where possible, it's sensible to save existing paving. It's a big job to break up paving and haul it away, and you pay for removal *and* replacement.

Inspect existing paving to make sure it drains properly. See if it has any structural cracks or if it is tilting and settling. When I say structural cracks I mean anything wider than 1/4 inch. If the paving appears sound, but doesn't look good, it might be *improved* rather than replaced. Where

part of the paving is good, rent a concrete saw and cut out the bad portion.

If a paved area is too small or a walk too narrow, add to it instead of starting over. Match it as closely as possible to avoid a patchy appearance. A better way is to choose a contrasting material

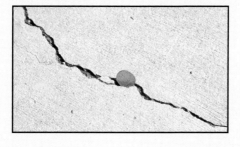

A crack large enough for this quarter to fall into may mean the concrete isn't structurally sound and should be replaced.

A concrete stain was used to give the sidewalk a brownish-rust color that ties in with the new wood landing. Stain reacts chemically with cement and, unlike paint, is permanent.

and make the addition a design feature. For example, a row of bricks on each side of a narrow concrete walk makes it more usable and better looking.

Acid stain can often transform dull, drab concrete into an attractive sur-

A power saw slices right through concrete so undesirable sections can be removed.

Left: The entrance to this Ohio home is enhanced by a curving walkway and heavy planting with a touch of color for added interest. Landscape Architect: Andrew L. Sparks, ASLA, with Land Techniques.

# ADDING CONCRETE

After concrete is poured, 3/4-inch stones are sprinkled on the surface to give a textured finish.

Adding concrete follows the same procedure as shown in Chapter 3, "Laying Concrete." Here Billy Becher lends a hand while his father installs forms for an addition to a narrow front walkway.

As soon as the concrete starts to harden, it is swept lightly with a broom to expose the stone.

The stones are pressed into the wet concrete until barely covered.

Left: The crucial decision is when to start washing the surface with a light stream of water. This concrete is just about "ripe."

Right: The exposed pebbles contrast subtly with the plain concrete of the old paving.

You can lay bricks in a mortar base over an existing concrete patio. Mortar joints are filled in later. These are split bricks, less than 1-inch thick.

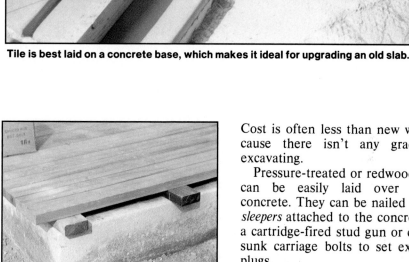

Tile is best laid on a concrete base, which makes it ideal for upgrading an old slab.

face with a minimum of expense and effort. This method is effective in solving the problem of glare. For stain to take properly, the concrete must be clean and free of paint, wax, oil and grease. Use trisodium phosphate or a dilution of 1 part muriatic acid to 20 parts water to remove whatever you can't scrub off with a broom and hose. The cleaner the concrete, the better the results.

Stain is brushed on in two coats. Allow time for the first coat to dry before applying the second. In most cases, stain soaks in unevenly for a pleasing, mottled effect. Don't expect it to be solid or to cover chips, cracks or other imperfections. Material cost is about 20 cents per square foot.

Another way to upgrade existing paving is to use it as a base for new paving. The trick here is to make sure the extra thickness doesn't create a drainage problem or a dangerous small step. New concrete poured over old concrete should be at least 3 inches thick. Thinner layers tend to crack. Roughen the old surface, and paint it with concrete glue to help form a bond. Usually the price is similar to new work, but you save the removal cost.

Common bricks or flagstone laid on a 1-inch-thick layer of sand or mortar bed on top of old paving raises the level about 3 inches. If this is too much, set split-bricks or patio tiles in mortar or mastic to keep the added thickness down to as little as 1 inch.

Here, 2x4 *sleepers* are glued to a concrete landing and redwood 2x4s nailed in place.

Cost is often less than new work because there isn't any grading or excavating.

Pressure-treated or redwood planks can be easily laid over existing concrete. They can be nailed to wood *sleepers* attached to the concrete. Use a cartridge-fired stud gun or countersunk carriage bolts to set expansion plugs.

Planks can also be laid directly in concrete glue. This works best on a small porch or landing where a single plank can be used without splicing. Figure about $1.50 per square foot for

A 2x8 trim board has been added and the wood bleached to blend with the house. Matching English hollies in wood barrels complement the lights. Landscape architect: Ken Smith, ASLA.

2-inch planking. You may have to do the work yourself. Finding a carpenter for a small job like this is unlikely.

It's easy to seal-coat asphalt when it looks shabby. Sweep sand into the cracks, then broom on the emulsion. Material cost is about 10 cents a square foot. If the surface is extremely bad, a paving company can add a 1-inch layer of new asphalt on top of old for less than tearing it all out and starting over.

## CONSTRUCTION

Your decision to keep existing walls, fences, shade trellises and other garden construction should be made the same way you decide about paving. If a structure is unsound or unsafe, remove it or look for ways to improve it. You can use the same acid stain on concrete-block walls, or use a cement-based paint or plaster. Stain wood fences, or keep the frame and install new paneling.

Make shade trellises attractive by applying *plant-ons*. Enhance a 4x4 post by nailing 1x2s on all four sides. Treat beams and rafters the same way. The key to success is a little ingenuity.

## SWIMMING POOLS

A pool represents a considerable amount of money. You'll want to keep the pool unless it is structurally unsound or you can't stand water. Call in a reputable pool company to check out the filter and heater for maximum efficiency. If there's a nearby south-facing roof, you may be able to add supplementary solar heating.

Unsightly plaster can be acid-washed and painted or replastered. Consider a dark color for a mountain-lake effect. Update the tile trim while you're at it. If there is concrete decking, follow the suggestions on page 167 to see if it is worth keeping or if it needs redoing. Replace old-style precast concrete copings with 12-inch-long bricks, or new concrete decking can be cantilevered over the edge for a clean look.

Add a sunbathing area if it's needed. Perhaps the problem is lack of shade. A shade trellis or gazebo is a good way to add comfort to a hot pool area.

Plants around swimming pools often need refurbishing. If there's too much paving, saw-cut and remove some concrete to introduce more

**Landscape architect Thomas W. Hill, ASLA, selected white picket fencing and appropriate plantings in the restoration of this historic house in Gates Mills, Ohio.**

**When I was called in on this job, the pool decking was cracked, concrete was gray and the wall was an ugly concrete block. We veneered the wall with used brick, carried it out with new coping and decking and replastered the pool in a dark plaster.**

Inviting entry is highlighted by a well-designed trellis that seems to lead you into the house.

Wood deck raises outdoor living area to floor level. Materials and colors appear to be part of the house. Design/build: Landscape Services Inc.

foliage. Add container plants and hanging baskets. Save, remove or transplant trees and shrubs as needed to balance and refresh the area. See this page for helpful transplanting tips.

## FRONT ENTRANCE

You might want to go a little overboard at the front entrance of the house or property. You can add a personal touch and get maximum return on your effort. This is an opportunity to upgrade the paving by laying brick, tile, flagstone or wood over the typically uninspiring slab of concrete at the front door.

Where the roof overhang is lacking or minimal, a well-scaled wood trellis can turn a dull entry into an exciting, gracious one.

Hillside gazebo was built for enjoying the view of the valley below.

Don't be afraid to be dramatic. Bring in a few boulders, or cluster some sawed-off telephone poles or railroad ties as accents. Add a few choice plants in containers and include some low-voltage lighting to complete the picture.

## VIEWS

Make the most of any nice view. It doesn't have to be a panoramic sweep of rolling hills, a winding river or rocky shoreline. Sometimes a pleasant glimpse is enough to make it worthwhile. Add a path to a secluded bench or hammock where you can relax. A gazebo makes a good destination point and offers shade in the absence of trees.

## PLANTS

It's difficult to decide which plants to save. If you're remodeling your own garden, it becomes an emotional issue to cut down an undesirable plant, especially if you're the one who planted it. A plant is expendable when it no longer serves its purpose. Take out dead and dying plants first. Then determine which remaining ones are still doing a good job and which ones are ill-chosen.

Transplanting is always a risk and is often attempted with the erroneous belief that all plants are valuable. Moving a small plant is one thing—any plant more than 4 feet high becomes a major task. In many cases, it's better to start with a new plant. If you decide to go ahead and move a plant, here are some general rules:

• Check with a nursery to see what a new plant of comparable size costs. Ask your nurseryman if the plant is easy to move.

• Decide if you have an actual need for the plant in your garden and if there is a place for it.

• Choose the best time of year to move plants. Late fall and early spring are best for most plants. Midsummer and midwinter are least desirable.

• Avoid clear, hot days for transplanting. Cool, overcast weather is best. Provide temporary shade protection if it turns hot. Use anti-dessicant sprays to reduce water loss.

• Take as much of the root system as practical. Move the plant directly into the new position. Prune back to reduce leaf surface. Apply a transplanting hormone, such as Hormex or Super-thrive, and keep the root area moist until established.

Now is a good time to correct previous mistakes and anticipate future problems. The most-common example of this is overgrowth. Rather than hacking away at a large shrub next to a walk or under a window, it might be better to remove it.

If there is enough space for a shrub to grow, don't be too hasty to take it out. Even when severely pruned back, many shrubs regrow to give many more years of service. An overgrown shrub can also be converted into a small tree by pruning lower branches.

## TREES

Where large trees are involved, it may be best to seek expert advice. It's sad to remove a beautiful old tree that might be rehabilitated with good pruning. The cost of professional pruning may be less than total removal. Check on the estimated value of a tree before cutting it down. You may be destroying a valuable specimen.

Most existing trees are sensitive to changes in grade. Do not add soil more than a few inches deep in the area between the trunk and the outermost spread of the branches. If deeper fill is unavoidable, a wall several feet from the trunk helps keep soil away from the trunk and saves the tree from almost certain death. Also avoid lowering the grade within the drip-line area.

Orchard trees, such as apple and pear, are difficult garden subjects. In fact, most fruit and nut trees are normally grown with natural rainfall and a minimum of supplemental irrigation. Typical landscape watering can lead to crown and root diseases, especially in poorly drained soil. A deep soaking during drought periods may be necessary, but it's best to avoid frequent sprinkling within the drip-line. This means that plantings requiring considerable moisture, such as a lawn, azaleas, ferns and pachysandra, are incompatible with most orchard trees. If underplanting is considered essential, use material that requires infrequent watering.

## CASE HISTORY

The 15-year-old garden above appeared overgrown and was too shady for the grass to thrive. Rather than remove any trees, they were severely thinned and lower branches removed. A new lawn shape was laid out on the ground with stakes and a hose. Permanent redwood edging was installed to emphasize the new flowing lines. Surface tree roots extending into the lawn area were removed, and a trench was filled with gravel to discourage future growth. To facilitate leaf raking, a ground cover of decomposed granite was used under trees. Boulders, with groupings of azaleas, provide interest and add beautiful color every spring.

**There are complex formulas for estimating the value of a tree, but I'd call this magnificent old London plane tree priceless.**

**It's a good idea to lay out proposed changes on the ground to see how they look before doing anything drastic. Photo: Fred Kahn.**

**Remodeled garden is more spacious and airy and easier to maintain. Photo: Fred Kahn.**

## INSTALLING RAILROAD TIES

You can cut through a few ties with a hand saw if you have muscle and patience. A two-man cross-cut is better than a carpenter's saw.

Telephone pole sections set vertically in the ground are used at the corners for support and appearance.

Left: A large circular saw is best to cut a lot of ties. A chain saw will also work if the blade has hardened tips.

Ties are combined with bricks for a stairway. A tie laid along the toe of the slope keeps soil in place.

These railroad-tie steps connect adjacent walks. Try to pick ties with smooth surfaces so people won't trip on rough spots.

## RAILROAD TIES

Railroad ties aren't limited to remodeling projects. However, they're so handy to add to an existing garden that it seems appropriate to include them here.

Prices have risen since the days when they were available for a $1 each. You may still find a bargain, but $10 to $15 is what you can expect to pay now.

They're expensive when used as paving—the cost of the ties alone can be as much as $2 per square foot. Best uses for ties are as steps and low walls.

Where frost heaving isn't a problem, they're heavy enough to hold themselves in place with only 30d nails to pin them together. Where winters are severe and for walls higher than two ties, reinforce them with 3/4-inch steel pipes driven through 1-inch-diameter holes below the frost line. You'll need a heavy-duty drill for the job.

A common use of railroad ties is in the rustic or natural garden. Ties fit in well with all but the most-sophisticated designs. Pressure-treated 6x6 timbers and poles can be used in a similar manner if ties are not available or if a neater effect is desired.

## OTHER CONSIDERATIONS

Don't forget to adapt site drainage, sprinklers and lighting to any changes you make. Evaluate what kind of maintenance situation you've inherited. Maybe you don't have the time or interest to take care of a rose or annual garden or to do extensive hand watering. As long as the place is torn up, correct problems and make changes where desired.

# Maintenance

The ideal garden requires care only on cool, sunny weekends when you have nothing special planned and when there's no important game on television. Unfortunately, plants are like kids and pets. They always seem to need the most attention when you have a million other things to do. You *can* have an enjoyable garden without being a slave. It takes careful planning and proper maintenance techniques along with a little ingenuity.

Nearly everyone wants a *low-maintenance* garden. But no one agrees what that means. You need to determine how many gardening hours are required to maintain the average yard. If you have a gardener, you may be less concerned than if you do all the work yourself. But good gardeners are hard to find, and they are costly. A good compromise is to hire a lawn-care service to mow, edge, fertilize and spray the lawn, and you do the rest.

It's important to reduce unnecessary consumption of fertilizer, chemicals and water. Whether you want a low-maintenance garden or a showplace, follow these suggestions to get the most out of your maintenance effort and materials.

• Limit manicured-lawn areas to visible and usable space. Use ground covers and shrub covers for slopes and non-traffic areas.
• Install convenient hose-bibbs or a permanent sprinkler system.
• Space plants with ultimate size in mind, and don't overplant. Use compact and dwarf varieties for small areas.
• Work with a plant's natural growth habit rather than fighting it.
• Select plants adapted to your specific climate that grow easily with little damage from insects and diseases.

I'd classify this well-tended garden in the medium-to-high maintenance category. Landscape architect: Roy Seifert.

## Maintenance Chart

| Category | Description | Hours per Month |
|---|---|---|
| High Maintenance | Large lawn area, annual flowers and roses. Meticulous trimming. The showplace of the neighborhood. | 24 and up |
| Medium Maintenance | Some lawn, a few annuals. Neat, but not perfect. Better than most. | 16 to 20 |
| Low Maintenance | No lawn or annuals. Paving and bark or stone mulches. Definite casual appearance. Can look run-down and shabby if not well-designed. | At least 8 |

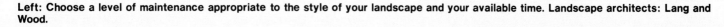

**Left: Choose a level of maintenance appropriate to the style of your landscape and your available time. Landscape architects: Lang and Wood.**

There's no denying the appeal of neatly clipped plants. For them to look their best, don't allow plants to get overgrown between shearings.

Large lawns require riding mowers. Besides, it's kind of fun.

Landscape designer Robert E. Morrell chose dwarf Japanese yew and compact Pfitzer junipers to minimize the need for trimming. Landscape contractor: Mavroff Inc.

If there's such a thing as perfect maintenance, this is it. Note the exquisitely pruned pine at the right. Design/build: Theodore Brickman Co.

● Plant properly. Build watering basins for deep soaking. Mulch plants to retain moisture and limit weeds.

● Use large areas of paving and semipaving.

Let's look at various jobs and explore ways to reduce the time they take. You don't have to approach maintenance like a professional who takes care of 10 places a day. The intent is to handle tasks you least enjoy as efficiently as possible. If you want to spend half the day pruning your favorite tree, caring for prize roses or getting out in the sun and pulling weeds by hand, you'll have time to do it.

## LAWN CARE

Lawns leave the most room for improvement. Use an efficient mower, and keep it sharp and in good repair. If exercise is desirable, a sturdy hand mower is fine for most grass. However, bermudagrass, zoysiagrass and buffalograss require power equipment. Areas larger than 2,000 square feet justify the need for a power mower. For large areas, a 25-inch riding mower becomes a necessity. Reel-type mowers are best for well-groomed lawns, bentgrass, hybrid bermudagrass and zoysiagrass. Rotary mowers are better adapted to general lawn care and rough conditions. For large properties, consider a multiuse yard tractor for mowing, tilling, snow removal, grading and hauling.

Reducing the size of your lawn shortens cutting time, but it may not help much. Once you have the mower out, it's not much effort to cut a few more square feet. To save time, eliminate narrow strips of grass and fancy

Hybrid bermudagrass requires frequent, low mowing with a front-throw mower to look its best.

ming next to paving. Use a spade, power edger or plastic-line trimmer to keep a definite edge. With no permanent line, the shape of the planting beds changes drastically through the years. Grass has a way of taking over ground covers and shrubs, especially creeping grasses, such as bentgrass, bermudagrass and zoysiagrass.

## MOWING STRIPS

Mowing strips are essential if neat, permanent edges are desired. They relate directly to the finish grade of the lawn. Install them in conjunction with that operation. The following are the most common types.

**Wood Edging**—This is satisfactory, except in constantly soggy soil. It is unobtrusive and relatively inexpensive. Use full, rough heartwood 2x4s of decay-resistant species, such as redwood, cypress or cedar, or pressure-treated lumber. Laminate 1x4s or 1/2x4s for curves because narrow strips break easily. Material cost is about 50 cents per linear foot. Installed, it costs $1.50 and up.

**Brick-and-Concrete Mowing Strips** —These edgings are more practical than wood. Lay the bricks flat and side-by-side for an 8-inch-wide strip. Brick and concrete are strong design elements. Lay them out carefully so they don't attract too much attention. Material cost is about 50 cents per linear foot. Installed cost is $3 and up.

**Steel Edging**—Steel edging is available with special splices and stakes at a

It takes twice as many bricks if you lay them side-by-side, but this strip of used brick is wide enough for the mower's wheel.

cost of about $1.25 per linear foot for 1/8-inch thickness. Steel stakes are an advantage in hard soil.

**Special Edgings**—Plastic lawn edgings are flexible but can be damaged by power edgers. Corrugated aluminum, bricks set on end, large stones and similar designs are more trouble to trim around than a plain edge. Most of them are obtrusive and unsightly.

edges that require lots of trimming. In some cases, you may be able to eliminate the lawn entirely. If so, be sure what you replace it with won't be more of a chore.

To further reduce lawn-care requirements, think of the lawn as a meadow rather than a putting green. Select a less-demanding type of grass. Cut it less frequently and higher than normal. You save mowing time, and most weeds are shaded out or at least hidden.

In a casual garden, let the lawn grow where it may, and eliminate some of the edging. It still needs trim-

Nylon string weeder is the way to go. Young, tender-bark trees must be protected from damage.

Plastic edging set flush with the grade is much easier to mow along than if the lawn went all the way up to the boulders. Design by Robert E. Morrell. Landscape contractor: Mavroff Inc.

## MOWING STRIPS

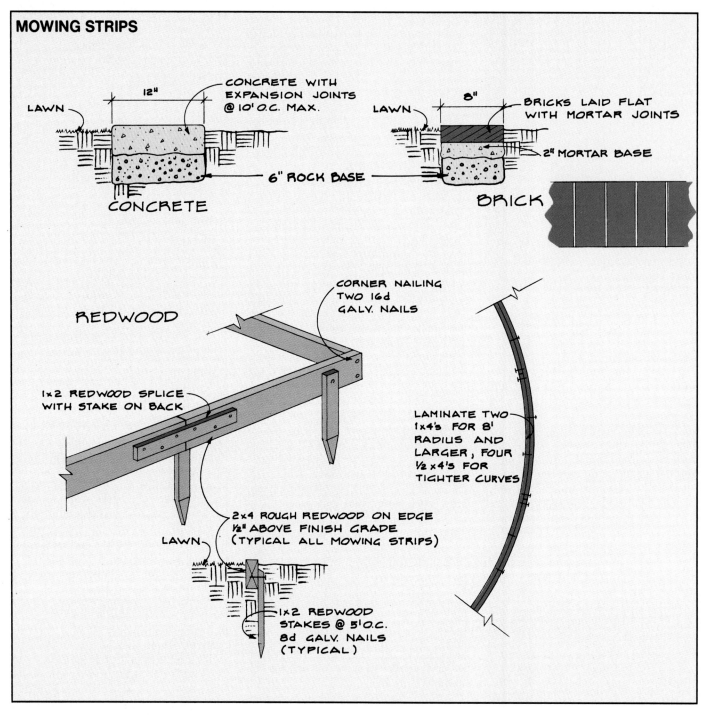

### WATERING

Water is no longer the cheap resource it used to be. The high cost of energy required for pumping has affected the price, and the rising population has affected the available supply. In areas of low rainfall, this has a direct impact on the landscape and how much it will cost to maintain it. Even where rain is plentiful, water companies often have difficulty meeting peak demands during droughts and water shortages.

We must do some serious thinking about what kind of garden is appropriate for present and future conditions. We must manage water use better than in the past. An obvious answer is to use plants that thrive on normal rainfall. Many plants can get by with minimum supplementary irrigation during dry spells, and there is little problem for the average-sized lot. Large properties with extensive lawns require a lot of water.

Another approach is to concentrate landscaping efforts on the areas adjacent to the house. Under extreme conditions, apply the golf-course concept of greens, fairways and rough. Plantings adjacent to the house and outdoor living areas are the greens. Give them the most care and water. Intermediate areas receive somewhat less attention and irrigation, similar to fairways. Fringe areas are the rough. Don't do anything to it that isn't absolutely necessary.

If you plan a new garden or make

Curved wood edging is made by laminating two strips of 1x4s for extra strength.

Gravel driveway is separated from lawn by a sturdy and unobtrusive steel edging.

Almost all large trees drop lots of leaves. This sycamore is in a natural setting where a pile of leaves doesn't matter.

A hand aerator is great for opening up those packed-down spots in a lawn where water won't penetrate.

inhibits growth of water-stealing weeds.

- Don't overplant. Space plants far enough apart so they have room to grow.
- Don't feel obligated to cover every square inch of your property with plants. There's nothing wrong with mulch or bare earth between shrubs and trees.
- Plant during the spring or fall so roots become established with minimal watering.
- Make extensive use of paving and semipaving.
- Preserve existing woods and native plants rather than converting your entire property to lawn.
- Place shrubs where they benefit from rainfall. Plantings under wide overhangs may require frequent watering.

Get to know how plants signal for water. Grasses tend to lie flat after being stepped on if moisture is low, and the color is duller than normal. Many plants lose their gloss and start to droop before going into wilt. Some plants can recover without losing a leaf after sprawling flat on the ground. Others defoliate, drop buds and flowers and may never be the same once they've dried out. Observation and experience are the best ways to learn which plants are sensitive and which are tough.

Don't water on a rigid schedule. The time to water is when plants *need* it. If in doubt, don't water until you make sure the soil is almost dry. The symptoms of waterlogged plants can sometimes be confused with symptoms of dryness. Dig down below the surface rather than just guess. Use a soil sampler for a deeper look.

Water early in the morning to avoid excessive evaporation loss. Evening is not good because fungus diseases have all night to attack moist foliage. Mornings are usually calmer and evaporation is less than when it is windy, and less spray gets blown onto paving.

Some plants, such as azaleas, rhododendrons, lily-of-the-valley, shrubs and most ferns have surface roots that benefit from frequent, light watering in addition to an occasional deep soaking. Most plants, including lawns, develop deeper root systems and tolerate drought better if watered deeply. Water penetrates easily in sandy soils. In clay soils, apply water

extensive changes to an existing one, several things can keep water requirements low. Use the tips on page 175, along with the plants listed on page 182. They will help you save water and reduce maintenance.

- Limit lawn in size and to areas that will be both beautiful and usable.
- Select a type of lawn that grows with less water and survives drought periods.
- Install an efficient sprinkler system if supplementary irrigation is required.
- Avoid plants with high moisture

requirements. A few thirsty ones tucked into a shady corner won't affect total water usage very much. An entire garden that needs constant watering consumes a lot of water.

- Properly prepare the soil for new plantings. Include earth watering basins where excessive rain is not a problem.
- Mulch to retain moisture. Plants with normal watering requirements do well during droughts when they have extensive root systems and are properly mulched. Mulching also

slowly so it soaks in. Earth basins help confine water to within the drip line of trees and shrubs and are helpful for new plantings.

## DIFFICULT SITUATIONS

Compacted soil is subject to run-off. *Vertical mulching* is a procedure used at the drip line of trees and shrubs to aid water penetration. Use an electric drill to make holes 1/2 to 1-inch in diameter, about 12 inches apart and 12 inches deep around the plant. Rent or buy extra-long drill bits. Make sure the drill is properly grounded. You can also use the holes to apply fertilizer.

A root-feeder device attached to the hose is another way to get water into hard soil. Consider using a canvas or plastic soaker coiled around a tree and allowed to run slowly for several hours.

Slopes are difficult to water without run-off and erosion. Use earth basins for individual trees and shrubs. Turn on sprinklers for short intervals and then repeat several times until penetration is achieved. Jute and plastic mesh, organic mulches and straw help retard erosion and are essential on steep slopes.

## LAWNS

The discussion of lawns, beginning on page 137 covers choosing a grass that is reasonably drought tolerant to reduce watering needs. Bluegrass, bentgrass and ryegrass require approx-imately 1 inch of water per week. Tall fescue, bermudagrass and zoysiagrass can get by on half as much, buffalo-grass even less.

*Thatch,* the layer of dead plant parts that accumulates at the soil level, is an enemy of good water penetration. Periodic verticutting reduces runoff and encourages healthier growth and deeper rooting.

*Aeration* also improves water penetration. Hollow tines remove cores of soil and reduce the effects of compaction. For small areas, this process can be done by hand. Large lawns call for a motorized aerator. Chemical soil penetrants can also help water soak into the ground better, but results are relatively short-lived.

Raise mowing height during hot weather. Roots are kept cooler by taller grass, and less water is needed.

If droughts are frequent occurrences in your region, a permanent, underground sprinkler system is worth considering. This is especially true if you have a large expanse of lawn. Obviously, turning on sprinkler valves takes less time than moving the hose around all day. With a sprinkler, water is applied more evenly and may use less water than a hose or portable sprinklers.

Many landscape contractors install sprinkler systems. Or if you want to do it yourself, some major manufacturers offer design and installation advice along with selling the equipment and materials.

## SWEEPING AND RAKING

Leaf and litter raking can be a time-consuming chore. Anyone who has dealt with a row of poplars along his property line, a giant sycamore in the front lawn or a mimosa in a paved area, knows how big a job it is.

Small or medium "clean" trees are best for paved areas, lawns and places where leaf accumulation is undesirable. Flowering dogwood, Bradford pear, American holly, Canadian hemlock, amur maple and katsura tree are in this category. Use "dirty" trees only if there is room for leaves to accumulate naturally, or if leaves can be raked infrequently instead of daily. Along with poplar, sycamore and mimosa, willow, beech, sugar maple, catalpa, mulberry, many pines and most large trees fall into the "dirty" class.

There are both deciduous and evergreen trees on the lists. Deciduous trees drop most of their leaves over a short period and seem "dirtier." Evergreen trees drop their leaves throughout the year, so you may not notice it as much. Some trees shed fruit, flowers, small twigs and bark that are more objectionable than leaves. Large trees are more of a problem because of their volume. Small leaves, such as variegated goutweed, common wintercreeper, Japanese spurge and English ivy, can filter into ground cover and eliminate the need for raking.

**Rather than constantly raking them up, pine needles are put to good use as a mulch.**

**Soil samplers give a good profile of underground conditions. They're available in 12- and 18-inch lengths.**

# FERTILIZING

Fertilization is a complex subject and is confusing to most homeowners and many professionals. The general intent is to maintain health and appearance, plus flower and fruit production for some plants. Usually, sturdy, rapid growth is desirable until ideal size is reached, with slower growth thereafter.

Don't pile on fertilizer once a year. Most plants respond to several light applications, and there is less danger of burning. Sandy soils usually have higher requirements than clay soils because leaching carries nutrients through the root zone. Soils rich in organic material retain and release nutrients better than those with low-organic content.

For most plants, a complete fertilizer supplying nitrogen, phosphorus and potassium is satisfactory when applied about four times a year. Certain plants, such as rhododendrons, azaleas, roses and vegetables, may respond better to special formulations. These are worth the additional cost unless large quantities are involved.

When green foliage is the goal, such as lawns and leafy vegetables, a high-nitrogen formula is more economical. A 3-1-2 ratio is considered the best balance. The first number indicates *nitrogen,* so a label that reads 15-5-10 is ideal. Lack of nitrogen shows on most plants as an overall pale-green leaf color. Apply the proper amount of nitrogen, and water immediately to avoid burning. Slow-release and time-released types are less apt to burn, last longer and reduce the number of necessary applications.

Lawn fertilizers that contain insecticides and herbicides are okay for special situations. There's no advantage to using them every time unless the need is indicated.

It makes no difference to the plant if the fertilizer is applied in chemical or organic form, in grains, pellets or liquid. Organic types are useful to enrich soil low in humus. Manures are good natural fertilizers but low in fertility. Use them with caution. Fresh manure can burn tender rootlets. Some manure sources contain weed seeds, and many have high salt content. Use these fertilizers in limited amounts, preferably composted and diluted with organic material.

*When* you fertilize is important.

If your Pyracantha or other plants have leaves that look like this, they may be suffering from lack of iron.

Spring is best for hardy deciduous trees and shrubs and coniferous evergreens. Make additional applications in fall. Fertilize cold-tender plants and most broad-leaved evergreens only in spring and early summer. Late-summer feeding promotes new growth that can be damaged by winter cold.

It's traditional to fertilize bluegrass, tall fescue, bentgrass and perennial ryegrass in early spring. A new practice is to make a main application in the late fall, skip the normal spring feeding and make another application in late spring. This helps the grass stand summer heat. The advantages are that disease-prone, excessive top growth in early spring is reduced, and strong root growth is encouraged.

Bermudagrass and zoysiagrass require most of their fertilization in late spring and summer. With all grasses, apply light feedings to keep grass green and healthy. Overfertilization results in faster growth, which means more mowing, more water and more fungus diseases.

Liming is not fertilization, but it makes some elements more available to the plant by reducing acidity. If a soil test indicates the need for lime during initial soil preparation, additional applications may be needed every 3 or 4 years. Another soil test at that time determines the amount required. At the same time, have your soil tested for fertility to pinpoint the type and quantity of fertilizer that may be needed. Don't apply high-nitrogen fertilizer to lawns or plants at the same time you apply lime.

*Iron chlorosis* is a common problem, often mistaken as a need for fertilizer.

The tomato horn worm is really difficult to see. Hand picking is an effective control. You can also handle snails this way.

The identifying symptom is yellowing of leaves as veins remain green. If left unchecked, the condition often ends with the entire plant turning yellow and dying. Sweet gum, rhododendron, azalea, pyracantha, holly, mugo pine and ginkgo are frequently afflicted. Iron chelates are more successful than iron sulphate. Apply these when symptoms first appear. Iron chlorosis is usually caused by high-alkaline soil, irrigation water or excess liming. Lowering the pH with soil sulphur or another acidifier makes the iron in the soil more available to the plants.

A shortage of magnesium or zinc causes symptoms similar to iron chlorosis, but this situation is less common. Dolomitic limestone and Epsom salts are effective in correcting magnesium deficiencies.

## INSECT AND DISEASE CONTROL

Control of insects and diseases is another complex subject. The main concern today is whether chemicals are necessary. There are dangers involved in using most chemicals, but they are indispensable in many situations. Observe safety precautions and follow manufacturer's instructions carefully. If you have any doubt about the advisability or safety of a product, call the Cooperative Extension Service before using it.

Biological controls that are harmless to beneficial insects, plants, humans, fish and other animals are worth trying if you want to avoid chemicals. *Bacillus thuringiensis*, called *Bt* and sold as Dipel, Biotrol and Thuricide, is effective against caterpillars, includ-

## WATER-SAVING PLANTS

*Below are some plants that withstand heat and do well with little water. Once established, they often survive on natural rainfall alone—no need to drag out the hose during dry spells. Arranged in approximate order of hardiness to cold. See the Plant Lists page 86, for descriptions.*

Siberian Pea Tree
Wooley Thyme
Russian Olive
Moss Pink
Crown Vetch
Cinquefoil
Goldmoss Sedum
Tatarian Honeysuckle
Hedge Cotoneaster
Japanese Barberry
Hall's Honeysuckle
Variegated Goutweed
Silvermound Artemisia
Silver-lace Vine
Adams-Needle
Goldenrain Tree
Smoke Tree
Purple-leaf Winter Creeper
Silk Tree/Mimosa

Silvermound Artemisia

Sibereian Pea Tree

Wooly Thyme

Cinquefoil

ing cabbage worms, gypsy moth and loopers. Milky spore bacteria, sold as Doom and Japonex, attacks Japanese-beetle grubs and other white grubs, including June-beetle larvae.

Select plants that are free from insects and disease. Some degree of prevention is possible with general good care because a healthy, vigorous plant is less susceptible to attack than a weak one. A clean garden also offers fewer breeding spots.

Hand picking and washing with the hose keeps some insect populations at an acceptable level. Manufactured and homemade traps are effective for many insects. Application of chemical control before a problem arises is possible in some instances. An example is applying a *systemic* to roses in early spring to control aphids and fungus. Systemics are absorbed into the plant and cannot be washed off.

Scatter bait *before* snails and slugs devour plants. Put cardboard or plastic collars around the stems of young transplants to protect against cutworms and other chewers. If fungus is likely to strike certain plants in your garden, apply a fungicide at the beginning of humid weather instead of waiting until it gets out of hand. Many insects and diseases can affect bluegrass lawns. Periodic preventive spraying, as practiced by most lawn-care companies, appears justified.

Constant vigilance is the best answer to pest and disease problems. Indiscriminate spraying can create more problems than it solves by interfering with the balance of nature. Prompt, proper treatment usually controls the problem before serious damage is done. A weekly walk through the garden to look for problems is a good way to avoid a nasty surprise. There's nothing that says you can't enjoy a little beauty while you stroll.

A knowledgeable nurseryman can help in problem situations. Take in a sample—a damaged leaf or twig—if you can't catch the culprit. The nurseryman can usually recommend the latest, most-effective means of control. Cooperative Extension Service agents are usually available for advice, as are tree companies and pest-control firms. If you don't know what the problem is, ask before it's too late.

Watch for new developments. Insecticidal soap is non-hazardous to people and pets. It's effective against aphids, earwigs, mealybugs, thrips and scales, and it doesn't harm many beneficial insects. *Pheromone,* a sex lure, is being tested for control of cabbage loopers, gypsy moth, apple maggots, Japanese beetles and various borers. Insects are enticed to their death, but at least they die happy.

Experiments are being done with decollate snails that attack common young garden snails, leaving foliage and fruit alone. Caterpillar nematodes destroy weevils, root maggots, armyworms, cutworms, lawn-moth and click-beetle larvae but are harmless to earthworms, plants and vertebrates. A new systemic fungicide, called Subdue, has produced dramatic results in the inhibition of root rot and water mold.

## WEED CONTROL

There are several ways to cut weeding time. These include eliminating weeds before planting and removing new ones while they're still small—before they go to seed. Mulching around trees, shrubs and ground covers helps prevent weed growth. Use herbicides judiciously when hand methods fail or are impractical. Here are some typical weed situations and what you can do about them.

**Broad-leafed Weeds**—This type of weed includes dandelion, ground ivy, plantain and chickweed. In an established cool-season lawn, treat it with 2,4-D, or a mixture of 2,4-D, MCPP and dicamba, sold as Trimec and Trex-San, without harming grass. Use 2,4-D carefully on most warm-season grasses and bentgrasses that are sensitive to it in varying degrees.

**Grassy Weeds**—This type of weed often invades a broad-leafed ground cover or shrub bed. It can be sprayed with a product containing dalapon, commercially sold as Dowpon, with little or no damage to most broad-leafed plants. Check the list on the label for tolerant and sensitive plants. Indications are that manufacture is being discontinued, and the supply will be available for only a few years. Several new, highly selective grass weedicides which serve the same purpose will be marketed soon. In the meantime, there is an alternative.

Glyphosate is a non-selective herbicide that controls a wide range of weeds. It is sold as Kleen-up, at about $15 a quart, or as higher strength Round-up, at $80 a gallon for large areas. By carefully wiping it on weeds with a special wick applicator and not touching the desirable plants, it is usable in established shrub and ground-cover areas. Other ways to apply it are with a small paint brush or by wearing poison-saturated cotton gloves over rubber gloves to wipe weed leaves.

This is more effective than trying to remove deep-rooting grasses, such as zoysiagrass and bermudagrass, by hand. Bentgrass, goosegrass, quackgrass and tall fescue can usually be pulled out, but glyphosate may be easier for large areas.

To control crabgrass in established cool-season lawns, apply bensulide, sold as Betasan, or siduron, sold as Tupersan, in spring to kill seeds as they germinate. Precise timing depends on climate zone and how early the soil warms. Some annual bluegrass and other annual grasses may also be killed if germination time coincides. Siduron can be applied when seeding a new bluegrass, ryegrass or tall-fescue lawn. However, bermudagrass and some bentgrasses are sensitive to siduron.

When crabgrass and annual grasses sprout in an established lawn, use a post-emergent treatment of DSMA. The older and tougher the weeds are, the more applications are necessary.

Yellow nut sedge, usually called *nutgrass,* in a lawn is a tough problem. Bentazon, sold as Basagran, DSMA or MSMA applied to actively growing, emerged foliage gives some control. Heavy stands are almost impossible to eliminate selectively. You either live

with it or have a professional applicator fumigate with methyl bromide, then replant.

**Future Weeds**—Weeds might come up in the bare earth in ground covers, shrub areas and flower beds not planted with seeds. They can be avoided by applying the following pre-emergent herbicides: EPTC, sold as Eptam; diphenamid, sold as Enide; trifluralin, sold as Treflan; or a similar pre-emergent herbicide that kills germinating weed seeds without harming established plants. A diphenamid and trifluralin mix is effective.

**Mixed Weeds**—Mixed weeds are often found in a non-planted area, such as semipaving, and bare earth between shrubs and trees. Spray mixed weeds with glyphosate, fortified weed oil, amino triazole, cacodylic acid or a similar non-selective, *knock-down* material. Where there are no existing plants and you don't want any, apply soil sterilants, such as borate/chlorate or simizine-amino-triazole combinations.

**Caution**—There's no reason to use chemicals if simple hand weeding takes little or no more effort than spraying. If you decide a weedicide is needed, take proper safety precautions. Carefully follow all manufacturer's directions. Spray when there is little or no wind to avoid drift onto desirable plants. Be careful that spray or granules aren't washed off or dissolved where they can run off into plant basins and root areas. Store all weedicides, insecticides and poisons in their original containers, locked away from children and pets.

## PRUNING AND TRIMMING

There seem to be two extremes when it comes to pruning. Either the homeowner is afraid to snip off the smallest branch, or he butchers the plant back to unsightly stubs. Some professionals are no better. They treat all plants as cubes or spheres and destroy the natural grace and form of the species.

When plants are selected with their natural growth habit and size in mind, you can throw away the hedge clippers. Regular pruning can guide the plant's growth, rather than waiting until the plant becomes unshapely and oversized.

There are a few general rules that can be helpful:

• Don't prune unless there is a need for it or you have a goal in mind. Reasons for pruning include limiting size, improving shape and appearance, increasing flower and fruit production, and protecting the health and vigor of the plant.

• Weak, damaged or dead wood is unsightly and a potential source of infection. Remove it.

• Usually, both broad-leafed and needle evergreens require less pruning than deciduous types. For most evergreen plants, light, frequent pruning is better than drastic measures after long intervals.

• Selective removal of stems and branches, sometimes called *feather* or *pick* pruning, is better than shearing. If you want dense foliage, cut back tips to induce growth. To feature a plant, clean out the inside to reveal the branch structure. This lets air pass through, lessening wind damage and weight from ice.

• Prune most deciduous plants in late spring, at the end of the dormant period. Some pruning throughout the year is okay, except for some, such as birch, sugar maple, red maple and American elm, that bleed excessively

A winter mulch of salt hay or similar material will minimize root damage and ground heaving.

Pruning large trees takes special equipment and expertise. Careful tree selection can save lots of money later on.

if cut when sap is flowing. Prune them in late summer only.

• Prune plants that bloom on last year's wood, such as forsythia, mock orange, hydrangea and deutzia, *after* they bloom. This leaves strong, new shoots for next year.

• Prune plants that bloom on new wood, such as rose-of-sharon, spirea bumalda, European cranberrybush and peegee hydrangea, in winter or early spring. This encourages new growth that produces flowers later in the season.

• Rejuvenate old, overgrown plants by removing suckers and cutting back close to the ground. Mock orange, lilac, privet, weigela and most viburnums respond well to this treatment.

• Nearly all vines need periodic thinning. Keep rampant types such as honeysuckle, wisteria and Boston ivy in-bounds by constant pruning. Prune clematis on the basis of whether it flowers on new or old wood.

• Prune hedges severely cut hedges when they are young to encourage bushy growth. Trim wider at the bottom to prevent shading of lower branches.

• Carefully prune shade trees when young to provide a sturdy framework for the years to come. Trim lower branches to the desired height, unless a low-branching effect is desired. Eliminate narrow V-crotches that are subject to breaking. If the appropriate-sized tree is selected, a minimum of pruning is required once it is properly shaped.

• Fruit and nut trees and berries require specific pruning techniques. Choosing the wrong time and method can result in losing the crop. Your Cooperative Extension Service has excellent pamphlets available on this subject.

• For roses, remove dead, weak, thin and crossing canes. Reduce height of remaining canes to 6 to 12 inches in late winter or early spring as buds begin to swell. Remove oldest canes of climbers to encourage new replacements. Drastically prune ramblers immediately after flowering to keep them under control.

## WINTERIZING YOUR GARDEN

The best way to insure against winter damage is to select *only* the hardiest plants suited for your climate zone. Place them in' the proper exposure. In severe climates, additional measures are still needed.

• Wrap young, newly planted, tender-bark trees, such as dogwood, crab apple, maple, linden and honey locust, with tree-wrap paper, burlap or a commercial plastic product. This prevents sun scald and frost cracks. Check wrapping in spring for nests of gypsy-moth caterpillars and other creatures.

• Stake young and newly planted shrubs and trees to prepare for strong winds. You can also guy them to keep them from blowing over and damaging roots.

• Wrap a circle of 1/4-inch wire mesh around tree trunks from below the ground to 24 inches above the anticipated snow level. This keeps mice, rabbits and other gnawing animals from stripping tree bark. Deer can reach low-hanging branches and are difficult to fence out. A repellent containing Thiram may be helpful or at least convince deer to feed elsewhere.

• After ground freezer, mulch roots of all plants with 4 to 6 inches of wood chips, bark, salt hay, straw, ground corncobs or small branches. This minimizes frost penetration and freezing and thawing of the soil. Stomp on the mulch occasionally to discourage mice tunnels. In Zones 4 and cooler, you may have to cover roses with mulch and soil for maximum protection. Gradually remove winter mulches in spring to prevent smothering. Using mulches deeper than 2 inches during the growing season can be detrimental especially to shallow-rooted plants, such as rhododendrons, azaleas, Japanese pieris, mountain laurel, leucothoe, yews and hollies.

• Wrap evergreens with burlap or construct a lath or burlap barrier if wind and sun damage is anticipated. Tie up loose branches of trees and shrubs with rope or strong cord and keep them from spreading out. Shake branches after a storm to dislodge heavy snow and keep them from breaking under the weight.

• Build a temporary cover for plants that is in the line of snow sliding off the roof. Conserve snow cover on plants by shading with branches. Small shrubs, ground covers, roses, bulbs and perennials benefit from the insulation.

• Keep evergreen trees and shrubs supplied with water during winter so wind and sun do not dry them out. Make sure there is a reserve moisture supply by soaking your garden in the fall if rainfall is inadequate. Spray with an anti-transpirant, such as Wilt-Pruf or Cloud Cover. It may protect against winter kill by reducing water loss through foliage.

Salt applied to roads and other paving for deicing purposes is harmful to most plants because of splashing onto and accumulating in the soil. If you have control over the application, use pure sand where plants are likely to suffer. In other areas, mix salt with cinders, ashes or sand. Apply *after* snow has been cleared from paving, and use a limited amount on critical areas only. Provide curbings, walls or drainage channels along paving, so salt water run-off is directed away from plant roots. Temporary screens of burlap, plastic, wood or other material may be necessary next to public roadways to protect foliage from salt spray.

Leach soil that has been contaminated with salt by applying large amounts of water in the spring. This only works if the soil drains well. Add gypsum to clay soil to improve drainage and facilitate leaching. Or remove several inches of salty soil and replace with clean topsoil.

A solar greenhouse can reduce heating bills and provide comfortable indoor space during winter and summer. Photo: Four Seasons Greenhouses.

# Sources of Information

Although I've tried to include as much information as possible in this book, additional questions will undoubtedly arise as you work on your landscape. A surprising number of questions will answer themselves with a little thought and common sense. Where do you get the answers to the more technical ones?

As mentioned earlier, a good way to learn how to do something is to watch a craftsman do it. Second best is to look at the finished results. I built an entire house this way, from the ground up.

The people who sell a product generally know a great deal about it. An experienced person at a nursery, lumberyard or building-supply company is a potential gold mine of information. Look for free or low-cost commercially prepared publications such as: nursery and garden catalogs; spa, hot tub and pool booklets; sprinkler and lighting pamphlets; decking and patio materials brochures; fertilizer, weed killer, insecticide and similar product-description sheets.

Now we come to the "experts." Landscape architects and designers were discussed in Chapter 2, along with landscape contractors, gardeners and nurserymen. Various sub-contractors really know their specialty, but they're not in the business of dispensing free advice. You have to hire them to do the work in order to benefit from their knowledge.

State agricultural extension offices usually have agents or specialists available to answer questions concerning plants, soil condition, insecticides and similar subjects. A list of addresses is found below. State universities often give advice. My experience has been that extension agents and university personnel are well-qualified, and their publications are excellent. Check under County Government in the phone book and look for Farm Advisor or Cooperative Extension Service. Check with the agricultural department of the nearest state university.

## COOPERATIVE EXTENSION SERVICES

**Connecticut**
University of Connecticut
Storrs, CT 06268

**Delaware**
University of Delaware
Newark, DE 19711

**Illinois**
University of Illinois
Urbana, IL 61801

**Indiana**
Purdue University
Lafayette, IN 47907

**Iowa**
Iowa State University
Ames, IA 50010

**Kansas**
Kansas State University
Manhattan, KS 66520

**Kentucky**
University of Kentucky
Lexington, KT 40506

**Maine**
University of Maine
Orono, ME 04473

**Maryland**
University of Maryland
College Park, MD 20742

**Massachusetts**
University of Massachusetts
Amherst, MA 01002

**Michigan**
Michigan State University
East Lansing, MI 48823

**Minnesota**
University of Minnesota
St. Paul, MN 55101

**Missouri**
University of Missouri
Columbia, MO 65201

**Nebraska**
University of Nebraska
Lincoln, NB 68503

**New Hampshire**
University of New Hampshire
Durham, NH 03824

**New Jersey**
Rutgers University
New Brunswick, NJ 08903

**New York**
New York State College
Ithaca, NY 14850

**North Dakota**
North Dakota State University
Fargo, ND 58102

**Ohio**
Ohio State University
Columbus, OH 43210

**Pennsylvania**
Pennsylvania State University
University Park, PA 16802

**Rhode Island**
University of Rhode Island
Kingston, RI 02881

**South Dakota**
South Dakota State University
Brookings, SD 57006

**Vermont**
University of Vermont
Burlington, VT 05401

**West Virginia**
West Virginia University
Morgantown, WV 26506

**Wisconsin**
University of Wisconsin
Madison, WI 53706

## GOVERNMENT, BOOKSTORES AND LIBRARY SOURCES

Don't overlook the federal government as a source. Write to the Superintendent of Documents, Government Printing Office, Washington, D.C. 20402 and ask for *List of Available Publications of the U.S.D.A.*—Bulletin No. 11. It costs 45 cents.

You may find what you're looking for faster and more easily in the library and bookstore than through the other sources. When plants are involved, some books ignore or only superficially recognize the tremendous differences in growing conditions in different climates. Look through the racks carefully to see if a book is written for your specific region and if it offers information that applies to your needs.

## PUBLIC GARDENS AND ARBORETUMS

The best way to find out what kind of garden you want and what plants you like is to look at as many good examples as possible. There are numerous beautiful public gardens and institutions with outstanding landscaping throughout the Northeast and Midwest. Make it a point to visit one or two whenever you're traveling. Check with local garden clubs for others, and for special tours of private homes and gardens.

Arnold Arboretum
Jamaica Plain, Massachusetts

Boerner Botanical Garden
Hales Corners, Wisconsin

Brooklyn Botanical Garden
Brooklyn, New York

Chicago Botanical Gardens
Glencoe, Illinois

Cornell Plantations
Ithaca, New York

Dawes Arboretum
Newark, Ohio

Des Moines Botanical Center
Des Moines, Iowa

Dow Gardens
Midland, Michigan

Duke Gardens
Somerville, New Jersey

Fernwood
Niles, Michigan

General Electric Appliance Park
Louisville, Kentucky

Hershey Rose Gardens
and Arboretum
Hershey, Pennsylvania

Hidden Lake Gardens
Tipton, Michigan

Holden Arboretum
Mentor, Ohio

Kingwood Center
Mansfield, Ohio

Leaming's Run Botanical Garden
Cape May Court House, New Jersey

Longwood Gardens
Kennett Square, Pennsylvania

Missouri Botanical Garden
St. Louis, Missouri

Morton Arboretum
Lisle, Illinois

New York Botanical Garden
Bronx, New York

Old Westbury Gardens
Old Westbury, Long Island,
New York

Planting Fields Arboretum
East Norwich, Long Island, New York

Sonnenberg Gardens
Canandaigua, New York

Stan Hywet Gardens
Akron, Ohio

U.S. National Arboretum
Washington, D.C.

Winterthur
Winterthur, Delaware

University of Minnesota
Landscape Arboretum
Chaska, Minnesota

# ACKNOWLEDGMENTS

**Horticultural and Technical Advisor**
Stephen M. Cohan, Ph.D.

**Regional Consultants**

Beauté la terre Designs
Carolyn J. Abel
Wichita, Kansas

CR3 Inc. Landscape Architects
Betsy Kaemmerlen
North Avon, Connecticut

Landscape Services Inc.
Terry S. Wallace
Hockessin, Delaware

Landshapes Inc.
Paul H. Barton, ASLA
Bloomington, Minnesota

Land Techniques Inc.
Andrew L. Sparks, ASLA
Delaware, Ohio

Mavroff Landscape Inc.
Robert E. Morrell
Waukesha, Wisconsin

Raymond J. Rolfe
Landscape Architect, ASLA
Centerport, New York

TKA Landscape Architects
John C. Thomas, ASLA
Indianapolis, Indiana

**Photographic Advisor**

William Aplin

# Index

Index

## Conversion to Metric Measure

| When You Know | Symbol | Multiply By | To Find | Symbol |
|---|---|---|---|---|
| **VOLUME** | | | | |
| teaspoons | tsp. | 4.93 | milliliters | ml |
| tablespoons | tbsp. | 14.79 | milliliters | ml |
| fluid ounces | fl. oz. | 29.57 | milliliters | ml |
| cups | c. | 0.24 | liters | l |
| pints | pt. | 0.47 | liters | l |
| quarts | qt. | 0.95 | liters | l |
| gallons | gal. | 3.79 | liters | l |
| board feet | bd. ft. | 0.002 | cubic meters | $m^3$ |
| cubic feet | cu. ft. | 0.03 | cubic meters | $m^3$ |
| cubic yards | cu. yd. | 0.76 | cubic meters | $m^3$ |
| **MASS (WEIGHT)** | | | | |
| ounces | oz. | 28.35 | grams | g |
| pounds | lb. | 0.45 | kilograms | kg |
| **LENGTH** | | | | |
| inches | in. | 2.54 | centimeters | cm |
| feet | ft. | 30.48 | centimeters | cm |
| yards | yd. | 0.91 | meters | m |
| acres | ac. | 0.40 | hectares | ha |
| miles | mi. | 1.61 | kilometers | km |
| **AREA** | | | | |
| square inches | sq. in. | 6.45 | square centimeters | $cm^2$ |
| square feet | sq. ft. | 0.09 | square meters | $m^2$ |
| square yards | sq. yd. | 0.84 | square meters | $m^2$ |
| **SPEED** | | | | |
| miles per hour | mph | 1.61 | kilometers per hour | km/h |
| **PRESSURE** | | | | |
| pounds per square inch | psi | 68974.76 | pascals | Pa |
| **TEMPERATURE** | | | | |
| Fahrenheit | F | 0.56 (after subtracting 32) | Celsius | C |